Electronic Resource Management
Report of the DLF Resource Management Initiative

August 2004

Timothy D. Jewell, Ivy Anderson, Adam Chandler,
Sharon E. Farb, Kimberly Parker, Angela Riggio, and
Nathan D. M. Robertson

DIGITAL LIBRARY FEDERATION

Digital Library Federation
Council on Library and Information Resources
1755 Massachusetts Avenue, NW
Suite 500
Washington, DC 20036

http://www.diglib.org

ISBN-13: 978-1-932326-14-7
ISBN-10: 1-932326-14-6
http://www.diglib.org/pubs/dlfermi0408/
http://purl.oclc.org/DLF/dlfermi0408

Additional print copies are available for $30 per copy. Orders must be placed through DLF's Web site.

♾ The paper in this publication meets the minimum requirements of the American National Standards for
Information Sciences—Permanence of Paper for Printed Library Materials, ANSI Z39.48-1984.

Library of Congress Cataloging-in-Publication Data

Electronic resource management : report of the DLF electronic resource management initiative / Timothy D. Jewell ... [et al.].
    p. cm.
    Includes bibliographical references.
    ISBN-13: 978-1-932326-14-7 (pbk. : alk. paper)
    ISBN-10: 1-932326-14-6 (pbk. : alk. paper)
    ISBN-13: 978-1-932326-16-1 (electronic version)
    ISBN-10: 1-932326-15-4 (electronic version) 1. Digital libraries--United States. 2. Libraries--United States--Special collections--
    Electronic information resources. I. Jewell, Timothy D.
ZA4082.U6E43 2005
025'.00285--dc22
                    2005009089

Contents

About the Authors

Timothy D. Jewell

Tim Jewell became head of Collection Management Services at the University of Washington in 1998, and has been involved in the coordination of electronic resources there since 1992, when he was appointed head of the UW Libraries' Electronic Information Program. He has been active in regional consortium activities for several years, and served as visiting program officer for Electronic Resources at ARL from 1996 to 1998. The research for his 2001 DLF report, "Selection and Presentation of Commercially Available Electronic Resources: Issues and Practices," led him and Adam Chandler to begin discussing ERM metadata and to initiate the "Web Hub" that brings together information about local and broader ERM initiatives. Tim has special interests in developing standards for license expression, e-metrics, and in developing practical systems to support collection management and evaluation. He holds an M.L.S. from SUNY-Albany and an M.A. in Sociology from the Pennsylvania State University.

Ivy Anderson

Ivy Anderson is the program manager, E-Resource Management and Licensing at the Harvard University Library, where she oversees the acquisition and ongoing management of Harvard's network-based resources, negotiates electronic information licenses, and serves as a consultant to other Harvard libraries on issues related to electronic publishing and the licensing of electronic information. In addition to her work on the DLF Electronic Resource Management Initiative, Anderson is chiefly responsible for the design of Harvard's local e-resource management system. Other recent professional activities have included conducting workshops for ACRL and the Medical Library Association on the subject of licensing and electronic resource management.

Adam Chandler

Adam Chandler is information technology librarian within the Central Technical Services department of the Cornell University Library, where his responsibilities include creation of new automated technical services processes, participation in library-wide technology initiatives, and management of the department's computers. His year 2000 assignment, to explore how to build a database to help manage the library's administrative metadata for electronic journals, led to his meeting Tim Jewell and creating the "Web Hub for Developing Administrative Metadata for Electronic Resource Management." That path led to his becoming a member of the ERMI steering group. Currently, Adam is technical lead for Cornell's implementation of III's ERM stand alone module. His ERMI standards involvement continues with work on the mapping of license terms to ERM systems; also, he has a growing curiosity about the potential relationship between electronic resource usage statistics and ERM systems.

Sharon E. Farb

Sharon E. Farb is the director of Digital Collection Management and Licensing for the UCLA Library, where she oversees the provision of centralized support, leads planning, coordinates shared resources, and develops and builds infrastructure and expertise in the selection, licensing, management, and persistent access and use of digital resources over time. She holds a J.D. and M.L.I.S. and is a candidate in the Ph.D. program in Information Studies at UCLA. Her research and professional interests focus on the intersection of key policy issues affecting libraries, law, and technology including intellectual property, copyright, privacy, and intellectual freedom. In addition to her work on the design and development of UCLA's local, home-grown e-resource management system, and the DLF Electronic Resource Management Initiative, Farb is also working on a project with the California Digital Library (CDL) to develop a rights framework that can be used as a generalizable framework that can be applied to the already large and growing streams through which an institution or digital repository acquires digital information. A further aim is to ensure that the framework explicitly secures for the institution or digital repository the rights it needs to manage and distribute the digital information it acquires in a manner that meets institutional needs, and to protect the rights of its content suppliers.

Kimberly Parker

Kimberly Parker is the head, Electronic Collections for the Yale University Library where, among other things, she coordinates the selection and acquisition of electronic resources including all kinds of difficult e-resource life-cycle issues. Kimberly graduated from the University of Michigan with an M.I.L.S. degree, and spent a year as an NLM associate before coming to Yale as the chemistry & geology librarian and science bibliographer at the Sterling Chemistry and Kline Science Libraries of Yale University. Science librarianship was a good place to develop skills with emerging electronic resources, and in 1997, Kimberly took the newly established position at Yale of electronic publishing & collections librarian that was later reworked into a department head position. Recently Kimberly has been working on issues of ensuring appropriate infrastructure to support electronic resources, staffing workflows for managing e-resources, and ways to make electronic materials easily available throughout the world.

Angela Riggio

Angela Riggio has worked for the UCLA Library for over twenty years. She earned both her undergraduate degree in English and her M.L.I.S. at UCLA.

Angela currently heads the Electronic Resources Cataloging and Metadata Section in the UCLA Library Cataloging and Metadata Center. Her responsibilities include the coordination of cataloging workflow in the department, troubleshooting and maintenance of electronic links in the catalog, advising staff involved in digital library project work on metadata, and providing mapping between metadata schemas. Angela participates in the Program for Cooperative Cataloging in support of UCLA's full BIBCO and CONSER membership. In addition to her work with the Electronic Resource Management Initiative, Angela has worked in conjunction with the Digital Collections Management and Licensing Department to support and define the infrastructure needed to manage the vast electronic collection at UCLA.

Nathan D.M. Robertson

Nathan D.M. Robertson is a database programmer/analyst and systems librarian at the Sheridan Libraries of the Johns Hopkins University.

Among many other responsibilities, he is a co-developer and the administrator of the Hopkins Electronic Resource Management System (HERMES). In addition to his work on the DLF Electronic Resource Management Initiative, he is a member of the NISO/EDItEUR Joint Working Party for the Exchange of Serials Subscription Information and is the chair of that group's Coverage Subgroup, working to develop simple and sufficient XML structures for the expression of coverage ranges in ONIX for Serials messages. Robertson is also the current chair of LITA's Standards Interest Group and a member of the Top Technology Trends committee. His research interests include information standards development and the design of information system architectures. He received his M.S.L.S. from the University of North Carolina at Chapel Hill in 1996, and holds a Bachelor of Arts in History from Davidson College.

Foreword

The Digital Library Federation (DLF) is a consortium of thirty-three members and five allied organizations that are pioneering the use of electronic information technologies to extend library collections and services. We pride ourselves on our ability to concentrate the talent of our librarians and technologists on issues of shared importance. The Electronic Resource Management Initiative (ERMI) is one such collaboration and has proved to be a timely and wide-reaching endeavor, finding a ready audience in libraries, systems vendors, and standards organizations.

The problem this initiative addresses is a pervasive one: when libraries acquire licensed electronic resources, they must comprehend, transmit, and inform others about the many financial, legal, and access aspects of these arrangements. The acquisitions and licensing processes are complex—publishers transmit this information to libraries in a variety of paper and electronic formats, and the number of licensed electronic products that libraries are collecting is increasing rapidly. Such situations tend to spawn local, ad hoc fixes. By contrast, the DLF ERMI has created a coordinated solution, developing the common specifications found in this important publication for the management of license agreements, related administrative information, and the internal processes associated with licensed electronic resources.

Even when it was in draft form, response to this work has been swift and gratifying. Major vendors of library systems have been informed by the recommendations of the ERMI report as they design license management capacities into their software suites. The developers of ONIX, the metadata scheme used widely by academic and trade publishers, are looking closely at adopting ERMI as they consider their license expression needs, and the United Kingdom's national serials union catalogue (SUNCAT) is exploring ERMI as it seeks to express and store licenses within this developing national service.

David Seaman
Executive Director
Digital Library Federation

Executive Summary

As libraries have worked to incorporate electronic resources into their collections, services, and operations, most of them have found that their existing integrated library systems (ILSs) are not capable of supporting these new resources. A 2001 study by Jewell[1] determined that a number of libraries had begun developing local systems to overcome these shortcomings. The Digital Library Federation (DLF) Electronic Resource Management Initiative (ERMI) was organized to support the rapid development of such systems by producing a series of interrelated documents to define needs and to help establish data standards.

A National Information Standards Organization (NISO) and DLF workshop in May 2002 led to the creation of a steering group that would guide the development of the ERMI. In addition, the DLF invited librarians, library-system vendors, and representatives of related organizations to serve on two project advisory groups. The steering group shared draft versions of the documents it was developing with members of these two reactor panels. The drafts were also made publicly available via Cornell University's Web Hub for Developing Administrative Metadata for Electronic Resource Management (available from http://www.library.cornell.edu/cts/elicensestudy/).

This publication contains the report and appendixes developed by the steering committee during the course of its work. The report itself is intended to serve as a road map for electronic resource management (ERM). It outlines ERM system needs and discusses and illustrates screens from systems that are already in place at such institutions as the Massachusetts Institute of Technology (MIT), University of California, Los Angeles (UCLA), and the Johns Hopkins University (JHU). Appendix A summarizes in detail some 50 functional requirements of an effective ERM. Appendix B provides a diagram that outlines some differences between workflows for print and electronic resources. This appendix also contains diagrams for more specific phases of the e-resource life cycle.

Appendixes C, D, and E are closely linked. Appendix C is an entity-relationship diagram that illustrates how groups of data elements relate to one another. Appendix D is a data dictionary encompassing more than 300 elements. Appendix E covers data structure, grouping the data elements by entity and keying them to the functional requirements. The concluding XML investigation discusses and compares some existing rights expression languages (RELs). It notes that while it is desirable for libraries, publishers, and vendors to have a standardized, XML-based way to describe key terms of license agreements, no current RELs or schemas seem practical or usable without major modification. To fill this need, the authors propose creation of a *native* ERM schema based on the ERMI data dictionary.

---

[1] Jewell, Timothy D. *Selection and Presentation of Commercially Available Electronic Resources.* Washington, D.C.: Digital Library Federation and Council on Library and Information Resources, 2001. Available at http://www.clir.org/pubs/abstract/pub99abst.html.

The work of the ERMI has been received very favorably by both librarians and vendors, several of whom are already developing systems based in large part on this report and appendixes. Among several areas needing additional work are functional requirements for consortia, specifications for incorporation and reporting of usage data, and further development of data standards.

1. Introduction: The Need for Comprehensive Electronic Resource Management Systems

A few years ago, Cornell University Libraries' strategic plan included the bold and startling prediction of a "mostly digital environment" for that library system by 2005 (Cornell Libraries 2000). Whether or not this prediction proves to be accurate for Cornell or would apply to most other libraries, it is clear from Association of Research Libraries (ARL) expenditure-trend data that spending for electronic resources (e-resources) has been growing much more rapidly than have the materials budgets of which such resources are usually a part. In the 2001–2002 academic year, at least a few ARL libraries were already spending half their materials budgets for e-resources (ARL 2002, 2003). Libraries are in the midst of a profound shift toward reliance on e-resources, and this reliance seems to have deepened within the last year or two as libraries have shed paper journal subscriptions to help pay for online access.

Meanwhile, user behavior and attitudes seem to be changing even more quickly. For example, nearly half of the undergraduates surveyed by Outsell, Inc., for a recent study of the scholarly information environment indicated that they used e-resources either exclusively or almost exclusively (Friedlander 2002). That study also showed that many faculty and graduate students would like to see more journals available to them electronically. However, as many librarians can attest, demand for expanded access to e-resources is only part of the story. Users now compare their libraries' services to such recent innovations as the Google search engine and Amazon.com, and they expect libraries to provide similar levels of simplicity, power, and convenience.

These developments provide the context for what many librarians find to be a daunting and increasingly complex challenge: successfully managing their collections of e-resources. In an earlier study of DLF-member library practices, Jewell (2001) identified some noteworthy trends in how these libraries selected and acquired licensed e-resources and presented information about them to users. Perhaps of greatest importance for the present discussion, most of the responding DLF libraries had found that their existing ILSs were incapable of supporting these functions and had begun to design and build local automated tools to fill the gaps.

One fundamental management problem that some of these systems were meant to address is the need to describe larger and larger numbers of bibliographic databases and to present that information to users. Another challenge lies in the nature and characteristics of some of the new resources. For example, most libraries now spend significant amounts of money on *aggregator* databases. Available from companies such as EBSCO, Gale, LexisNexis, and ProQuest, these databases provide access to the contents or partial contents of large numbers of periodicals. Although such collections often provide substantial benefits, reliably and routinely determining which journals they provide—for what periods of time, in what format, and with what degree of currency or completeness—has been an elusive goal. The growth of electronic journals (e-journals) and databases has heightened this problem while complicating and transforming the processes associated with acquiring and servicing library materials.

The 2001 DLF report cited above noted that users were often presented with special alphabetical or subject lists of e-resources to help meet this descriptive or resource-discovery need. Aggregator databases had become a staple within this group, and many of the libraries had begun to experiment with listing their contents along with subscribed e- journals. Since the research for the DLF report was conducted, companies such as Serials Solutions, TDNet, and EBSCO have begun to offer services aimed at filling these needs, but few ILSs that can fully support or interact with them have become available. In recent years, libraries have also begun linking their indexing and full-text resources through proprietary database vendor solutions and broader, standards-based tools Ex Libris's SFX, thus not only providing greater user convenience but also adding a layer of complexity to the management of e-resources.

Other changes that are much less visible to users have also been taking place. As e-resources have become pervasive, formal license agreements have come to supplement or supersede copyright law as the basis for defining and determining their appropriate use. Despite the welcome and promising appearance of model licenses (Cox 2000; Council on Library and Information Resources 2001) and other efforts to standardize license terms, libraries have been investing substantial time and effort in the review and negotiation of license terms. Local license negotiations may become complex and protracted, involving staff at multiple levels of both licensor and licensee organizations. As a result, some libraries had begun making special efforts to track the status of a particular negotiation, describe its important license terms, and present those terms to users and staff.

At the same time, libraries have been entering into complex, consortium-based purchasing arrangements with other libraries. These arrangements are characterized by ongoing financial commitments and new communication, evaluation, and decision-making processes. Once acquired, these resources must be supported through specialized skills and new kinds of information. Recognizing the complexity of some resources and user expectations for convenience, some libraries have begun to provide instructional and other specialized information directly to their users via their Web sites.

Another defining facet of the new electronic environment revealed in the 2001 DLF study is that large numbers of staff from disparate units of larger libraries had begun playing new and important specialized roles in the selection, support, and evaluation of e-resources. Most of these staff had needs for a wide range of specialized information. For example, staff members in different areas might need to know the status of a given resource within the local acquisition and licensing process. Others might need to know access details, whether access problems related to a particular resource had arisen, and who was involved in what specific troubleshooting activities. Several libraries were also implementing planned, cyclical reviews of their e-resources, and—with that in mind—beginning to systematically gather and report all available information on their use.

2. Current Efforts to Create Electronic Resource Management Systems

Libraries' emerging interest in ERM systems prompted Jewell and Adam Chandler at Cornell to establish in 2001 a Web *hub* to exchange information about local systems and foster communication among interested librarians. As local systems were identified, librarians involved in developing them were systematically asked about their systems' functions and data elements, and the elements were analyzed and summarized in the DLF report previously mentioned (Jewell 2001, p. 26). Seven functional areas were identified: listing and descriptive, license-related, financial and purchasing, process and status, systems and technical, contact and support, and usage. Informal discussions were also begun concerning the value of standardizing functional descriptions, element names, and definitions to support these functions.

Within a year or two, some 20 libraries and vendors had announced that they had produced or were planning to produce such systems (table 1).

Table 1. Library-Based ERM Initiatives

- California Digital Library
- Colorado Alliance (Gold Rush)
- Columbia University
- Griffith University (Australia)
- Harvard University
- Johns Hopkins University (HERMES)
- Massachusetts Institute of Technology (VERA)
- North Carolina State University
- University of Notre Dame
- Pennsylvania State University (ERLIC)
- Stanford University
- University of Texas (License Tracker)
- Tri-College Consortium (Haverford, Bryn Mawr, and Swarthmore)
- University of California, Los Angeles
- University of Georgia
- University of Michigan
- University of Minnesota
- University of Virginia
- Willamette University
- Yale University

Each system developed by a library reflects particular local requirements and development constraints, and many systems exhibit creative and noteworthy features. Rather than provide an exhaustive review of these systems, this discussion focuses on features of just a few of them. Its purpose is to begin to identify elements of an ideal, but achievable, system for managing e-resources.

The Pennsylvania State University (Penn State) Libraries' ERLIC (Electronic Resources Licensing and Information Center), established in 1999, is a good example of a system that was designed to address a fairly limited need but whose functions have been expanded substantially (Penn State Libraries 2001). Developed using Microsoft Access to track the status of orders and to anticipate renewals, ERLIC, and now ERLIC², have evolved into centralized sources of ordering, access, authentication, and licensing information (Stanley et al. 2000; Alan 2002). The MIT Libraries' VERA (Virtual Electronic Resource Access) system was developed about the same time as Penn State's and also exhibits a wide spectrum of functions (Duranceau 2000a; Duranceau 2000b; Hennig 2002). It offers both extensive support for "back-office" staff functions and requirements and numerous noteworthy public Web page-design features. Yale University's schematized treatment and public presentation of license terms serves as an interesting supplement to MIT's approach to the same problem.

Like ERLIC and VERA, UCLA's ERDb system was developed to provide a wide range of functionality. While its functionality and screen designs are of substantial interest and will be explored in the following pages, related working documents (Farb 2002) also articulate useful guidelines that could be generally applied to ERM-system development. Under these guidelines, a system should

- accommodate growth
- design for flexibility
- be offered "one database, but many views"
- avoid unnecessary duplication
- be capable of phased implementation

Similarly broad in scope is JHU's HERMES, which stands for Hopkins Electronic Resource Management System (Cyzyk and Robertson 2003). Based on PostgreSQL and Cold Fusion, HERMES has recently been made available on an open-source basis. While intended to support such functions as the dynamic generation of public Web pages, HERMES is of special interest because of the careful analysis of staff roles, workflows, and associated functional requirements that have gone into it. Also worthy of mention is Gold Rush, developed by the Colorado Alliance of Research Libraries (Stockton and Machovec 2001). Gold Rush was the first commercially available system to incorporate substantial functionality for e-resource subscription management. Reasonably priced and offering support both for individual libraries and library consortia, Gold Rush enables a central consortium administrator to "push" out to member libraries a record with a range of information pertaining to an e-resource.

3. Functions and Examples

3.1. A LIFE CYCLE–BASED OVERVIEW

Records management has been defined as the "systematic control of all organizational records during the various stages of their lifecycle: from their creation or receipt, through their processing, distribution, maintenance and use, to their ultimate disposition" (Robek et al. 1996). Effective management of e-resources depends on the execution of a wide range of functions that follow a slightly different life cycle. For example, while libraries at present generally do not have to deal with the creation of licensed e-resources, they do need to evaluate new products and services, and there are other fairly close parallels between a simplified records management life cycle model and one for e-resources.

Table 2 outlines many of the tasks involved in managing e-resources and the staff who may be involved in different life cycle phases. The table is based on the functions and reports available to staff users of HERMES and largely follows the DLF Electronic Resource Management Initiative (ERMI) workflow sequence (see Appendix B).The column headings refer to five roles that Hopkins staff play in the process: *selector* and *superselector, acquisitions administrator, library computing systems administrator,* and *public display administrator.* Each of these roles is described in the following paragraphs.

1. Product consideration and trial process. At JHU, a selector is responsible for identifying a resource, determining whether a trial is necessary, and gathering preliminary license information. The acquisitions administrator is responsible for negotiating a trial license, if needed. The selector recommends whether to proceed following a trial, which the superselector then approves or disapproves. Additional details, such as trial URLs, passwords, and publicity, are established and recorded during this phase.

2. Acquisition processes. These processes involve three fairly distinct subprocesses that may take place simultaneously. At JHU, the acquisitions administrator is responsible for license negotiation and for entry of related information into HERMES, and the computing services administrator determines technical feasibility and gives or withholds permission to proceed. Remaining tasks, also the responsibility of the acquisitions administrator, relate to funding and purchase.

3. Implementation. During this phase, authentication details are worked out and recorded, any necessary database configuration is performed, and the resource and any appropriate components are cataloged and incorporated into public Web pages. The descriptive tasks during this phase can be difficult and time-consuming, particularly if the resource in question is an e-journal or aggregator package containing large numbers of journals or other content. Public Web page presentations can be provided in a number of ways and, as will be shown later, could include the provision to staff and users of information about licensing terms. It may also be necessary to make the resource known to a link resolver or proxy server.

4. Product maintenance and review. One of the important tasks within this phase is subscription renewal, which can be triggered by date-configurable reminders to staff and could involve price or license-term renegotiation. Another task is maintenance of the holdings, or *coverage*, information encountered during the implementation phase. Additional tasks that could figure in the renewal process include acquiring and making usage data available to staff and identifying and resolving problems relating to access and other technical issues.

Electronic Resource Management: Report of the DLF ERM Initiative

Table 2. Johns Hopkins University's HERMES Selection/Acquisition Tasks, Roles, and Reports

Function/Role	Selector	Superselector	Acquisitions Administrator	Cataloger	Library Computing Services Administrator	Public Display Administrator
1. Product consideration and trial						
Select a resource	•					
Determine if trial required	•					
Gather preliminary license information	•					
Negotiate trial license			•			
Decide to proceed, after trial	•					
Gain approval to proceed		•				
2. Acquisition						
Receive negotiated license and approval to proceed			•			
Insert a new license			•			
Ensure project is technically feasible/Gain approval to proceed					•	
Check funding			•			
Gain approval from purchasing			•			
Generate and send purchase order			•			
Confirm final order			•			
3. Implementation						
Identify items recently imported to HERMES			•			
Identify items awaiting final review and secure approval of catalog records				•		
Hold recently imported items waiting for final review and approval of catalog records				•		
Add resource to public Web pages						•

Electronic Resource Management: Report of the DLF ERM Initiative

Table 2. Continued

Function	Selector	Super-Selector	Acquisitions Administrator	Cataloger	Library Computing Services Administrator	Public Display Administrator
4. Product maintenance and review						
Determine whether license is up for renegotiation			•			
Reset the "days-before" expiration value			•			
Determine whether license is being renegotiated			•			
Gain response from purchasing for renegotiated license			•			
Update an existing license			•			
Attach a new resource to an existing license			•			
Attach an existing resource to an existing license			•			
View possible problem records				•		
5. Administrative functions and reports						
Check status of open items	•					
Reassign open items		•				
Assign budget codes to selectors		•				
Administer budget codes			•			
Administer provider look-up table			•			
Administer vendor look-up table			•			
Administer the subjects module				•		
Administer the Library of Congress/MESH heading mappings				•		
View workflow order	•	•	•	•		
Search e-resources and/or licenses	•	•	•	•		
Run standard reports	•	•	•	•		

3.2. SAMPLES OF ERM SYSTEM AND PUBLIC WEB PAGE SCREENS

3.2.1. Product Consideration and Trial Processes

The preceding life cycle, task, and role inventory may not correspond closely with the screen displays that staff actually see when using ERM systems or their derivatives. For example, the functions listed on table 2 could be reorganized and presented according to staff role—as they are within the HERMES. This underscores the value of one of UCLA's aforementioned design principles: "One database, many views." Another example of multiple views and an alternative organization of similar information is this screen from MIT's VERA (figure 1).

Fig. 1. MIT Libraries' VERA Staff Display Showing Range of Functions

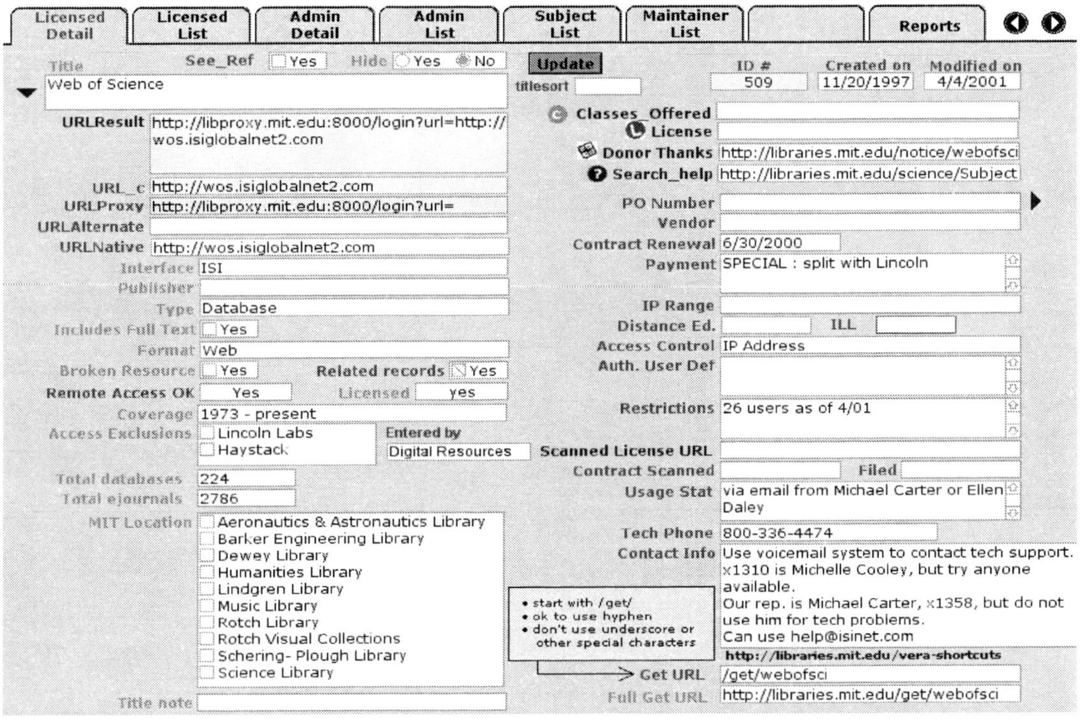

In this view, information from different life cycle phases, such as acquisition (purchase order number and vendor), implementation (URL, location), and product maintenance and review (renewal date, technical support contact, information about usage data) is presented together, presumably because the staff who use this screen need to see it simultaneously.

Figure 2 shows a view from UCLA's ERDb system. Called a Resource Screen, it includes information relevant to multiple e-resource life cycle phases. In addition to basic identifying or descriptive information that will be useful and used throughout the resource life cycle, selection information (e.g., sponsoring unit and selector), as well as acquisitions information (e.g., vendor and purchase order number) can be seen.

Fig. 2. UCLA Resource Screen

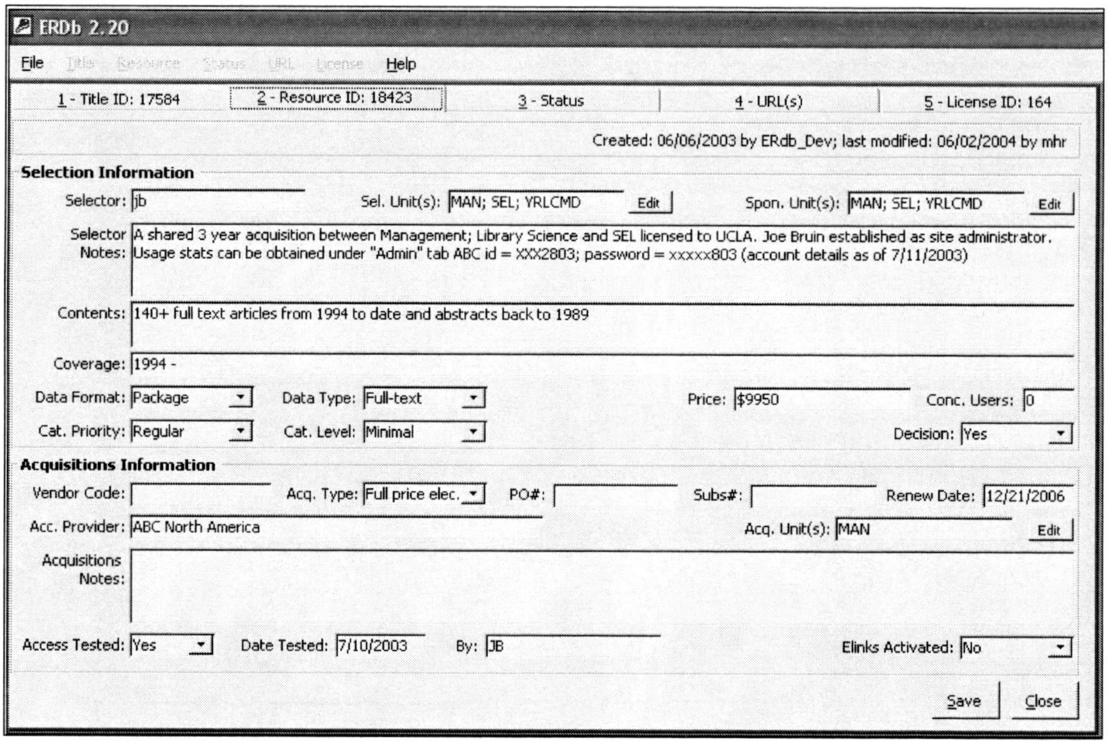

Figure 3 depicts the License Screen, another view of ERDb information related to the same resource. In addition to identifying the *licensor*, or *negotiator*, for UCLA and a link to a redacted version of the relevant license, this screen provides space for a detailed analysis of the specific rights and other details included in the license.

Fig. 3. UCLA License Screen

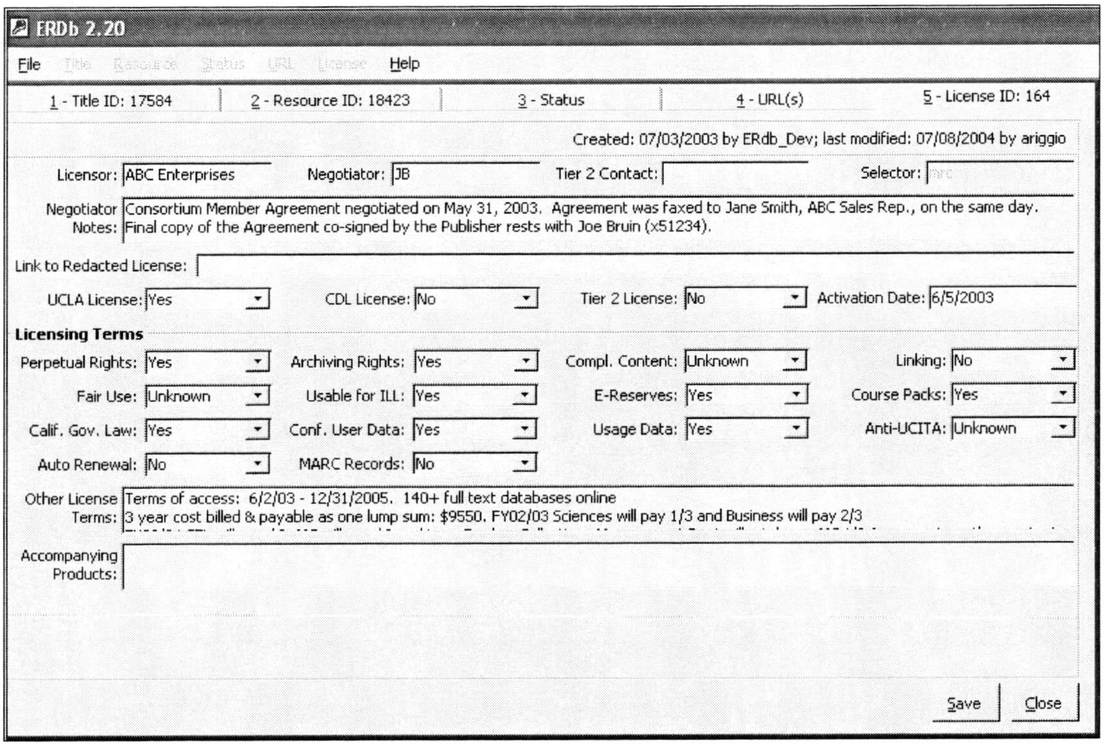

3.2.2. Implementation Processes and Public Web Pages: Alphabetical and Subject Presentations

Libraries commonly present users with multiple routes to licensed resources, including OPAC catalog entries, alphabetical and subject Web page listings, e-reserve links, and links connecting index or abstract entries to the corresponding full text. The mechanisms used to provide these presentations are generally hidden from public view. Figure 4 shows what UCLA users encounter when they follow a link from the library's gateway page to Online Materials.

Fig. 4. UCLA Online Materials Web Page

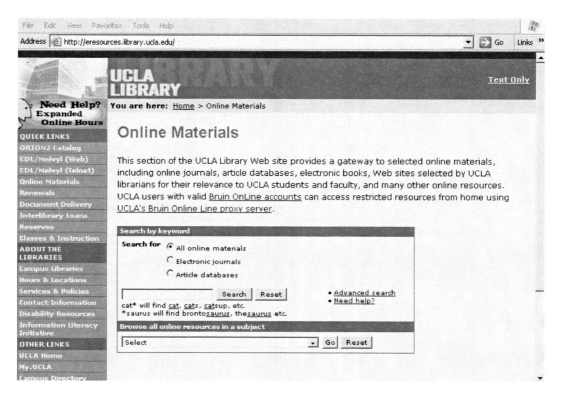

As many other libraries do, UCLA distinguishes between e-journals and article databases. Accordingly, those distinctions need to be made within its database. UCLA's alphabetical and subject presentations (figures 5 and 6, respectively) are similar to those of many other libraries.

Fig. 5. UCLA Online Materials Web Page Title List

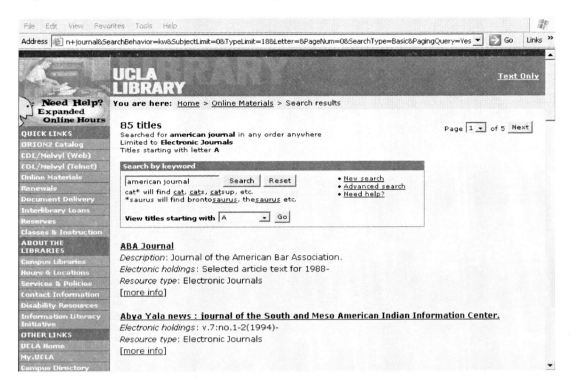

Fig. 6. UCLA Online Materials Web Page Showing Drop-Down Subject List

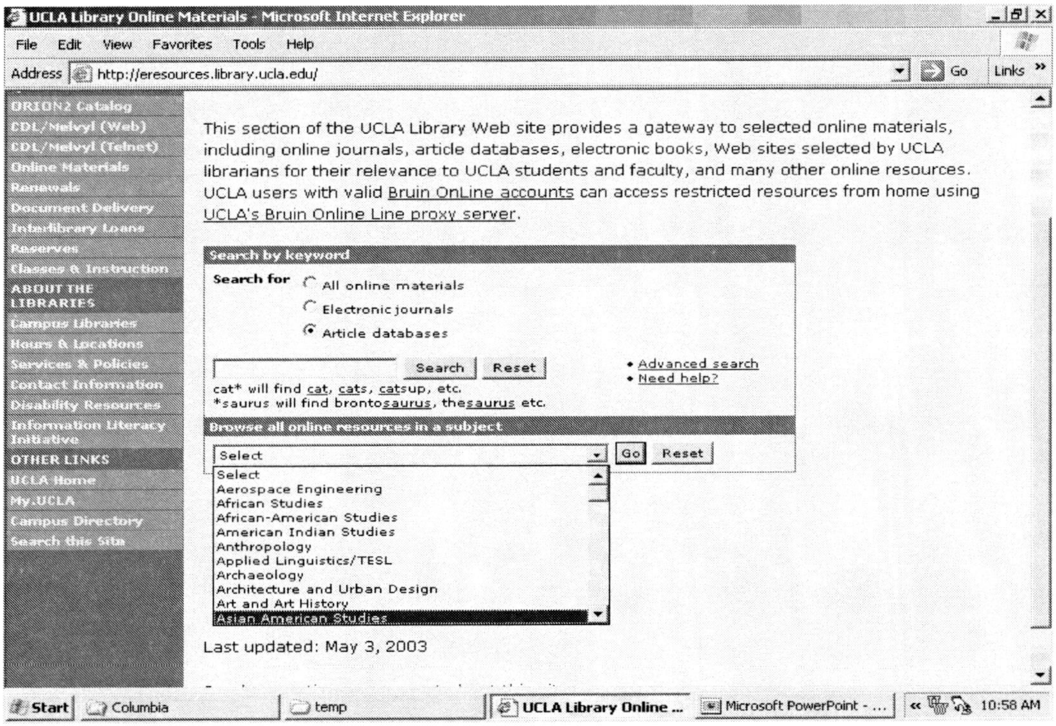

Helping drive and support these presentations is information gathered and maintained via the ERDb Title View (figure 7), such as the basic bibliographic data for the resource. Another view, to be released shortly, relates the component titles of a particular e-journal package to a parent record that is necessary for a number of functions, such as linking license terms to particular titles. The Title View also enables the association of a resource with both Subjects (figure 8) and Types of Resources (figure 9).

Fig. 7. UCLA Title View Screen

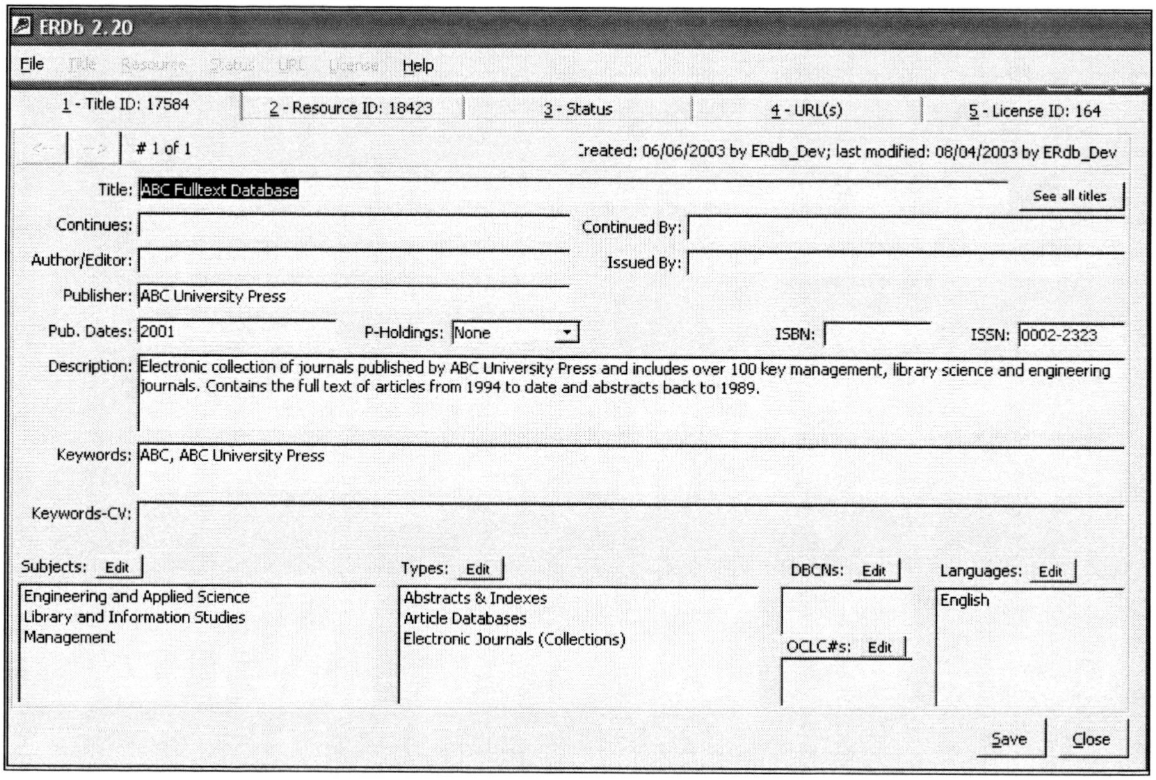

Fig. 8. UCLA Title View Screen, Showing Drop-Down Subject List

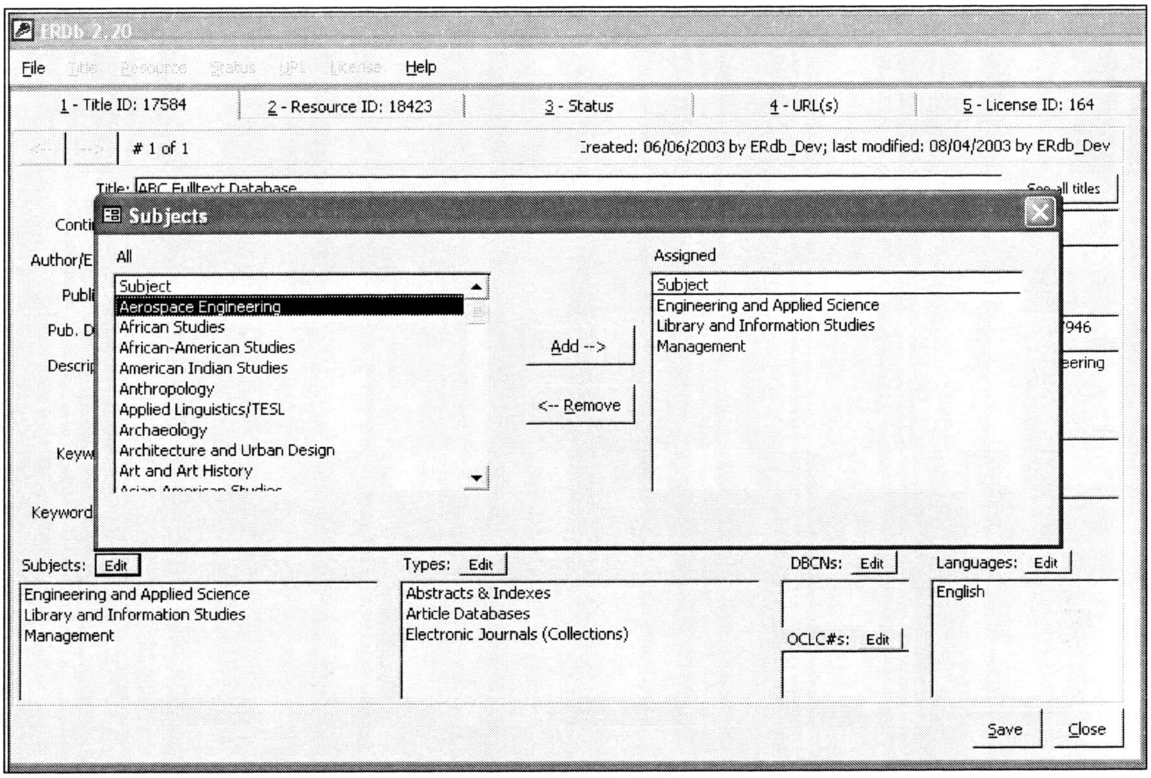

Fig. 9. UCLA Title View Screen, Showing Drop-Down Resource Type List

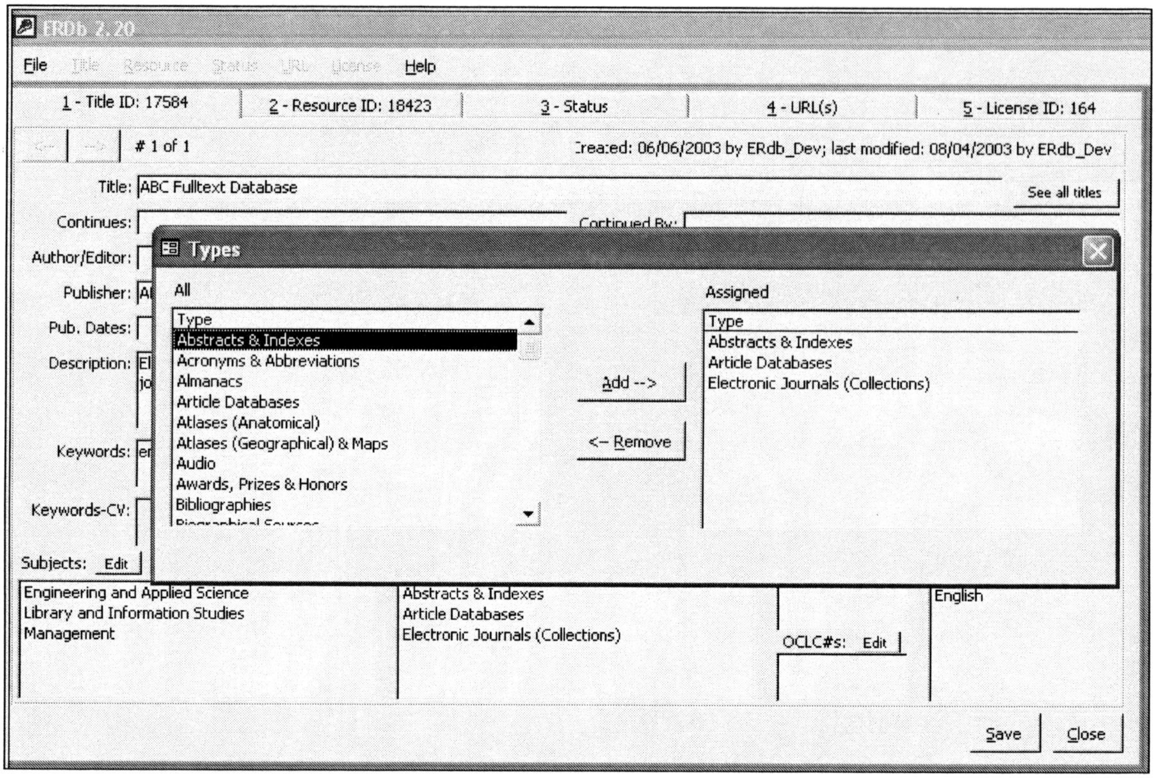

3.2.3. Implementation Processes and Public Web Pages: Extended Information

Like UCLA's ERDb system, MIT's VERA is used to generate subject (figure 10) and alphabetical (figure 11) Web pages for databases and e-journals. VERA is also used to describe e-resource availability by specific location and to manage and generate resource-specific URLs.

Fig. 10. MIT Libraries' VERA Subject Listing of Electronic Resources

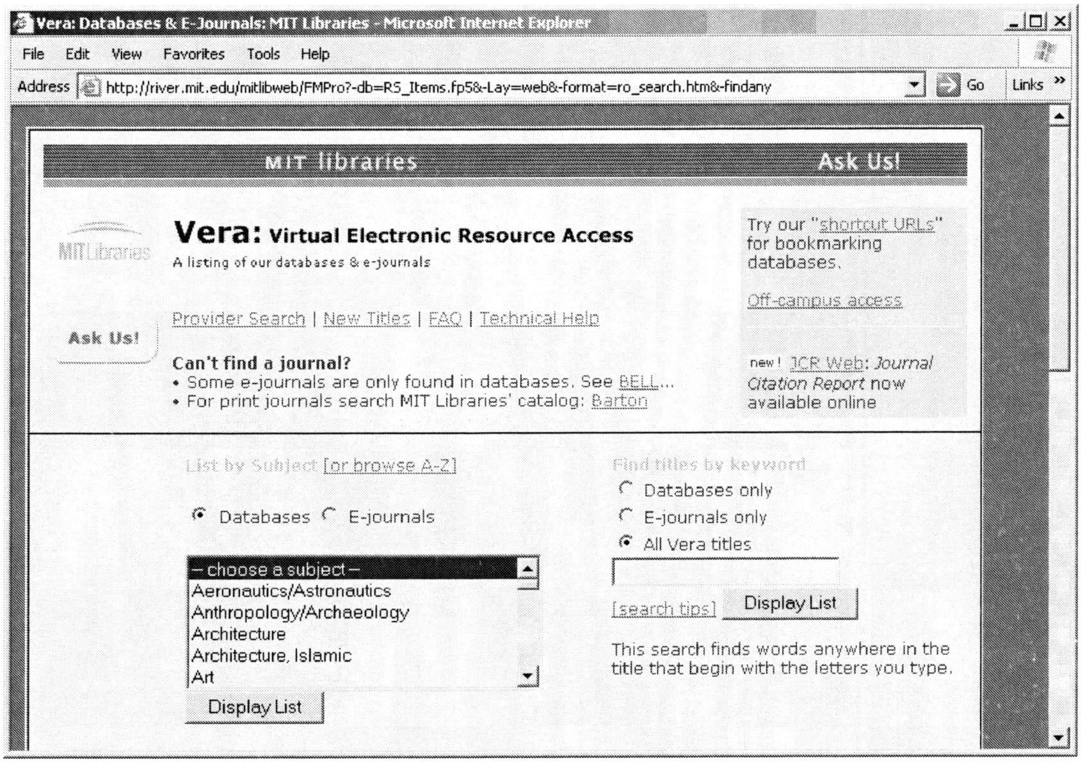

Fig. 11. MIT Libraries' VERA Alphabetical Display Showing E-Resource Details
Provided and Key to More Information

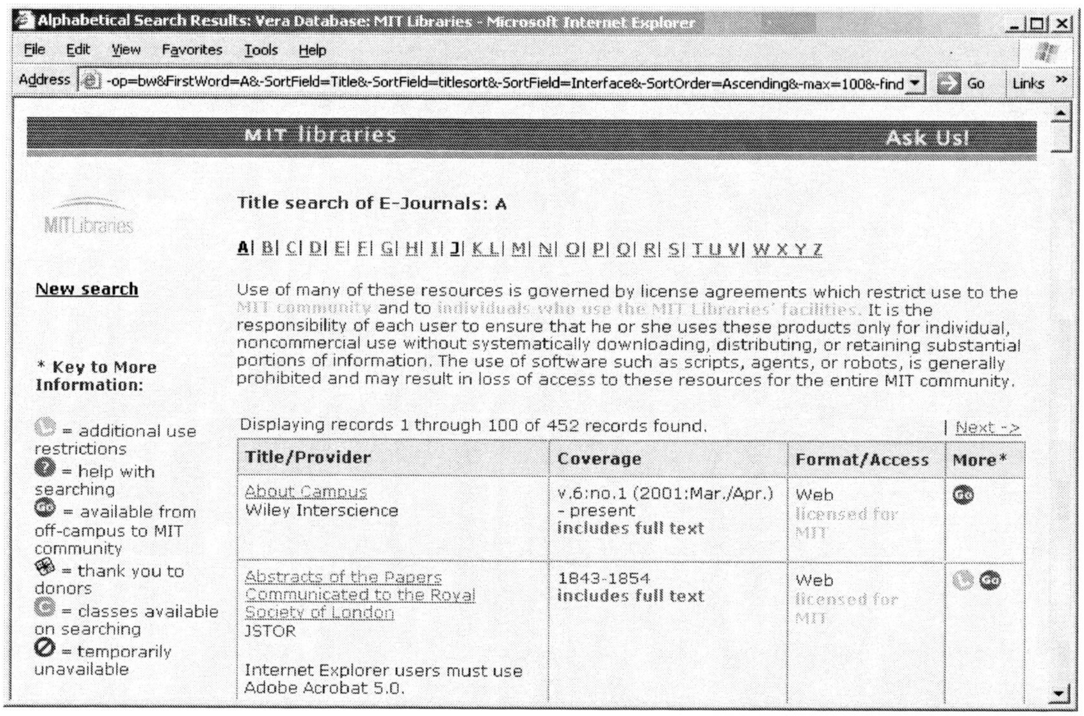

The way in which VERA incorporates and presents a wide range of other information
using special-purpose icons is especially noteworthy (see the lower left corner of fig. 11).
For example, the "Go" button indicates that a resource is available to the MIT community
from off-campus, the "?" icon leads to search tips and other documentation, and the "C"
icon leads to information about upcoming classes on using the specific resource. The
universal "Not" symbol also indicates the existence of resource-specific access problems.
Of even greater interest is the way in which VERA incorporates license information. In
addition to the generic message about appropriate and inappropriate use of resources that
precedes the resource list, the "L" icon indicates when more specific license-related
information is available. For example, figure 11 shows an entry for the Abstracts of the
Papers Communicated to the Royal Society of London—provided by JSTOR. The "L"
icon leads the user to a summary of key provisions of the JSTOR license (fig. 12) that
governs its use.

Fig. 12. MIT Libraries' VERA System: Summary of JSTOR Use Restrictions

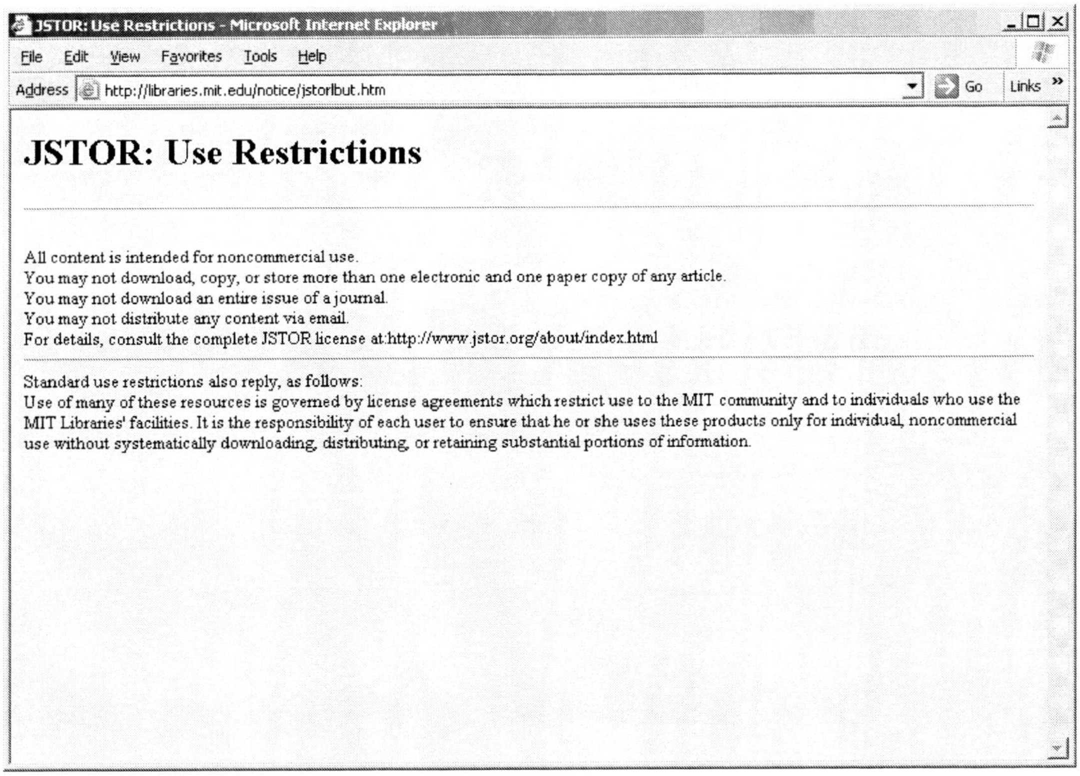

Yale University Library's public e-resource pages also integrate instructional and licensing information in clear and understandable ways. For example, figure 13 shows an alphabetical listing of databases in the social sciences, including Academic Universe.

Fig. 13. Yale University Library's Social Science E-Resource Subject List Showing
Entry for Academic Universe

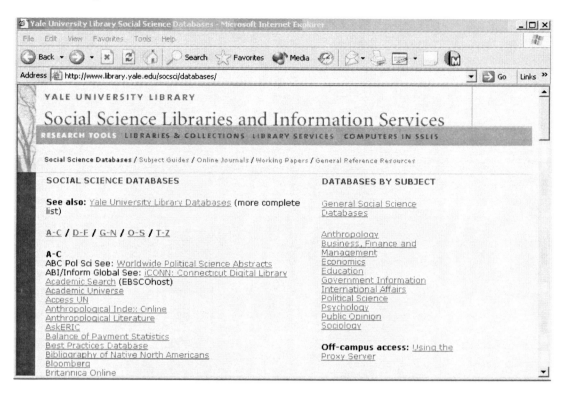

When users click on the Academic Universe entry, they are taken to the display of additional information shown in figure 14, which includes a group of Help tools as well as a link to Permitted Uses of Databases.

Fig. 14. Yale University Library's E-Resource List Entry for LexisNexis Academic Universe

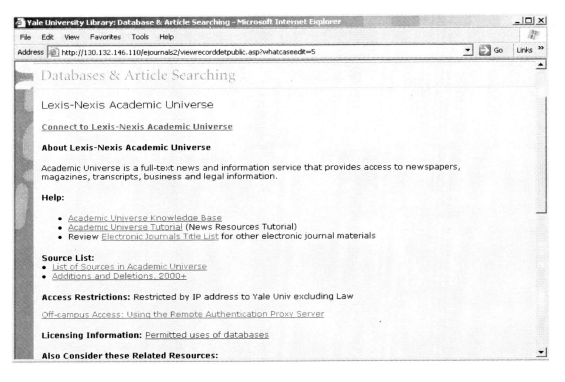

The Permitted Uses of Databases link takes users to the appropriate section of a lengthy document summarizing permitted uses for many or most of the library's licensed resources (fig. 15).

Fig. 15. Yale University Library's License Information Summary for
LexisNexis Academic Universe

Lexis Nexis Academic & Library Services
    Academic UNIVerse
    Congressional Universe
    Statistical Universe

Licensing Information

Yes	Copy	
Yes	Download	
No	ILL	
No	ILL (Partial)	General Terms and Conditions for Use of the Lexis-Nexis Services
Yes	Limited sharing for scholarly purposes	
Yes	Course & Reserve Packs	
Yes	Print	
Yes	Use by Walk-ins	For educational use only; May not actively promote walk-in use.

This presentation is noteworthy for at least three reasons. First, the resources' licenses have been analyzed to determine their provisions in eight key areas, with a simple "yes" or "no" indicating whether or not a particular use is permitted. Second, the summary grid provides space to expand where needed on any of the key terms. Third, the presentation allows for a link to the full Terms and Conditions. In this case, the link takes users to the LexisNexis Web page (fig. 16), but it could just as easily take them to a locally digitized version of an institution-specific license.

Fig. 16. LexisNexis Academic Terms and Conditions page (linked to from Yale
      University Library's Academic Universe License Information Summary Page)

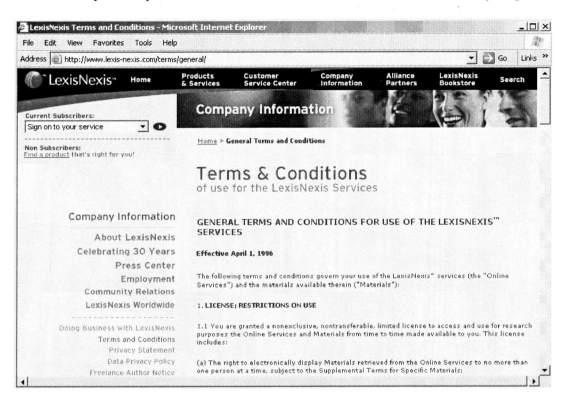

An interesting contrast to the MIT and Yale license-information presentations is provided
by the simple Terms of Use section from the Colorado Alliance's Gold Rush Staff
Toolbox (fig. 17). Whereas MIT's and Yale's summaries are designed for use by those
library systems alone, Gold Rush can provide summary license terms to all libraries
sharing the system and particular resources.

Fig. 17. Terms of Use Area from Colorado Alliance's Gold Rush Staff Toolbox

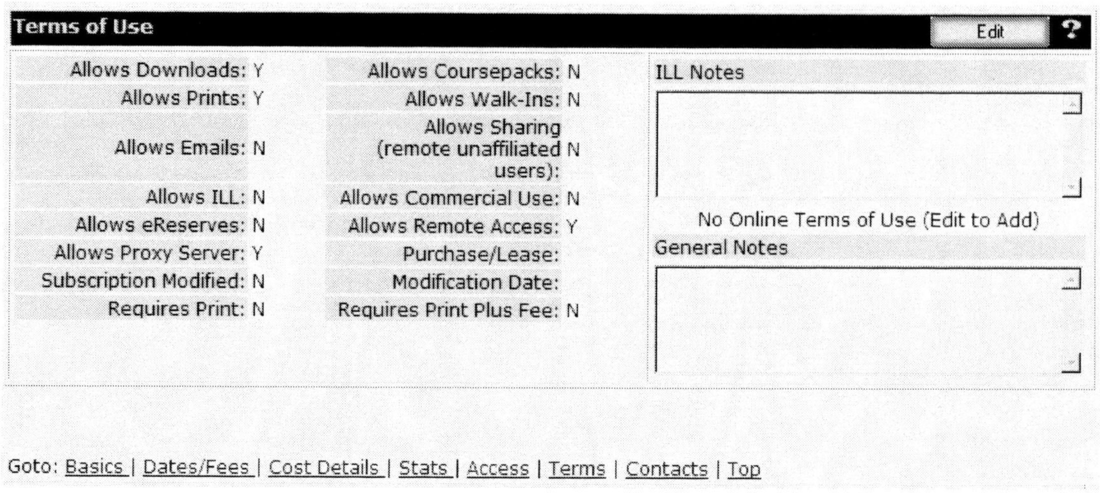

3.2.4. Product Maintenance and Review

Once access to a product has been established and its availability made known to staff and users, any number of problems may arise. For example, a vendor or another information provider may need to take a product offline for brief or extended periods for planned maintenance or to correct unanticipated technical difficulties. Occasionally, vendor files of a subscriber's IP addresses may fail to reflect recent changes or become corrupted, and this will affect access to subscribed services. Delays in product invoicing and payment may lead to outages, especially at the beginning of a month. These problems may manifest themselves in a variety of ways, such as prompts for usernames and passwords or other messages that may be difficult to understand. Still more vexing may be that an access problem related to a particular publisher's package of e- journals or an aggregator service can affect all its component journals—entries for which may be dispersed through an online catalog or Web list of journals available online.

When any of these circumstances arise, it may be difficult or impossible for a library to effectively manage communication with staff and affected users. One promising approach to staff communication is shown in figure 18, which depicts a Status screen from UCLA's ERDb system. The upper half of this screen displays basic information about the resource in question, while the lower half provides space to record information about a reported incident, such as a user's name, IP address, Internet service provider, and browser; a description of the problem; the action required; and the present status of the problem.

Fig. 18. UCLA Library's Status Screen

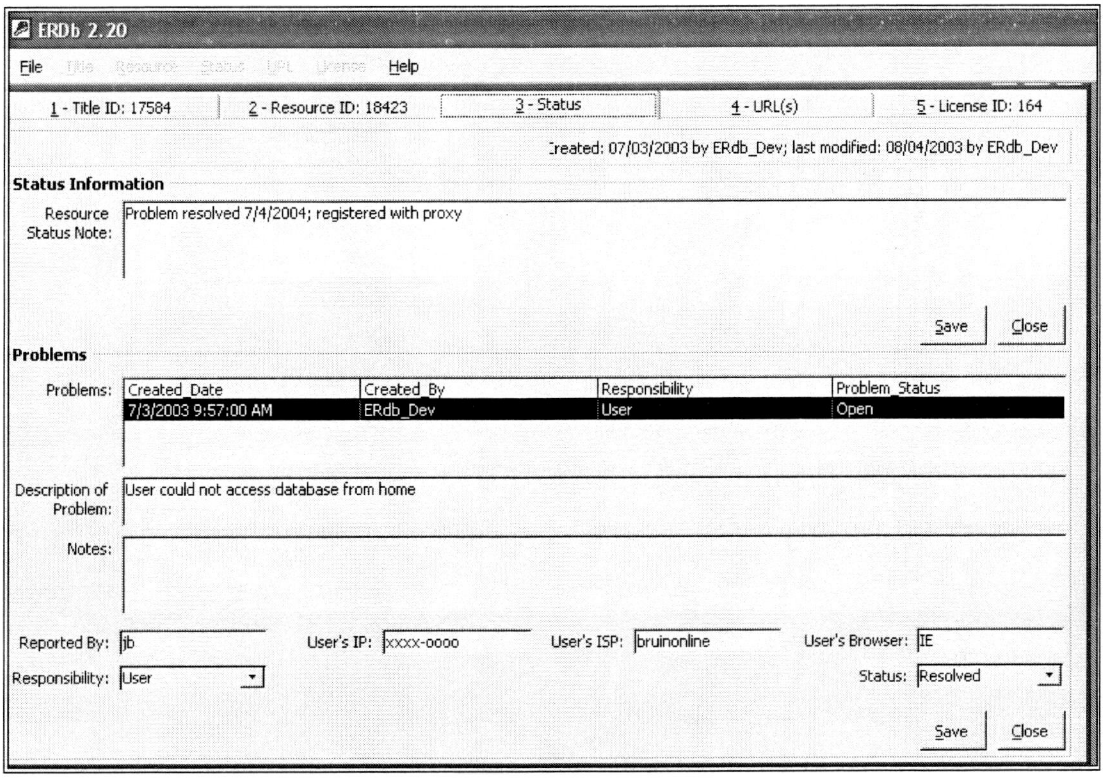

Another approach to communicating problems such as some of those mentioned above is shown in figure 19, which is a mock-up of a Billboard function envisioned for Penn State's ERLIC[2]. This feature would allow users or staff to quickly identify any resources to which access was likely to be a problem at a particular time.

Fig. 19. Penn State University Libraries ERLIC^2 System Prototype of E-Resource
   Billboard Function

Electronic Resources Licensing & Information Center (ERLIC²)

Today's Billboard:

5/28/02	Elsevier	Access (V)	Access problem with selected Elsevier titles; Serials Dept working to resolve
5/27/02	ERDS	Trial	New Database Trial "ERDS"
5/26/02	E-Journal List	Access (L)	ITECH working on Cold Fusion Server problem; e-journal list not working **more...**

4. The DLF ERM Initiative

4.1. BACKGROUND: EVOLUTION AND ORGANIZATION OF THE PROJECT

The project that eventually became the DLF ERMI began with the Web hub developed by Jewell and Chandler. At the time the hub was created, the ALCTS Technical Services Directors of Large Research Libraries Discussion Group developed an interest in ERM and agreed to sponsor an informal meeting on the topic at the June 2001 American Library Association (ALA) annual conference. That meeting attracted some 40 librarians and led to further discussions of functions and data elements. Shortly thereafter, an informal steering group was formed that included Jewell, Chandler, Sharon Farb and Angela Riggio from UCLA, Nathan Robertson from JHU, Ivy Anderson from Harvard, and Kimberly Parker from Yale. This group worked with Patricia Harris and Priscilla Caplan at NISO and Daniel Greenstein (then at the DLF). These individuals undertook discussions of possible standards that ultimately led to the presentation of a NISO/DLF Workshop on Standards for Electronic Resource Management in May 2002. The workshop was attended by approximately 50 librarians and representatives from a number of vendors and publishers, including EBSCO, Endeavor, Ex Libris, Fretwell-Downing, Innovative Interfaces, SIRSI, and Serials Solutions.

At the workshop, in addition to presentations and discussions concerning the nature and extent of ERM, a proposed entity relationship diagram (ERD) and several lists of data elements were presented and discussed. One important outcome of this meeting was the formation of a consensus that standards to help guide the development of ERM systems were indeed desirable. This affirmation led the workshop steering group to consider a more formal, collaborative approach to the establishment of related best practices and standards. Such an effort, the steering group members maintained, might reduce unnecessary costs and duplication at the institutional level, support interoperability and data sharing among diverse systems and organizations, and provide extended benefits to the wider library community.

Accordingly, the steering group developed and submitted to the DLF a proposal for an ERMI. The aim of this project was to formalize and provide further shape and direction for efforts that had previously been very informal and ad hoc. Its primary goal was to foster the rapid development of systems and tools for managing e-resources—whether by individual libraries, consortia, or vendors—and, more specifically, to

- describe the functions and architectures needed to enable systems to effectively manage large collections of licensed e-resources;

- establish lists of appropriate supporting data elements and common definitions;

- write and publish experimental XML Schemas/DTDs for local testing;

- identify and promote appropriate best practices; and

- identify and promote appropriate standards to support data interchange.

The DLF accepted the proposal in October 2002. The seven librarians who organized the May 2002 NISO/DLF workshop became the steering group for the new initiative. The steering group's task has been to continue the efforts already begun and produce the documents, or deliverables, described below.

The steering group held weekly conference calls for two years. In addition, to provide for ongoing expert advice, two reactor panels, or advisory groups, were formed. One panel (table 3) consisted of librarians deemed specially qualified by their experience and interest in ERM systems to provide the kinds of feedback needed.

Table 3. DLF ERMI Librarian Reactor Panel

- Bob Alan (Penn State)
- Angela Carreno (New York University)
- Trisha Davis (Ohio State University)
- Ellen Duranceau (MIT)
- Christa Easton (Stanford University)
- Laine Farley (California Digital Library)
- Diane Grover (University of Washington)
- Nancy Hoebelheinreich (Stanford University)
- Norm Medeiros (Haverford College)
- Linda Miller (Library of Congress)
- Jim Mouw (University of Chicago)
- Andrew Pace (North Carolina State University)
- Ronda Rowe (University of Texas)
- Jim Stemper (University of Minnesota)
- Paula Watson (University of Illinois)
- Robin Wendler (Harvard University)

Members of the steering group and the librarian reactor panel communicated in a number of ways. First, several members of the panel and of the steering group attended a special meeting held in conjunction with the DLF Spring 2003 Forum in New York City. Steering group members established a groupware site at UCLA using Microsoft's SharePoint software. This facilitated sharing of draft documents, task lists, and information on upcoming meetings and deadlines. The site was also used to post questions for the panel members and to provide space for responses and replies. Since not all members of the reactor panel were able to use the SharePoint site, questions and responses were also distributed via e-mail. As needed, the steering group invited panel members who posted comments and questions to participate in the conference calls. The steering group members found that the discussions and feedback substantially enhanced their understanding of the problem, and many comments and questions led to refinements of the deliverables.

The second panel, the vendor reactor panel, consisted of representatives from a range of other organizations with interests in the problems to be addressed by the initiative. This group comprised representatives from a number of integrated ILS providers and other companies serving the library market (table 4).

Table 4. DLF ERMI Vendor Reactor Panel

- Tina Feick (SWETS Blackwell)
- Ted Fons (Innovative Interfaces, Inc.)
- David Fritsch (TDNet)
- Kathy Klemperer (Harrassowitz)
- George Machovec (Colorado Alliance)
- Mark Needleman (SIRSI)
- Oliver Pesch (EBSCO)
- Chris Pierard (Serials Solutions)
- Kathleen Quinton (OCLC Online Computer Library Center, Inc.)
- Sara Randall (Endeavor)
- Ed Riding (Dynix)
- Jenny Walker (Ex Libris)

Communication patterns between the steering group and the vendor panel differed from those used with the librarian panel. While the vendor group was provided with versions of the draft documents and the questions being posted to the librarians, there was relatively little further communication about those documents at the time. Nevertheless, many of the companies represented on the vendor panel have continued to express strong interest in the project. ILS vendors have been especially responsive. Many discussions have involved steering group members. For instance, Innovative Interfaces, Inc. (III) has pursued development of an ERM module since spring 2002. Tim Jewell has been involved in related discussions and has kept the company informed of ongoing work on data elements (see below) so that III's elements could be as consistent with them as possible. Ex Libris has also performed substantial analytical work preparatory to product development; Ivy Anderson has contributed heavily to those efforts, especially to the statement of functional requirements that has helped guide it. More recently, Dynix held predevelopment meetings in which Nathan Robertson was involved, and the company has now developed an internal white paper describing the architecture of a future system that references the steering group's work.

4.2. PROJECT DELIVERABLES AND USE SCENARIOS

The ERMI has developed and made available a number of deliverables. An overarching goal has been to control costs and save time by providing a series of interrelated documents on which libraries and vendors could base their efforts. It was expected that the documents might be put to a variety of other uses as well. The documents and some of their anticipated uses are as follows:

- Problem Definition and Road Map. The purpose of the road map was to offer an overview of the ERM problem, provide examples of the creative approaches some libraries have taken to solving it, and highlight problems needing resolution.

- Workflow Diagram. Devising a detailed but generic workflow diagram was expected to help the steering group understand work processes and thereby help ensure that other documents would be developed appropriately and completely. A workflow diagram could provide a reference point for analyzing local workflows, which could lead to improved internal communication and more streamlined processes.

- Functional Specifications. This document was intended to clearly and comprehensively identify the functions that an ERM system would serve. Libraries could use it to support discussions of the features they might wish to purchase or incorporate into a locally developed ERM system or use the specifications in a draft request for proposals from vendors.

- Entity Relationship Diagram. An ERD is a standard system-development tool that can help designers conceptualize and present groups of data elements, or entities, and their interrelationships. As noted earlier, a draft ERD was presented during the DLF/NISO workshop, and a revised version was expected to help clarify discussions during the initiative and to assist future system designers.

- Data Elements and Definitions. Providing a standardized list of entities and data elements was projected to save developers substantial time. Such a list could also be helpful in the development of data standards. Draft lists of data elements were discussed at the NISO/DLF workshop, and it was intended that the final, single list would be keyed to, and organized to reflect, the ERD. To invoke a naturalistic comparison, the ERD (as a sketch of a whole system), could be likened to a tree, while the data elements could be compared to its leaves.

- XML Schema. The XML schema was intended to extend the value of a standardized list of entities and elements by providing a means for exchanging data. Such a schema could provide partners a platform upon which to test the sharing of license information across different systems while giving an additional boost to local library and vendor development efforts.

- Final Report. A final report would integrate these documents and present them as a whole.

The importance and potential value of standards to ERM systems is fundamental. A primary motivation for establishing standards in this case is to lessen vendor development costs and risks and thereby accelerate the development process. In addition, although it is conceivable that ERM systems might be developed and marketed as standalone systems, it seems likely that they will need to be overlaid on or otherwise linked to existing tools, such as serials or acquisitions systems, online catalogs, and e-resource gateways (Warner 2003). It is therefore critical to establish predictable pathways among variant data streams. Libraries that have developed their own systems or that wish to do so in the short term, might hope ultimately to transfer their data to a vendor system. If agreement on standards could be reached, those libraries could develop, modify, or align their systems with the standards, thus paving the way toward data and system migration. Finally, it is conceivable that, provided they had standard ways of doing so, libraries could exchange license information with trading partners or create systems that would describe the availability of specific e-resources for specified uses such as interlibrary loan.

These considerations led the steering group to survey and monitor the status and development of standards that might dovetail with or otherwise have relevance for its work. Farb and Riggio (2004) summarized the results of that investigation as follows:

> Increasingly, we are learning about new metadata schemata, structures, and standards designed to address various communities and constituencies. To date, however, none exist that address the dynamic, multidimensional, and legal aspects of acquiring and managing licensed e-resources over time.

Table 5 provides a rough mapping of the planned DLF ERMI metadata schema coverage against several others designed to address specific aspects of ERM. The first seven column labels indicate general functional areas that need to be addressed by standards, and the right-hand column shows whether or not a particular effort is proprietary, which the steering group regarded as an important determinant of potential value to libraries and other interested parties. The row labeled "DLF ERMI" indicates the steering group's assessment that its work addressed all seven functional areas in a significant way, although attention to the "Usage" category was less extensive than for the others. While related standards efforts are shown as having focused on fewer areas—such as identification and description—it should not be assumed that the steering group expected its work to take the place of other efforts. Instead, the intent was to identify areas of common interest and avoid duplication of effort.

Table 5. Metadata Standards Comparison: E-Resource Management

Metadata Standards Comparison: E-Resource Management								
	ID/ Description	Acquisition	Licensing	Access/ Trouble	Usage	Preservation	Authenti- cation	Non- Proprietary
DLF ERMI	●	●	●	●	○	●	●	●
Dublin Core	●	○	○					●
A-Core	●						●	●
ONIX	●	○	○					●
ONIX for Serials	●	●						●
<indecs>	●	●	●					●
METS	●		●	●		●		●
COUNTER	●		○		●		○	●
Shibboleth							●	●
ODRL	○	○	●	●				●
XrML	○	○	●					

- ● Substantial coverage
- ○ Some coverage

4.3. PROJECT RESULTS

This section reviews what has been learned in the process of developing the various ERMI documents and the results of the XML investigation. The documents themselves may be found in the appendixes.

4.3.1. Functional Requirements (Appendix A)

In spring 2003, staff from Harvard's and MIT's libraries met with staff from Ex Libris to discuss possible work on an ERM tool. While lists of likely data elements were available and discussed, attention quickly turned to the question "But what is the functionality?" To answer that question, Harvard and MIT libraries' staff, led by steering group member Ivy Anderson and MIT's Ellen Duranceau, collaborated to write a description of the functionality needed in an ERM system. This document was subsequently broadened for use as a DLF ERMI deliverable.

The functional requirements identify and describe the functions needed to support e-resources throughout their life cycles, including selection and acquisition, access provision, resource administration, staff and end-user support, and renewal and retention decisions. The requirements are based on the following guiding principles:

• Print and e-resource management and access should be through an integrated environment.

• Information provided should be consistent, regardless of the path taken.

• Each data element should have a single point of maintenance.

• ERM systems should be sufficiently flexible to make it possible to easily add new or additional fields and data elements.

In addition, a few core requirements for ERM systems were identified. For example, systems should be able to represent the relationships among individual e-resources, packages, licenses, and online interfaces; associate the characteristics of a given license, interface, or package with the resources to which it applies; and provide robust reporting and data-export capabilities.

This document encompasses 47 requirements, more than half of which discuss functionality needed to support staff. The scope of the requirements can be seen from the following category summary.

• General (4 requirements). These include the three core requirements in more precise language, and state that "security features to control staff views and maintenance rights" are also required.

- Resource Discovery (7 requirements). These requirements address the need for making resources available through, or pass information about them to, OPACs and Web presentation services and for contextual presentation of license information at the point of access.

- Bibliographic Management (2 requirements). These address the need for a single point of data entry, maintenance for bibliographic information, and the ability to import aggregator holdings and subscription-management data.

- Access Management (5 requirements). This group covers the management of basic access-related information such as Uniform Resource Identifiers (URIs), User IDs and passwords, and lists of institutional IP addresses, as well as the requirement to interoperate with or submit data to related technical systems such as proxy servers and persistent naming services.

- Staff Requirements (29 requirements)

  - General Interface Requirements (4 requirements). The staff interface should be organized into views that are optimized for particular areas of staff activity or interest such as resource acquisition, troubleshooting, license administration, or administration and statistics.

  - Selection and Evaluation Processes (9 requirements). An ERM system should support the recording of actions and other information at various steps in what may be decentralized processes. It also must have the capability to perform specified actions or to send alerts in defined circumstances. The library should be able to customize actions and triggers to support a site-specific workflow.

  - Resource Administration and Management (11 requirements). This group describes functionality related to administrative user names and passwords, local configuration options, hardware and software requirements, problem-solving and troubleshooting support, the ability to flag resources as unavailable, and the ability to store information about usage data.

  - Business Functions (5 requirements). This group covers pricing models, cancellation restrictions, renewal and termination activities, and cost-sharing and consortial-relationship information.

To help make the functional requirements as universally applicable as possible, the steering group reviewed and discussed them with members of the librarian reactor panel, who were asked to distinguish between the requirements they saw as core or essential, and those that were not. The steering group found it gratifying (although vendors may find it dismaying) that every requirement was considered core by at least one member of the reactor group. Nevertheless, it is possible to identify some of the functions that this group viewed as most critical.

One of the most important requirements was the ability to manage the relationships among bibliographic entities (i.e., individual titles) and the packages, licenses, and interfaces through which they are made available. Another important requirement was the ability to store access-related information such as URLs, user IDs and passwords, and institutional IP addresses. The ability to record authorized-user categories and other license permissions, restrictions, and metadata about the agreement itself was viewed as equally important. Not surprisingly, the ability to store license permissions and associated metadata was one of the most frequently cited requirements, and the ability to link to an online version of a redacted license was also desired by most panelists. Offering a single point of maintenance for bibliographic and other descriptive data and facilitating electronic transfer of holdings and other subscription data from external providers were also identified as essential, as was supporting institutional workflows via customized routing and notification tools.

Other core or essential features included the ability to store information about administrative IDs and passwords and information about and access to usage statistics.

The following themes also emerged in the reactor panel discussions:

- Most libraries want to be able to use their existing ILSs for core acquisitions functions such as ordering, budgeting, and fund accounting. However, these systems must be enhanced to accommodate the additional functionality required by e-resources. If ERM is implemented in a stand-alone application, libraries will generally choose to continue to perform core acquisitions activities in their ILSs but may want to export some data to the ERM system for analysis and reporting.

- The relationship of the descriptive data in an ERM system to other descriptive systems such as the OPAC, federated search tools, and link resolution services is a matter of concern for many libraries. All agreed that minimizing duplicative data and enabling these systems to "talk to" one another was important. As one reactor said, the OPAC should be recognized as the home of MARC bibliographic data.

- Usage statistics are an increasing focus of interest for many libraries. In addition to relying on vendor-provided usage data, many libraries collect such data locally. The steering group asked the panel members whether an ERM system should store usage data or merely point users to external data sources. Although most respondents found pointers to be adequate, a number felt that a common framework for storing and presenting statistics from disparate sources should be provided.

- Many large libraries use persistent URIs. Support for them can be critical to the library's operation. In general, libraries that assign persistent URIs want to be able to record them in the ERM system. Many agreed that being able to generate persistent URIs was both desirable and feasible since the algorithms by which they are assigned tend to be highly formulaic.

4.3.2. Workflow Diagram (Appendix B)

The purpose of the workflow diagram was to provide a detailed overview of the activities associated with managing the life cycle of electronic products (e-products). A starting point was the realization that while there are some similarities between the acquisition and management processes for traditional, physical library materials and those for e-products, many issues are unique to e-products.

Some of these differences are obvious from the overview flowcharts in Appendix B. For example, e-products routinely require a licensing process and may pose technological challenges for implementation. Activities associated with acquiring and activating a networked product are substantially different from those associated with the receipt and processing procedures for physical items. Maintenance, troubleshooting, and license renewal for e-products are quite unlike the circulation, physical storage, and repair issues for physical objects.

The flowchart for the project, developed primarily by Kimberly Parker and Nathan Robertson, reflects these complex realities by breaking down a model workflow into the four main subprocesses identified for HERMES in section 3.1. Each subprocess is depicted through its own diagram. The first subprocess, Product Consideration and Trial Processes, traces typical steps from the point at which library staff become aware of the availability of an e-resource of interest, through trial and evaluation steps, to the "Proceed/Don't proceed" decision point. A decision to proceed would trigger three other processes shown in the diagram (since they typically occur concurrently)—License Negotiation, Technical Evaluation, and Business Negotiation.

Once all these processes reach the "approval to proceed" point, the third major set of processes is triggered. These are labeled Implementation Processes and encompass such disparate steps as product registration and configuration, cataloging and inclusion in appropriate Web pages, and activities related to availability and handling of usage data. The final set of processes is Product Maintenance and Review. Among the functions included in the routine maintenance category are the capture of usage statistics, troubleshooting and problem resolution, routine product changes from the vendor (e.g., URL revisions), and revisions to public documentation.

4.3.3. Data Entities, Elements, and Structure (Appendixes C, D, and E)

Three of the deliverables are tied especially closely to one another: the ERD, the data element dictionary, and the data structure. The ERD is a visual representation of ERM concepts and the relationships between them. The data element dictionary identifies and defines the individual data elements that an ERM system must contain and manage, but leaves the relationship between the elements to be inferred by the reader. The data structure associates each data element with the entities and relationships defined in the ERD. Together, the three documents form a complete conceptual data model for ERM.

An ERD is often used as a way to visualize a relational database. Each entity represents a database table, and relationship lines represent the keys in one table that point to specific records in related tables. ERDs may also be more abstract, not necessarily capturing every table needed within a database but simply diagramming the major concepts and relationships. The ERD developed for the ERMI is of the latter type. It is intended to present an abstract, theoretical view of the major entities and relationships needed for management of e-resources, but does not identify every table that would be necessary for an ERM database.

The data element dictionary, which now includes roughly 300 elements, grew out of a data dictionary developed for UCLA's ERDb. It lists the elements alphabetically by data element name and includes an identifier, definition, and, where deemed necessary, comments. To the extent possible, element naming and definitions were based on guidelines provided by International Standards Office (ISO) 11179. In addition, an effort was made to identify and use element names already included in other relevant metadata schemas such as Dublin Core, ONIX, ONIX for Serials, and METS. A more detailed discussion of these standards and schemas and of how the work of the initiative relates to them is provided in Appendix F.

The data structure document integrates the ERD and the data element dictionary by mapping the data elements from the dictionary to the approximately two dozen entities depicted in the ERD. In addition to the names and definitions, the data structure indicates element type (e.g., logical, pointer, text), use or functionality (including references to specific points in the functional requirements document), suggested values, optionality (whether optional or mandatory), repeatability (whether the element carries a unique value or can be repeated), and selected notes or examples for additional clarity.

Some of the two dozen defined entities, such as the entities for Electronic Resource and for Interface, could be characterized as serving a primarily descriptive function. A large number of data elements are required to summarize license terms. For example, a Terms Defined entity includes groups for identification, user group, and terms of use—which itself contains some 30 elements covering such license provisions as fair use, scholarly sharing, interlibrary loan, and course packs.

There are also entities for Acquisition and Processing Workflow, and for Access Information and Administrative Information. Some entities can be used for a variety of purposes. For example, the Organization entity can be used to record information about any business, vendor, provider, publisher, licensor, etc., with which a library does business related to e-products.

Since the elements identified, named, and defined for this part of the project were seen as possibly forming the core for an emerging data exchange standard, the lists have been available via the Web hub for some time. Communication with two ILS vendors (Innovative Interfaces and Ex Libris) that have been actively working on ERM systems has been especially close, and both have undertaken substantial work to see that their data elements are consistent with those of the initiative.

4.3.4. XML Investigation (Appendix F)

The final proposed deliverable was an XML schema that would foster the development of metadata standards for the exchange of information about e-resources, e-resource packages, and licenses. During fall 2003, a group was formed to pursue this work. Coordinated by Adam Chandler, it included fellow steering group members Sharon Farb, Angela Riggio, and Nathan Robertson, plus Robin Wendler (Harvard), Nancy Hoebelheinrich (Stanford), and Simon St. Laurent (O'Reilly & Associates). Rick Silterra (Cornell) joined the effort later. Because this part of the project depended on finalizing work on the data entities, elements, and structure, it was impractical to get very far ahead of that part of the project. The desire to complete the project in a timely way and make it available for comment and use also meant that time available for this part of the project was fairly limited. The data element work was informed and affected by what the steering group knew of emerging work elsewhere on standards, including the work of the NISO/EDItEUR Joint Working Party for the Exchange of Serials Subscription Information.

The XML investigation began with a consideration of the uses to which an ERM schema might be put. These possible uses included

- exchange among vendors and libraries of data for use in link resolvers, including user group license terms;

- publisher e-resource title lists;

- packaging actionable license terms with associated objects in a preservation archive (e.g., using METS);

- dissemination of license and administrative data to members of a consortium; and

- exchange of license data with a contracting partner.

With these many possibilities in mind, XML group member Wendler developed a draft schema for general use that included Dublin Core and MODS name space and schemas, and a slot or placeholder for rights expression. As the group discussed the draft and as the NISO/EDItEUR and XrML/ODRL dynamics further unfolded, it became clear that a more fruitful approach would be to concentrate on a limited number of practical scenarios. Since license terms have been of substantial concern to libraries for several years, but no directly related, known XML work had yet taken place within that community, it was decided to focus on license terms. The group focused on two sets of elements:

- a short *quick-fix* set that would best describe license terms that staff and users would most need to know; and

- a broader *license* set of elements that could be most usefully shared by two libraries or other entities such as a publisher or consortium and a library.

Members of the group selected the required elements from the DLF ERM system data structure document and created instance documents with data that were then used to develop a schema optimized to these narrow uses.

Because of the many potential advantages of relying on existing schemas, the group looked for work that was closely related or that might be adapted to the purposes it had in mind. Apparent similarities led to investigation of work on digital rights management (DRM), and rights expression languages (RELs). As Karen Coyle has described in her recent report for the Library of Congress (Coyle 2004), two well-established RELs currently vie for recognition as the standard for media products such as movies in DVD format. The first of these, now referred to as MPEG-21/5, grew out of the XrML language developed by a company named ContentGuard. The second is called the Open Digital Rights Language, or ODRL. These initiatives are intended not only to enable a rights holder to describe what a user may do with a particular resource but also to confer substantial control of user behavior on the implementing party. The XML group learned of the existence of extensive patent claims related to MPEG-21/5, and its strong preference for open standards led it to focus on ODRL.

A third initiative that sparked interest is from Creative Commons and is based on the resource description framework (RDF). The intent of the Creative Commons approach, unlike that of the MPEG-21/5 and ODRL, is to provide a means for authors to declare the terms on which they are making works available free of charge via the Internet, rather than to exert control. The group elected to focus some of its attention on the Creative Commons schema, and four schemas (corresponding to the two use cases described above) were developed: one for ODRL, another based on the Creative Commons RDF, and two for native ERMI, which were based on ERMI project elements and values.

The attempt to use ODRL met with mixed results. While ODRL proved to be extensible and flexible, learning to use it effectively was time-consuming and would have taken much longer without the generous assistance of Renato Iannella and Susanne Guth of the ODRL initiative. For example, the group found that only the form of the XML documents could be validated in the ODRL schema that the group developed, meaning that any value (including invalid ones) would be accepted. (Iannella told us subsequently that it is possible to validate a document more completely, but time did not allow us to alter our demonstration ODRL schema to incorporate that feature.) In addition, it is necessary to describe all permitted uses under ODRL; this is clearly inconsistent with libraries' expectations that they should be able to make reasonable uses of resources that are not prohibited by licenses.

A greater degree of success was hoped for with the Creative Commons RDF, because it was not designed to support direct control of use and its ethos is consistent with open access and fair use. While less constraining and more extensible than the ODRL, it unfortunately also lacks provision for validating structure and data types. The group consequently concluded that the Creative Commons RDF could not provide a basis for license description and communication.

These discoveries led to work on the third alternative, the aforementioned native ERMI license-expression development. In essence, this would entail establishing a name space for license expression on the basis of elements and values from the ERMI data dictionary and data structure documents. Its benefits include the ability to simply use any of those elements and values, to avoid time required to adapt other existing RELs to purposes for which they may be ill suited, and to have greater syntax and value validation. One added benefit that was found in the process of creating the two test native ERMI schemas is that they were more compact than those created using either ODRL or the Creative Commons RDF. Because of this "best fit," the group believes that discussion of standardized license expression within the library and scholarly publishing communities should focus on the native ERMI alternative in the near term.

5. Response to the Initiative and Future Considerations

Now that the results of the DLF ERMI have been fully described, it is time to briefly consider responses to the work from the library and vendor communities and to review selected areas where members of the steering group feel that additional work is most needed.

5.1. LIBRARIAN AND VENDOR RESPONSE

The main reason behind the development of the ERMI was the realization that few libraries had the tools needed for successful management of e-resources and that developing such systems would be time-consuming and complex. From the beginning, the members of the ERMI steering group felt that solving such a problem would require extensive collaboration and investment. It is consequently very satisfying to report that librarians and vendors have had very positive reactions to the initiative.

Most important, at this writing, several vendors either have already begun developing ERM systems or services or have announced plans to do so, and most of this work has drawn heavily from the project's draft functional requirements and data elements. These organizations and their ERM-related products and services include the following:

o   The Colorado Alliance plans to improve and enhance the Gold Rush product in 2004.

o   Dynix announced development of an electronic management module during the 2004 ALA annual conference.

o   EBSCO has developed an electronic journal service that incorporates significant ERM functionality and uses an e-resource life cycle diagram in its literature.

o   Endeavor has announced plans to develop a full-function ERM product named Meridian for release in 2005.

o   Ex Libris has announced development of a product named Verde that will draw upon the SFX knowledge base. Initial release is planned by the end of 2004.

o   Harrassowitz has announced plans for HERMES 2.0, a service that will incorporate ERM features.

o   Innovative Interfaces, Inc. has developed an ERM module that is moving from development and beta testing into production.

o   Serials Solutions has an ERM product in its near-term plans.

o   SIRSI has developed a prototype system that was shown at the 2004 ALA annual conference.

o   VTLS announced plans this spring to develop an ERM product called Verify (VTLS 2004).

5.2. OUTSTANDING ISSUES

As these vendors develop their products and services, they and the libraries they serve inevitably will find places where the ERMI products will seem lacking or incomplete. Accordingly, they will devise new and helpful approaches to solving some of the problems sketched out in this report or to problems not yet identified. In that spirit, we would like to identify some problems that we were unable to solve within our time constraints, but that merit further work.

5.2.1. Consortium Support and Functionality

The ERMI has focused on the needs of individual libraries rather than on those of the library consortia to which so many libraries now belong. That has allowed rapid headway to be made, but a broader view that takes consortial support functions into account is highly desirable. Doing so is complicated by the fact that library consortia differ substantially from one another. Some, such as Ohiolink and CDL have significant amounts of central funding and a broad service mandate, while others function more as buying clubs and have correspondingly more limited missions, staffing, and goals. Nevertheless, some steps in this direction have been taken within the last several months. The extent of consortial support desired at the "central funding/broad mandate" end of this continuum was suggested in an assessment conducted for CDL (Wright 2003), which referenced the work of the ERMI. In March 2004, the University of California (UC) system libraries' System-Wide Operations and Planning Advisory Group (SOPAG) followed up on this assessment with a retreat to discuss ERM needs. Each library in the UC system sent representatives to this meeting. Although the functionality and architecture described in the ERMI documents was discussed and endorsed, attention was also given to SOPAG requirements seen needing a higher profile or not addressed in the DLF initiative. For example, CDL expends significant effort tracking which member libraries participate in which voluntary buy-in purchases and what cost shares apply. Additionally, evaluation and negotiation of e-journal packages requires the ability to track current print and e-journal subscription information at both the individual campus and consortial levels and to link to it other information such as cost, usage and Thompson ISI (Institute for Scientific Information) "impact factor." Given the likelihood that CDL libraries will continue to use different ILSs and ERM systems, the need for data standards and interoperability noted above is especially acute.

Following the SOPAG ERM retreat, two relevant sessions were held at the International Coalition of Library Consortia (ICOLC) meeting. The first session focused on consortial *administrivia* and offered an opportunity for consortium managers to discuss the kinds of information they must track and communicate to vendors and member libraries and related support tools they have devised. Librarians who have followed the ERM discussions would have recognized many themes, including the diversity of data needed (such as library and vendor contacts IP ranges, and renewal dates, and reliance on various spreadsheets and databases to do that work). The second session was on managing e-resources across the consortium. It featured descriptions of the work of the DLF, the UC system, and the Gold Rush product. Attendees expressed substantial interest in vendor developments, their support of consortia, and data standards. A subsequent ERMI steering group discussion of points raised during these ICOLC sessions concluded that the ERMI data model supports, or can be extended to address, key consortial requirements, but that a more careful review was needed. Since CDL is engaged in analyzing its requirements, it is conceivable that a document resulting from that process could be developed into a more generic statement of consortial ERM requirements and released under ICOLC auspices.

5.2.2. Usage Data

Although there is some provision for usage data within the ERMI data model, it would be desirable to better describe both the analyses libraries will perform on the data available to them and how such data might be passed more easily to libraries for incorporation into their ERM systems. Important sources for analyses of functionality are model usage-data programs such as the Data Farm developed at the University of Pennsylvania (Zucca 2003; University of Pennsylvania Libraries 2004) and ARL's E-metrics initiative (Association of Research Libraries 2004). Project COUNTER's code of practice for the "recording and exchange of online usage data" will undoubtedly become an increasingly important standard in this area, and the recently announced availability of an XML DTD for COUNTER usage reports is particularly welcome, as it will pave the way for smoother and more effortless transport of usage data.

5.2.3. Resource Succession

One issue related to the ERMI data model is that individual journals frequently pass from one publisher to another, or from platform to platform. As this happens, it may be difficult to keep track of the particular license terms, archival rights, and access information related to each change.

5.2.4. Data Standards

As important as these efforts are, they seem unlikely to succeed in the long run unless work to develop and maintain relevant data standards continues along with them.

- Serials Description and Holdings. Knowing that the NISO/EDItEUR Joint Working Party for the Exchange of Serials Subscription Information was working to develop a standard exchange format for serials subscription data, the ERMI steering group decided to rely on that group's work rather than to develop a competing standard. The steering group regards the work of the joint working party as fundamentally important and looks forward to further developments.

- Standard Identifiers. The steering group concluded that a single global e-resource identification system or registry for packages, providers, and interfaces could make it possible to exchange certain kinds of information far more reliably and precisely than at present.

- License Term Expression. Resolving issues related to standardized communication about intellectual property, licensing, and permitted use will also require additional work. Luckily, there is evidence of interest in this problem. For example, discussions at the recent CONSER Summit on Serials in the Electronic Environment suggested that some publishers may be ready to experiment with providing public versions of their licenses to libraries, and there was interest in establishing a test-bed of licenses marked up in XML for importing into local ERM systems. There have also been discussions of the possibility of establishing a standard data dictionary for publisher licensing and rights expression, using the ERMI data dictionary as a starting point.

- Interoperability. It seems reasonable to question whether or not stand-alone ERM applications can be developed that are truly capable of integration into ILSs from other vendors. While the steering group believes that standardizing data elements is an important step in this direction, it is possible that a new initiative called VIEWS, which is aimed at "enabling web services between disparate applications used in libraries," may be another (Dynix 2004).

Resolving these issues will require organized, cooperative efforts from libraries, consortia, publishers, serial agents and support companies, and library system vendors, as well as effective structures for communicating about them.

6. Conclusion

The new electronic environment in which libraries, publishers, and vendors operate has evolved quickly and become quite complex in relatively short order, but the complexities we now recognize could pale in comparison to those that may be just around the corner—as investments in e-resources grow, technical innovation continues, and business models evolve. No matter how the environment evolves, new tools, standards, smart choices, and collaboration will be needed. We hope that the DLF ERMI has enabled all these activities to happen more quickly and to be more efficient and effective.

References

Alan, Robert. "Keeping Track of Electronic Resources to Keep Them on Track." PowerPoint presentation, 17th Annual North American Serials Interest Group (NASIG), Williamsburg, VA, June 20-23, 2002.

Association of Research Libraries. "Collections and Access for the 21st-Century Scholar: Changing Roles of Research Libraries. *ARL: A Bimonthly Report on Research Library Issues and Actions from ARL, CNI, and SPARC,* no. 225 (December 2002), http://www.arl.org/newsltr/225/index.html.

———. ARL Supplementary Statistics 2001-2002. Washington, D.C.: Association of Research Libraries, 2003. http://www.arl.org/stats/pubpdf/sup02.pdf.

———. E-Metrics: Measures for Electronic Resources. Washington, D.C.: Association of Research Libraries, 2004. http://www.arl.org/stats/newmeas/emetrics/.

Cornell University Library. "Cornell University Library Digital Futures Plan: July 2000 to June 2002." Ithaca, NY: Cornell University Library, 2000. http://www.library.cornell.edu/staffweb/CULDigitalFuturesPlan.html.

Cornell University Library. "Digital Library Federation Meeting, November 2002." Summary, 2002. http://www.library.cornell.edu/cts/elicensestudy/dlf2002fall /home.htm.

Counter Online Metrics. "COUNTER: Counting Online Usage of Networked Electronic Resources," Web site, 2004. http://www.projectcounter.org/.

Cox, John. "Model Generic Licenses: Cooperation and Competition." *Serials Review* 26, no. 1 (2000):3-9.

Coyle, Karen. "Rights Expression Languages: A Report for the Library of Congress." White paper, 2004. http://www.loc.gov/standards/Coylereport_final1single.pdf.

Cyzyk, Mark, and Nathan D.M. Robertson. "HERMES: The Hopkins Electronic Resource Management System." *Information Technology and Libraries* 22, no. 3 (2003): 12-17.

Digital Library Federation. "DLF Electronic Resource Management Initiative." Project description, 2002. http://www.diglib.org/standards/dlf-erm02.htm.

Duranceau, Ellen Finnie. "License Compliance." *Serials Review* 26, no. 1 (2000):53-58.

———. "License Tracking." *Serials Review* 26, no. 3 (2000):69-73.

Dynix. Web site. Dynix. http://www.dynix.com/

Farb, Sharon E. "UCLA Electronic Resource Database Project Overview." PowerPoint presentation, ALA Midwinter 2002, New Orleans, LA, January 18, 2002. http://www.library.cornell.edu/cts/elicensestudy/ucla/ALAMidwinter2002.ppt.

Farb, Sharon E., and Angela Riggio. "Medium or Message: A New Look at Standards, Structures, and Schemata for Managing Electronic Resources." *Library Hi Tech* 22, no. 2 (2004):144-152.

Friedlander, Amy. *Dimensions and Use of the Scholarly Information Environment: Introduction to a Data Set Assembled by the Digital Library Federation and Outsell, Inc.* Washington, D.C.: Digital Library Federation and Council on Library and Information Resources, 2002. http://www.clir.org/pubs/reports/pub110/contents.html.

Hennig, Nicole. "Improving Access to E-Journals and Databases at the MIT Libraries: Building a Database-Backed Web Site Called 'VERA'." *Serials Librarian* 41, no. 3/4 (2002):227-254. http://www.hennigweb.com/publications/vera.html.

International Standards Office. International Electrotechnical Commission. *International Standard 11179*, Information Technology, "Specification and Standardization of Data Elements." Geneva, Switzerland: ISO/IEC, 1995–2000.

Jewell, Timothy D. *Selection and Presentation of Commercially Available Electronic Resources.* Washington, D.C.: Digital Library Federation and Council on Library and Information Resources, 2001. http://www.clir.org/pubs/reports/pub99 /pub99.pdf.

Johns Hopkins University Libraries. "HERMES—Hopkins Electronic Resources ManagEment System." Web site. Johns Hopkins University Libraries. http://hermes.mse.jhu.edu:8008/hermesdocs/.

National Information Standards Organization and Digital Library Federation. "NISO/DLF Workshop on Standards for Electronic Resource Management, May 2002." Notes, slides, and other materials. Ithaca, NY: Cornell University Library, 2002. http://www.library.cornell.edu/cts/elicensestudy/nisodlf/home.htm)

National Information Standards Organization. "NISO/EDItEUR Joint Working Party for the Exchange of Serials Subscription Information." Web site. http://www.fcla.edu /~pcaplan /jwp/.

Nawrocki, Robert F. 2003. "Electronic Records Management," in *Encyclopedia of Library and Information Science.* New York: Marcel Dekker, 2003.

Okerson, Ann S., principal investigator, Alex Edelman, Georgia Harper, Earl Hood, and Rod Stenlake. "CLIR/DLF Model License," Liblicense: Licensing Digital Information, 2001. Council on Library and Information Resources, Digital Library Federation, and Yale University Library. http://www.library.yale.edu/~llicense /modlic.shtml.

Robek, M.F., G.F. Brown, and D.O. Stephens. 1996. *Information and Records Management*, 4th ed. New York: McGraw Hill, 1996.

Stanley, Nancy Markle, Angelina F. Holden, and Betty L. Nirnberger. "Taming the Octopus: Getting a Grip on Electronic Resources." *Serials Librarian* 38, no. 3-4 (2000):363-368.

Stockton, Melissa, and George Machovec. "Gold Rush: A Digital Registry of Electronic Journals." *Technical Services Quarterly* 19, no. 3 (2001):51-59.

University Libraries, The Pennsylvania State University. "Data Farm." Web page, 2004. Pennsylvania State University. http://metrics.library.upenn.edu/prototype /datafarm/.

University Libraries, The Pennsylvania State University. "ERLIC Shareware: Electronic Resources and Licensing Information Center." Pennsylvania State University Libraries, 2001. http://www.libraries.psu.edu/tas/fiscal_data /electronicresources.htm.

Visionary Technology in Library Solutions. "'VIEWS': A Newly Created Vendor Initiative for Enabling Web Services Announced. Online article. VTLS, 2004. http://www.vtls.com/Corporate/Releases/2004/21.shtml.

Warner, Beth Forrest. "Managing Electronic Resources in Today's ILMS Environment." PowerPoint presentation, ALCTS Managing Electronic Resources: Meeting the Challenge Symposium, ALA Midwinter Meeting, Philadelphia, PA, January 24, 2003. http://kudiglib.ku.edu/Personal_prsns /ALA_Preconf_2003MW.htm.

Cornell University Library. "Web Hub for Developing Administrative Metadata for Electronic Resource Management." Web site. Cornell University Library. http://www.library.cornell.edu/cts/elicensestudy/.

Wright, Alex. "California Digital Library Electronic Resource Management Assessment: Final Report." Oakland, CA: California Digital Library, 2003.

Zucca, Joseph. "Traces in the Clickstream: Early Work on a Management Information Repository at the University of Pennsylvania." *Information Technology and Libraries* 22, no. 4 (2003):175-179.

Appendix A: Functional Requirements for Electronic Resource Management[2]

Ivy Anderson, Sharon E. Farb, Adam Chandler, Timothy Jewell, Kimberly Parker, Angela Riggio, and Nathan D. M. Robertson

Introduction

The goal envisioned in these requirements is a system that supports management of the information and workflows necessary to efficiently select, evaluate, acquire, maintain, and provide access to e-resources in accordance with their business and license terms. Such a system should support the service requirements of e-resources while building on existing investments in library technology, through seamless interaction and efficient sharing of data with traditional MARC-based online catalogs, Web portals, federated searching tools, local resolution services, local authentication and access-management systems, and traditional library-management functions. Whether implemented as a stand-alone system or as part of an existing library-management system, the ERM functions should complement, rather than duplicate, the capabilities of other systems deployed by the library.

This document outlines the broad areas of functionality that are required in such an ERM system. It is not intended, at this stage of development, to be a detailed description of every function needed, but rather to provide an overview of the main functions required of the system. The examples under each functional area are representative and illustrative, rather than exhaustive.

Guiding Principles

The ERM system should offer an integrated environment that supports both management and access, without maintaining duplicate systems. The system should offer a capacity for global updating and flexible addition of fields. It should offer the ability to hide fields and records from public view and have a single point of maintenance for each data element. It should support interoperation and dynamic data sharing with existing OPACs, Web portals, library-management systems, and link resolution services. It should offer users consistent information, regardless of the path they take in seeking it. Finally, the ERMS should, over time, support the ability to store, access, search, and generate reports of the information that it contains.

FUNCTIONAL REQUIREMENTS

General Requirements

---

[2] This document is based on specifications originally developed by Ivy Anderson, Harvard University, Ellen Duranceau, MIT, and Robin Wendler, Harvard University.

The ability to support complex, multiple-to-multiple relationships that accurately map how resources, business terms, licenses, and other components interrelate is an essential building block for supporting the functionality described throughout this document. The companion Entity Relationship Diagram for Electronic Resource Management (see Appendix C) presents a schematic representation of these relationships.

For all areas of functionality described in this document, it must be possible to

1. Identify what bibliographic entities (electronic and print) are covered by or provided through a given license, set of business terms, package, or online interface platform (hereinafter "interface");

2. Associate the characteristics of a given license, set of business terms, package, or interface with all the bibliographic entities (electronic and print) to which they apply;

3. Offer security features to control staff views and maintenance rights
   3.1. hide confidential information from certain staff
   3.2. restrict the ability to add, update, or delete certain data (field by field) to designated staff
   3.3. provide the ability to construct simplified data views by hiding unused fields; and

4. Perform ad hoc queries and generate reports across a broad range of fields and table values.

Resource-Discovery Requirements

While adequate facilities for searching and browsing for e-resources already exist in OPACs and portals at many libraries (through searches of author, title, alternate titles, cross-references, subjects, keywords, and other descriptors), facilities to cull e-resources for resource-discovery purposes are lacking at other institutions. Ideally, the ERM system should provide a user interface for libraries that require one as well as a means of integrating appropriate license data into the results of searches within externally deployed systems.

The ideal system should also provide Web developers database table- or view-level access and the ability to bypass the native interface to query and present data to the user in any number of custom-configurable ways. An ERMS implementation should include a dedicated user interface that is able to capture appropriate data in other systems or to share its information with elements in other supported systems to create unified user displays, including the capabilities described below.

It should be possible to:

5. Make resources available through or pass on information about resources to OPACs and Web-presentation services using traditional resource discovery methods, including the ability to search and browse by author, title, alternate titles, cross-references, subject, and keywords, facilitate the generation of dynamic, database-

driven Web pages that constitute pathfinders, course- or discipline-specific pages, or lists of selected e-resources in a given subject area and of a given type (e.g., e-journals, article databases) while supporting fully customizable presentation templates that are not limited to the branding and look and feel of the native interface;

6. Offer contextual presentation of relevant license information to the user at the point of access, regardless of the access path taken through any supported tool,

   6.1. make apparent to users whether or not they are authorized for access under the license
   6.2. display relevant permitted uses, use restrictions, and special requirements such as:
      6.2.1. permission to use in course packs, course Web sites, and distance education
      6.2.2. unusual prohibitions, such as record download limits and time of day restrictions
      6.2.3. citation requirements;

7. Support site-defined and auxiliary descriptive data. Such data might include:

   7.1. locally defined fields for descriptive needs not covered in existing MARC records
   7.2. a free-form note
   7.3. locally defined lists and descriptors;

8. Make available information about and provide access to other versions of the resource being viewed, including links to catalog holdings information for physical manifestations and direct links to all accessible electronic versions;

9. Make available information about issues particular to the online interface, such as inaccessible or nonsubscribed portions not marked as such at the site, unusual log-on and log-off requirements, and navigation or accessibility features;

10. Flag resources as unavailable in real time, with an optional explanatory note (see also Administrative and Management Functions); and

11. Offer advisory notices of planned downtime and other time-sensitive information.

Bibliographic Management Requirements

In many libraries, both traditional and auxiliary bibliographic data may be distributed among a variety of systems, including the library-management system, a federated searching portal, and a link resolution service. Nevertheless, to the extent possible, each unique data element should have to be maintained only once. Updates in one system should be automatically reflected in corresponding systems, either through the dynamic sharing of data or, where redundant storage cannot be eliminated, by propagation to other systems. Loading of data from external systems should also be supported.

Specifically, it should be possible to:

12. Provide a single point of maintenance for bibliographic and auxiliary descriptive data that can be exchanged or shared between the OPAC, portal lists, federated search tools, local resolution services, and other bibliographic systems and services; and

13. Import subscription-management data from external providers using standard software and developing protocols,
    13.1. lists of titles, ISSNs, and uniform resource identifiers (URIs) delivered in Excel or delimited format
    13.2. changes to titles and dates of coverage in aggregated databases communicated via any XML-based or standards-based data transfer protocol, such as ONIX for serials
    13.3. holdings updates supplied by a publisher or subscription agent to facilitate electronic check-in.

Access-Management Requirements

All libraries rely on authentication and access-management systems that are external to the systems and tools described in this document. These external systems may be as straightforward as reliance on the remote-authorization mechanism of an online provider (via IP addresses or user names and passwords) or as complex as a locally developed access-management service that assigns persistent identifiers to resources, passes connection requests to a system that validates users according to a local authentication scheme (e.g., Kerberos), and routes valid users through a proxy server. Institutions with complex local environments can be expected to have customized systems and tools with which to perform these functions, and the ERM system must interoperate with them.

The ERMS should accommodate both simple and complex environments with a disparate range of needs. To accomplish this, the following generalized requirements are necessary:

- Management of basic access-related information, such as URIs, user IDs and passwords, and lists of institutional IP addresses;
- Support for the creation of persistent URIs and for additional data elements required to support complex local access management services, such as proxy servers; and
- A set of export functions by which an ERMS can communicate its information to a local system or service.

Specifically, it should be possible to:

14. Store and maintain access URIs and make these actionable for end users, according to local requirements:

14.1. store vendor-supplied primary and secondary URIs (e.g., for mirror sites) used for access to the resource

14.2. support the creation, storage, and updating of persistent URIs and/or integration with external systems for managing persistent identifiers

14.3. support authentication and access systems (such as proxy servers or statistics-generating scripts), allowing for URIs to be constructed on the fly on the basis of stored data elements

14.4. generate notifications and/or exports of URI information to appropriate linked or external systems according to local requirements (e.g., notification or export to cataloging and information technology departments or systems)

14.5. provide seamless functional integration with external systems that record this information (e.g., through a shared pointer);

15. Integrate proxy server/access management with other functionality

15.1. provide a means for seamless integration of proxy server access for all or selected users and all or selected resources;

16. Store lists of IP addresses used to register access to specific resources and provide automated e-mail notification to online providers when IP addresses are updated,

16.1. support the creation and maintenance of multiple lists of IP addresses that can be associated or disassociated with one or more licensed locations and linked to one or more bibliographic entities

16.2. for a given resource or online provider, indicate whether IP addresses are/were registered online and record the registration URI

16.3. send automated e-mail notifications to vendors and providers when IP addresses are updated and record the date on which notifications are sent. Include the ability to record an acknowledgment date. This implies the ability to designate a vendor or provider contact address for IP address-notification purposes;

17. Store one or more user IDs and passwords and provide the ability to generate secure screen displays of this information for authorized users and staff, with associated text or for JavaScript autosubmission; and

18. Implement access restrictions,

18.1. record authorized user categories and authorized sites, including the ability to associate specific actions with those elements, such as:
18.1.1. generating staff and user displays
18.1.2. implementing access controls
18.1.3. exporting information to a local access-management system (technical system in use at your institution such as an authentication system and/or proxy server (see also Resource Administrative and Management Functions).

STAFF REQUIREMENTS

Staff Interface

An ERM system requires a staff interface that enables library staff to efficiently carry out the work described in the sections that follow. The interface should be organized into views that are optimized for particular areas of staff activity or interest, such as resource acquisition, troubleshooting, license administration, or administration and statistics. Details of appropriate interface design are not addressed in these requirements; these are left to the art and discretion of system developers.

Through this interface, staff should be able to:

19. Search, browse, and retrieve records by attributes unique to e-resources, such as license, vendor, interface, record status, licensed site, consortium, and library selector or other local contact individual;
20. View the full range of information appropriate to the staff member's security profile and functional role;
21. To the extent possible, link to other relevant information stored in library management systems, portals, or related systems; and
22. View records that are hidden from the public.

Selection and Evaluation Process

During the selection and evaluation process, it is typically necessary for a decentralized group of individuals to coordinate a complex and iterative series of steps. The ERM system should provide support for recording actions at each of these steps and be capable of performing specified actions upon completion of a given task and of sending alerts when anticipated actions do not occur.

A typical selection and evaluation process might involve the following steps and require the following reminders and notifications, all built from stored action dates and locally definable status fields:

- Build request record for trial;
- Flag resource as trial;
- Notify interested parties that trial is live and provide the access instructions and expiration date (triggered by trial start date and e-mail address[es] input into request record);
- Allow staff (and, optionally, users) to access the trial via stored URL;
- Send reminder to those notified of a trial that expiration date is near (triggered by trial end date and e-mail address[es] input into request record);
- Record opinions of key players and final purchase decision, allowing for both central and local input of opinions and funding commitments into notes fields in request record;

- Prompt licensing/acquisitions contact to report purchase decision (triggered by decision date input into request record). The most common options are "Approve," "Reject," or "Put on Hold"; and

- For resources that are approved for purchase, additional statuses and actions would be required, including
  - notify licensing contact to obtain and negotiate license, and remind this contact if license is not completed by a given deadline (triggered by stored licensing contact, notification of approved status, and deadline input at time of approval)
  - notify access contact if status has not changed to "live" by deadline (triggered by inputting likely access date into system at time of approval)
  - notify cataloging and selector/product sponsor, as well as other interested parties, when access is available (triggered, for example, by changing status to "Live" and by stored e-mail address[es] related to this purchase).

The companion Electronic Resource Management Workflow Flowchart provides a detailed diagrammatic view of workflow decision and action points (see Appendix B).

To support these processes, it should be possible to:

23. Create provisional records for resources that may or may not be permanently acquired and track the selection and evaluation process through acquisition or rejection;

24. Assign locally definable status fields to request records and associate particular actions with those statuses. Examples of such fields include "New Request," "On Trial," "Trial Expired/Decision Pending," "Approved," "Rejected," and "On Hold";

25. Assign locally definable fields to request records for license routing and status and associate particular actions with those fields. Site should be able, for example, to define a list of individuals from whom sign-off is required, send reminders to license reviewers, and record approval or rejection status, with notes;

26. Assign multiple local contact individuals and site-defined roles to both request records and permanent resource records;

27. Send e-mail notifications to individuals designated as local or licensing contacts;

28. .Make trial resources available in a secure manner through the library's resource tool of choice to authorized users (if wanted) and staff
    28.1. store trial URIs and passwords and make these available, securely if necessary
    28.2. flag items unambiguously as trial resources, with associated public and staff notes
    28.3. record a trial expiration date and, optionally, send an alert to designated recipients n days prior to trial expiration;

29. Record a decision due date and, optionally, send an alert to designated recipients n days prior to decision date;

30. Establish a site-defined routing workflow for resources that are approved for purchase. For example, it should be possible to send notifications to designated staff or departments or to place resources in a queue for further action by those units to trigger actions such as the placing of an order, completion of cataloging, and implementation of access management by designated staff; and

31. Purge rejected records from the system, sequester into a history archive, or retain such records with notes about the decision process (including a link to written evaluations if wanted), at the library's discretion.

Resource Administration and Management Functions

The functions described in this section pertain to activities required to fulfill license obligations and to administer and support resources that have been acquired. Some of the data and functions pertain to the license itself, while others pertain to the management of individual resources. The system should be able to record data at the most efficient level required to avoid redundancy, relying on the relationships among entities to make the information available at other applicable levels (e.g., individual resource, package, or interface).

It should be possible to:

32. Store license rights and terms for reference, reporting, and control of services

    32.1. for services including, but not limited to, interlibrary loans, reserves, distance education, course Web sites, and course packs,
        32.1.1. identify whether a given title may be used for the service and under what conditions
        32.1.2. generate reports of all materials that may or may not be used for the service with notes about under what conditions, and
    32.2. include a mechanism for adding new services, allowing staff to specify the name of the service and associated actions such as public displays, reports, and alerts;

33. Record the categories of users and sites that are authorized for access to a given resource and generate displays for end users and staff on the basis of this information (see also Access Management Requirements);

34. Support breach investigation and cure activities and other activities that may be required to fulfill license obligations

34.1. record the cure period for breach and generate alerts at library-specified intervals on the basis of this information when a breach has been reported

34.2. provide a breach-incident log in which to record reports of alleged breaching activity, including date and source of initial report, open/closed status, resolution date, and actions taken. This should have the capability of generating reports on commonalities of breaches (e.g., type of breach, department showing regular breaches)

34.3. include a mechanism for adding fields in which to record unusual compliance requirements that the library may want to track, including implementation status and date and the ability to generate reports or alerts on the basis of this information. Examples might include a requirement to post notices to end users or to destroy locally held copies upon termination (see also Termination Activities);

35. Record additional license terms and metadata for contract management and auditing purposes, such as license commencement date, duration of agreement, confidentiality provisions, and other site-definable key terms;

36. Provide the ability to display or link to an online version of a license agreement;

37. Manage the library's archival rights in electronic content,

37.1. record whether permanent rights to the year level exist in a given resource and, if so, their source, dates of coverage, manner of execution, and the applicable license through which rights are provided. It should be possible to associate multiple archival field clusters with a given resource to track successive rights with multiple providers

37.2. retain archival versions of license terms and conditions if desired, so that preexisting terms of agreement can be mapped to the bibliographic entities and dates for which such terms applied;

38. Support the administration of e-resources,

38.1. store administrative URIs, IDs and passwords, and associated notes and make them available to authorized staff

38.2. store subscriber numbers used to register online journals that are tied to print

38.3. provide the following capabilities for configuration options, including but not limited to features such as institutional branding, hooks to holdings, Z39.50 and OpenURL support,

38.3.1. identify whether a given title supports the feature and whether it has been implemented, with associated notes

38.3.2. generate reports of all materials that do or do not support the specified feature, including implementation status

      38.3.3. include a mechanism for adding new features, allowing staff to specify the name of the feature, implementation status, notes, and associated actions such as report generation,

    38.4. record the number of licensed concurrent users for a given resource, interface, or pooled user group (including pooled consortium users)

    38.5. record cataloging-related data such as,

      38.5.1. the availability and quality of MARC records for package items that include individual entities, including the status of loading or prioritization and additional notes

      38.5.2. the person or unit responsible for cataloging, if applicable

      38.5.3. related specifications, such as specific entries or other data to be included in cataloging records;

39. Support library instructional activities,

    39.1. store information about training accounts (URIs, IDs and/or passwords) and other user instruction arrangements and make these securely available to staff arranging for training classes and (optionally) to end users

    39.2. record information about and/or provide links to available documentation for staff and end users

    39.3. record information about and/or provide links to training classes;

40. Support management of and access to usage statistics,

    40.1. indicate whether usage statistics are provided, and record associated data such as frequency, delivery method, and available format(s)

    40.2. record URIs and IDs and passwords for access to online statistics

    40.3. store or provide information about and/or links to locally stored data

    40.4. if local storage of usage statistics is supported, provide the ability to download locally stored data into a spreadsheet for manipulation purposes

    40.5. generate staff displays for access to usage data

    40.6. provide a note field for special information pertaining to usage statistics (e.g., missing time periods or data errors)

    40.7. generate reports or notifications indicating when usage statistics should be available, based on the frequency parameter established in 40.1;

41. Support the troubleshooting of access and performance-related problems,

    41.1. record the amount or percentage of allowable downtime provided in the license agreement for performance monitoring purposes

    41.2. store information about the provider's normal maintenance window, and include the ability to display this information to the end user

    41.3. store information on locally defined notes for local performance monitoring Web sites/programs

41.4. display URI of server status provided by vendor

41.5. display to staff who perform troubleshooting elements such as URI and proxy information, hardware and software requirements, number of licensed concurrent users, subscription expiration dates, local contact information (site-defined), and vendor contact information

41.6. provide the ability to flag resources as temporarily unavailable, with both staff and public notes. It must be possible to apply the flag to individual titles, to all titles in a given package, or to all titles that use a given online interface (see End-User Requirements)

41.7. integrate a support incident log into the system to record and track problems, including date and source of initial report, category and description of problem, open/closed status, resolution date, and a record of actions taken,

> 41.7.1. provide the ability to route open problem reports to appropriate local contacts for further action including email capability for routing of problem/troubleshooting reports
>
> 41.7.2. generate alerts for unresolved problems at site-defined intervals
>
> 41.7.3. generate incident history reports on demand by resource, package, interface, and vendor for performance monitoring and auditing purposes,

41.8. [Desirable]: calculate the duration of downtime incidents based on data recorded in the log, and generate an alert if downtime exceeds the amount or percentage of allowable downtime provided for in the license agreement; and

42. Facilitate communication with vendors,

42.1. record multiple vendor contacts, including name, title, e-mail address, phone, and fax numbers, including the ability to assign site-defined contact roles. It should be possible to assign multiple roles to a single contact (technical support, customer support, sales, billing support)

42.2. provide the ability to generate standard notifications of IP addresses and changes to vendors

42.3. record official contract notice address and associated requirements (e.g., delivery requirements)

42.4. provide the ability to generate email messages to designated technical support contacts from data in the incident log.

Business Functions

Many of the business activities described here are related to, and may already be accomplished through, functionality that exists in a traditional library learning management system. Although item 44 in this section affirms the general requirement to support traditional acquisitions-related functions, such as ordering, fund accounting, and the ability to commit and expend budgets and to generate budget reports, it does not attempt to describe these requirements in detail, on the assumption that full acquisitions functionality will continue to reside within a library management system. These specifications concentrate instead on the functions and elements that are uniquely required to manage e-resources.

It should be possible to:

43. Make complex business information available to staff,
     43.1. store a description of the pricing model applicable to the resource
     43.2. know what license agreement is applicable to a given set of business terms
     43.3. know what print resources are subscribed to that are part of a package
     43.4. where there are restrictions on cancellation of print subscriptions
         43.4.1. record this information
         43.4.2. if the system is integrated with a library management system that supports print resources, warn (or block with override by authorized staff) attempts to cancel print subscriptions
     43.5. where price caps exist for multiyear agreements
         43.5.1. record this information
         43.5.2. calculate renewal invoices to ensure that price caps are not exceeded, where possible
     43.6. if the system is integrated with a library management system that supports print resources, prompt the library to evaluate retention of associated print subscriptions at renewal;

44. Facilitate the acquisitions process,

     44.1. perform traditional acquisitions functions such as:
         44.1.1. fund accounting
             44.1.1.1. commit, expend, and update budgets
             44.1.1.2. Produce budget and expenditure reports
         44.1.2. ordering
             44.1.2.1. ability to assign and issue purchase orders in any standardized format or protocol. For example, print, e-mail, or EDI transactional transmissions such as X.12, EDIFACT, or other XML-based suites
             44.1.2.2. purchase orders should accommodate site-defined data elements unique to e-resources, such as IP addresses and activation instructions
         44.1.3. invoice payment
     44.2. support cost sharing among departments and fund lines based on fixed numbers, percentages of some characteristic such as use, total budget or population, or special formulas
     44.3. support the ability to pay from one fund and charge costs against multiple funds belonging to distinct budget or administrative units according to the above algorithms;

45. Facilitate cooperation with consortial partners in a license agreement,

45.1. for resources acquired through a consortium, record the name of the consortium, relevant notes, and, optionally, the names of other participating institutions or the materials available as a result of participation of consortial partners

45.2. store name and contact information for key consortial contacts;

46. Facilitate the renewal process,

46.1. record the expiration date and update this date automatically upon renewal

46.2. record the advance notice period for renewal (in the form n days prior to expiration), and calculate a renewal notification date based on this information

46.3. generate a report or send an alert to designated recipients n days prior to renewal-notification date, with associated note. It should be possible to assign a system default period that can be overridden for a given resource (similar to existing claim functions)

46.4. record whether renewal is automatic or explicit and generate an action report and/or alert N days prior to renewal or notification date for resources requiring explicit renewal

46.5. record renewal action or decision and date

46.6. provide pointers or links to written evaluations associated with renewal decisions; and

47. Facilitate termination actions and decisions,

47.1. record whether termination by the library during the contract term is permitted, and if so, record the advance-notice period and applicable conditions (e.g., breach, specific nonperformance, any)

47.2. record whether termination by the licensor during the contract term is permitted, and if so, record the advance-notice period and applicable conditions (e.g., breach, specific nonperformance, any)

47.3. store the termination date and reason for termination

47.4. provide pointers and/or links to written evaluations associated with termination

47.5. record license conditions to be fulfilled upon termination (such as the requirement to destroy locally held copies) and generate alerts based on this information (see also Resource Administrative and Management Functions)

47.6. provide the ability to archive licensing information for noncurrent licenses whose terms remain applicable to previously licensed material

47.7. provide the ability to manage, record, and report on permanent or perpetual access rights following termination of a current agreement.

Appendix B: Electronic Resource Management Workflow Flowchart

Kimberly Parker, Nathan D. M. Robertson, Ivy Anderson, Adam Chandler, Sharon E. Farb, Timothy Jewell, and Angela Riggio

Introduction

The Electronic Resource Management Workflow Flowchart provides a detailed overview of the activities associated with managing the life cycle of electronic products, and is intended to be generally applicable to the processes followed at most institutions. The flowchart highlights functions and processes that are necessary for the acquisition and ongoing management of electronic products. While there are some similarities between the acquisition and management processes for traditional physical library materials and those for electronic products, there are many issues and complexities unique to electronic products. The following overview diagrams of physical resource and e-resource workflows highlight the similarities and differences between the two processes:

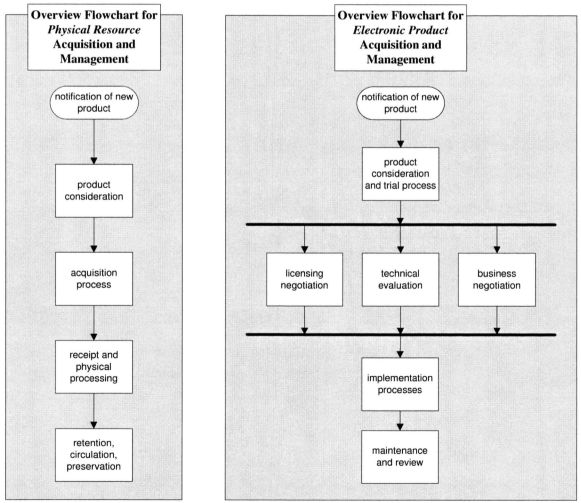

As the diagrams illustrate, there are substantial differences between physical and electronic product management. Electronic products routinely require a licensing process, and may pose technological challenges for implementation. Acquiring and activating an electronic product differs substantially from the receipt and physical processing procedures for physical items, and ongoing maintenance, troubleshooting, and license renewal for electronic products are quite unlike the circulation, physical storage, and repair issues for physical objects.

Throughout the flowchart a number of processes are depicted in detail while others are not. The processes with detailed workflow representations are those where most institutions proceed in a similar fashion and where the processes for electronic products diverge fairly significantly from physical formats. Processes without great detail in the workflow are either those where different institutions have differing processes or those where traditional workflows (with perhaps minor variations) are employed in processing the electronic products.

Flowchart Symbols

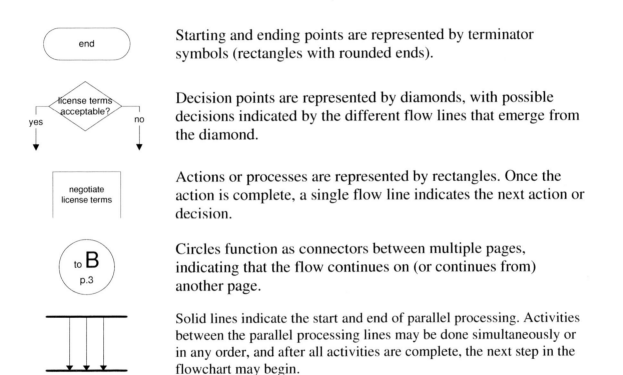

Starting and ending points are represented by terminator symbols (rectangles with rounded ends).

Decision points are represented by diamonds, with possible decisions indicated by the different flow lines that emerge from the diamond.

Actions or processes are represented by rectangles. Once the action is complete, a single flow line indicates the next action or decision.

Circles function as connectors between multiple pages, indicating that the flow continues on (or continues from) another page.

Solid lines indicate the start and end of parallel processing. Activities between the parallel processing lines may be done simultaneously or in any order, and after all activities are complete, the next step in the flowchart may begin.

Electronic Resource Management Workflow Flowchart

The following diagram is the complete Electronic Resource Management Workflow Flowchart. (Note that page references within the flowchart refer to chart pages, not pages of this appendix). Explanatory endnotes follow the diagram.

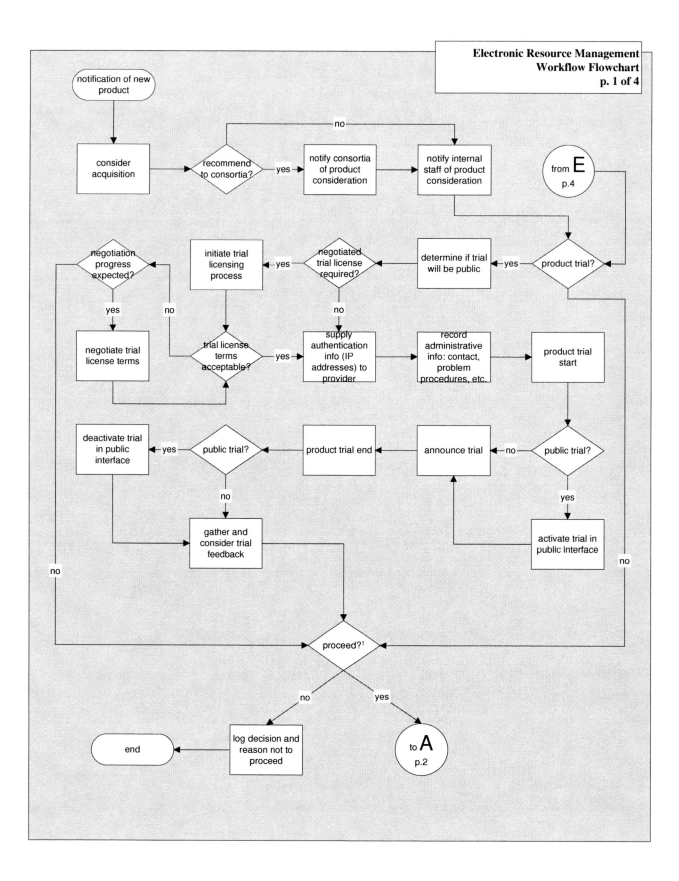

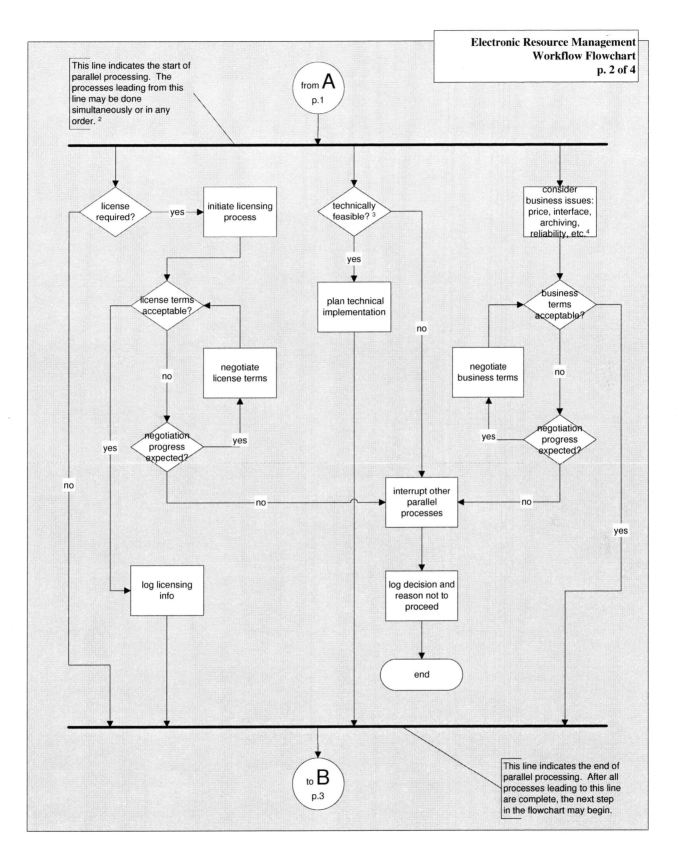

This line indicates the start of parallel processing. The processes leading from this line may be done simultaneously or in any order. [2]

Electronic Resource Management
Workflow Flowchart
p. 2 of 4

from A
p.1

license required?　—yes→　initiate licensing process

technically feasible? [3]

consider business issues: price, interface, archiving, reliability, etc. [4]

yes

plan technical implementation

license terms acceptable?

business terms acceptable?

no

negotiate license terms

negotiate business terms

no

negotiation progress expected?　yes

negotiation progress expected?

yes

no

no

interrupt other parallel processes

no

yes

log licensing info

log decision and reason not to proceed

end

to B
p.3

This line indicates the end of parallel processing. After all processes leading to this line are complete, the next step in the flowchart may begin.

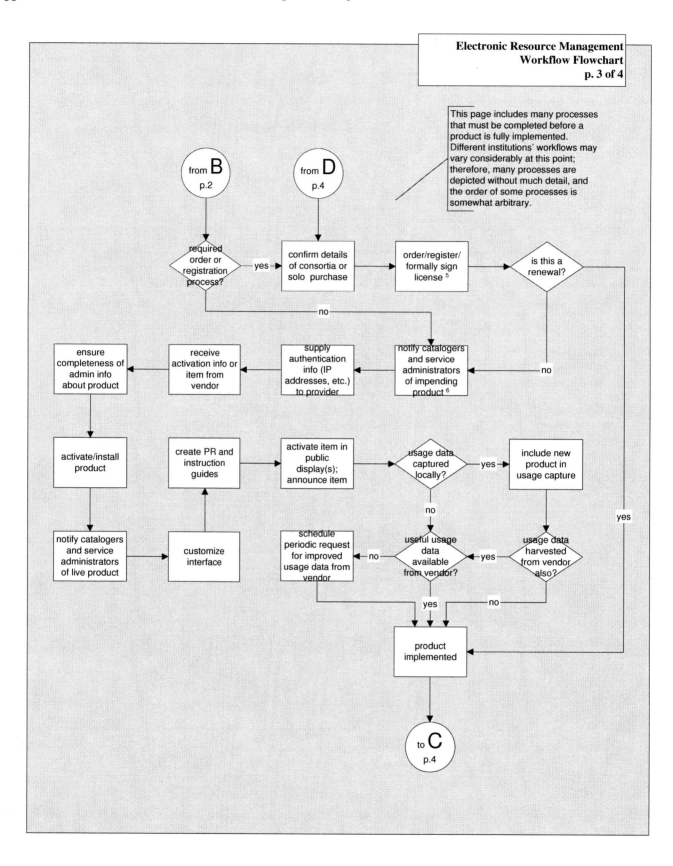

Electronic Resource Management
Workflow Flowchart
p. 3 of 4

This page includes many processes that must be completed before a product is fully implemented. Different institutions' workflows may vary considerably at this point; therefore, many processes are depicted without much detail, and the order of some processes is somewhat arbitrary.

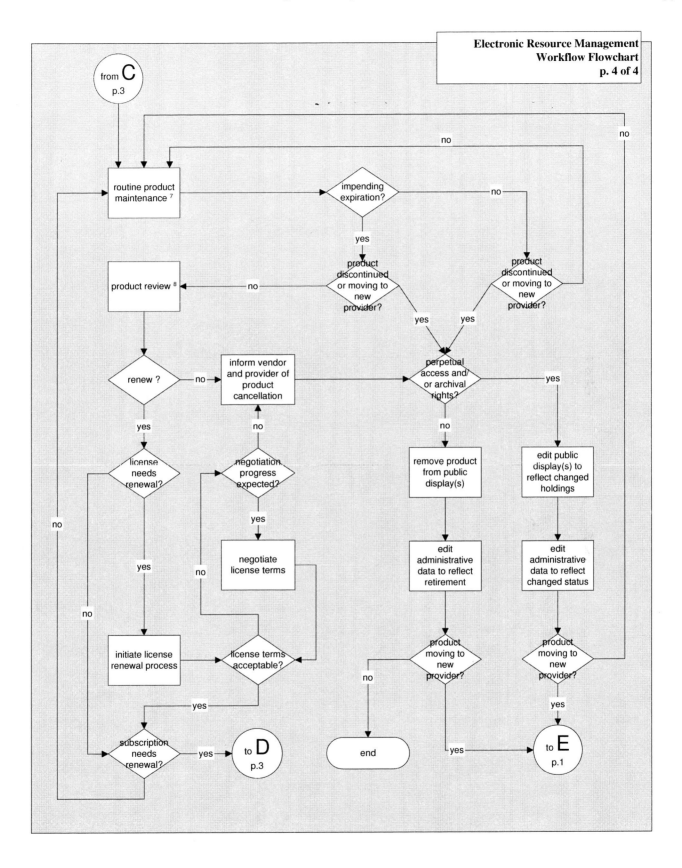

Notes

1. A decision to "proceed" indicates that the product's content has been evaluated during the preceding consideration process and a serious effort to acquire the product should begin.

2. While the parallel processes represented on page 2 are shown as following after a trial period if one takes place, in some cases the parallel processes may begin during the trial period if one is held, and the trial will assist in answering questions raised during the parallel review processes.

3. "Technically feasible?" represents a review of whether the product will function without difficulty within the institution's technical environment, or, if not, whether an acceptable level of effort will allow the product to function.

4. "Business issues" embodies an extensive list of important concepts. Among the items that might be investigated in this grouping are: price, archival needs, interface trajectory, vendor quality, branding capability, usage statistics, MARC record availability and price (if appropriate), instructional ports/accounts (if appropriate), OpenURL compliance, deep-linking capability, etc.

5. It is entirely possible that the license will already be signed by this point, or that the license signing process is completely divorced from the order process. The "order/register/formally sign license" action point is completed when the institution has formally committed to acquiring the product in every way necessary.

6. The action of notifying catalogers and service administrators (e.g. proxy server manager, OpenURL resolver manager, broadcast search service manager, etc.) may occur at any number of points. This item was placed early in the workflow diagram to emphasize that some products are problematic for service managers and early notification is often very beneficial.

7. "Routine product maintenance" encompasses a large array of functions not detailed here. Among the functions included in this concept are the capture of usage statistics, troubleshooting and resolving problems, routine product changes from the vendor (such as URL revisions), revisions to public documentation, etc.

8. "Product review" on page 4 is simply a truncated form of the review of a new product that occurs on page 2. The extent of the review may vary from product to product and from institution to institution.

Appendix C: Entity Relationship Diagram for Electronic Resource Management

Nathan D. M. Robertson, Ivy Anderson, Adam Chandler, Sharon E. Farb, Timothy Jewell, Kimberly Parker, and Angela Riggio

Introduction

This document is an entity relationship diagram (ERD) for a system to manage e-resources. An ERD is a model that identifies the concepts or entities that exist in a system and the relationships between those entities. An ERD is often used as a way to visualize a relational database: each entity represents a database table, and the relationship lines represent the keys in one table that point to specific records in related tables. ERDs may also be more abstract, not necessarily capturing every table needed within a database, but serving to diagram the major concepts and relationships. This ERD is of the latter type, intended to present an abstract, theoretical view of the major entities and relationships needed for management of e-resources. It may assist the database design process for an ERM system, but does not identify every table that would be necessary for an e-resource management database.

This ERD should be examined in close consultation with other components of the *Report of the DLF Electronic Resource Management Initiative*, especially Appendix D (Data Element Dictionary) and Appendix E (Data Structure). The ERD presents a visual representation of e-resource management concepts and the relationships between them. The Data Element Dictionary identifies and defines the individual data elements that an e-resource management system must contain and manage, but leaves the relationship between the elements to be inferred by the reader. The Data Structure associates each data element with the entities and relationships defined in the ERD. Together, these three documents form a complete conceptual data model for e-resource management.

Understanding the Model

There are several different modeling systems for entity relationship diagramming. This ERD is presented in the "Information Engineering" style. Those unfamiliar with entity relationship diagramming or unfamiliar with this style of notation may wish to consult the following section to clarify the diagramming symbology.

ENTITIES

Entities are concepts within the data model. Each entity is represented by a box within the ERD. Entities are abstract concepts, each representing one or more instances of the concept in question. An entity might be considered a container that holds all of the instances of a particular thing in a system. Entities are equivalent to database tables in a relational database, with each row of the table representing an instance of that entity.

Remember that each entity represents a container for instances of the thing in question. The diagram below has an entity for *student* and another for *school.* This indicates that the system being modeled may contain one or more students and one or more schools.

```
STUDENT            SCHOOL
```

So far, no relationship between students and schools has been indicated.

RELATIONSHIPS

Relationships are represented by lines between entities. Relationship lines indicate that each instance of an entity may have a relationship with instances of the connected entity, and vice versa.

```
STUDENT —————————— SCHOOL
```

The diagram above now indicates that students may have some relationship with schools. More specifically, there may be a relationship between a particular student (an instance of the student entity) and a particular school (an instance of the school entity).

If necessary, a relationship line may be labeled to define the relationship. In this case, one can infer that a student may attend a school, or that a school may enroll students. But if necessary, this relationship could be labeled for clarification:

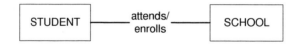

Read the first relationship definition, *attends,* when tracing the relationship left to right or top to bottom. Read the second definition, *enrolls,* when tracing the relationship right to left or bottom to top.

OPTIONALITY AND CARDINALITY

Symbols at the ends of the relationship lines indicate the *optionality* and the *cardinality* of each relationship. Optionality expresses whether the relationship is optional or mandatory. "Cardinality" expresses the maximum number of relationships.

As a relationship line is followed from an entity to another, near the related entity two symbols will appear. The first of those is the optionality indicator. A circle (○) indicates that the relationship is optional—the minimum number of relationships between each instance of the first entity and instances of the related entity is zero. One can think of the circle as a zero, or a letter "O" for optional. A stroke (|) indicates that the relationship is mandatory—the minimum number of relationships between each instance of the first entity and instances of the related entity is one.

The second symbol indicates cardinality. A stroke (I) indicates that the maximum number of relationships is one. A crow's-foot (<) indicates that many such relationships between instances of the related entities might exist.

The following diagram indicates all of the possible combinations:

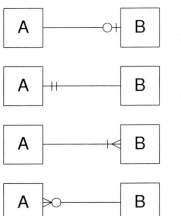

Each instance of A is related to a minimum of zero and a maximum of one instance of B

Each instance of B is related to a minimum of one and a maximum of one instance of A

Each instance of A is related to a minimum of one and a maximum of many instances of B

Each instance of B is related to a minimum of zero and a maximum of many instances of A

In our model, we wish to indicate that each school may enroll many students, or may not enroll any students at all. We also wish to indicate that each student attends exactly one school. The following diagram indicates this optionality and cardinality:

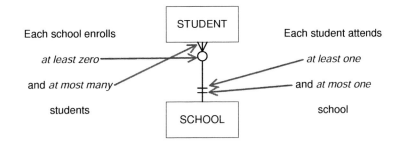

It is important to note that relationship optionality and cardinality constraints apply specifically to the system being modeled, not to all possible systems. According to the example modeled above, a school might not enroll any students—that relationship is optional. A school without students is not much of a school, and indeed if the system being modeled were a school system enrollment database, the relationship would probably be mandatory. However, if the system being modeled is an extracurricular honors program, there may be schools that have no students currently participating in the program. Consider the function of the system and consult the other documents in the data model to clarify modeling decisions.

BRIDGE ENTITIES

When an instance of an entity may be related to multiple instances of another entity and vice versa, that is called a *many-to-many relationship*. In the example below, a supplier may provide many different products, and each type of product may be offered by many suppliers:

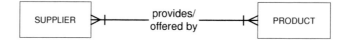

While this relationship model is perfectly valid, it cannot be translated directly into a relational database design. In a relational database, relationships are expressed by keys in a table column that point to the correct instance in the related table. A many-to-many relationship does not allow this relationship expression, because each record in each table might have to point to multiple records in the other table.

In order to build a relational database that captures this relationship, it is necessary to build a bridge between the two entities that uniquely expresses each relationship instance. This can be modeled in an ERD with a *bridge entity*, an entity box containing a diamond, which may replace the many-to-many relationship. (The diamond is used in other ER modeling systems to indicate relationships, or may be viewed as the joining—the bridge—of the many-to-many crow's-feet).

This diagram expresses the same relationship as the diagram above. Each instance of the *provides* bridge entity indicates that a certain supplier can provide a certain product.

In addition to explicitly depicting a relational database structure that can capture a many-to-many relationship, the bridge entity has an additional function in abstract entity-relationship modeling: A bridge entity may capture attributes that are specific to the relationship between instances of the bridged entities. In the supplier and product example, a product does not have an inherent cost; it only has a cost in relation to the supplier who sells it. Similarly, a supplier may not have a uniform delivery time; delivery times may vary in relation to the product being delivered. Any attributes that are dependent on the relationship would be associated with the relationship's bridge entity.

RECURSIVE RELATIONSHIPS

Instances of entities may have relationships with other instances of the same entity. These relationships may be drawn with relationship lines that begin and end connected to the same entity. Common occurrences of these recursive relationships include parent/child relationships:

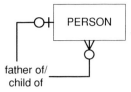

The diagram above indicates that a person may be the father of zero or many persons, and that a person may have zero or one father. (Not every person's father will be recorded in the system, so the relationship is modeled as optional).

MULTIPLE RELATIONSHIPS BETWEEN ENTITIES

An entity may have multiple relationships with another entity. These are depicted in the ERD with multiple relationship lines connecting the two entities:

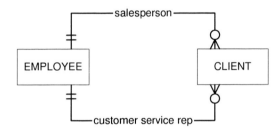

The diagram above indicates that an employee may be the salesperson assigned to zero or many clients, and an employee may be the customer service representative for zero or many clients. Each client has exactly one salesperson and exactly one customer service representative. Each client's salesperson may or may not be the same employee as the client's customer service representative; each relationship is treated independently.

ENTITY SUBTYPES

There are times when it is convenient to depict relationships that apply to an entire class of things, as well as depict relationships that apply only to certain types of the larger class. Entity subtypes accommodate these relationship depictions. In the ERD, entity subtypes may be depicted by entity boxes shown within larger entity boxes. The large entity represents the class, and the smaller boxes depict the subtypes.

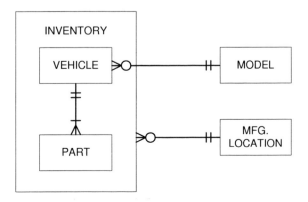

The example above depicts an *inventory* entity, with the subtypes of *vehicle* and *part*. A vehicle has one or many parts, and every part is associated with one and only one kind of vehicle (according to this diagram, there are no interchangeable components). All items in inventory, whether they are vehicles or parts, have a manufacturing location, but only vehicles are of a particular model.

EXCLUSIVE-OR RELATIONSHIP

If an entity instance may have either one relationship or another, but not both, the constraint may be modeled with an *exclusive-or relationship,* represented as a tree with a solid dot where the tree branches. The entity attached to the trunk of the tree is the one subject to the exclusive-or constraint. No relationship is indicated between entities attached the branches.

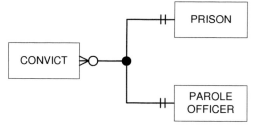

The diagram above indicates that each convict is assigned to a prison, or to a parole officer, but not both. A prison may have zero or many convicts, a parole officer may have zero or many convicts, and there is no relationship between prisons and parole officers.

INCLUSIVE-OR RELATIONSHIP

If an entity instance may have either one or more relationships, but must have at least one of the possible relationships, the constraint may be modeled with an *inclusive-or,* represented as a tree with a hollow dot where the tree branches. As with the exclusive-or constraint, the entity attached to the trunk of the tree is the one subject to the constraint, and the entities attached to the branches are not related to one another by this construction.

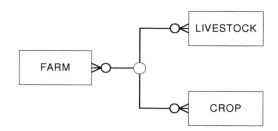

The diagram above indicates that a farm must have either livestock or a crop, or may have both. Any given type of livestock may belong on zero or many farms, and any given type of crop may be grown on zero or many farms.

Entity Relationship Diagram for Electronic Resource Management

The following diagram is the complete Entity Relationship Diagram for Electronic Resource Management. It presents an abstract, theoretical view of the major entities and relationships needed for management of e-resources:

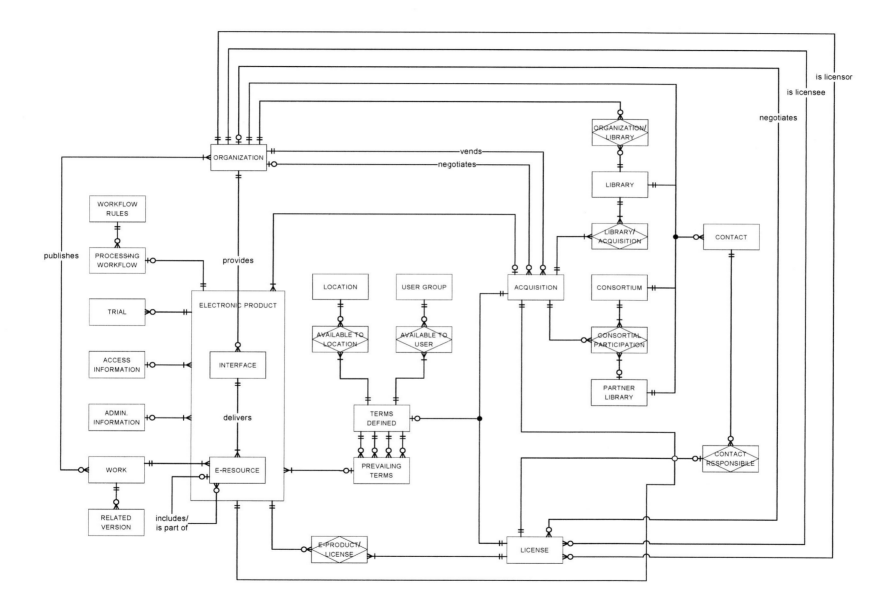

Additional Inheritance Constraints

Unlike other modeling systems, entity relationship diagrams (ERDs) do not explicitly depict situations in which entity instances are expected to inherit attributes or relationships of related entity instances.

This data model assumes the following relationship inheritance constraints:

• An e-resource may inherit its interface's relationship with an acquisition, administrative information, or access information. Alternatively, the e-resource may have a separate acquisition, administrative information, and/or access information from its interface.

• An e-resource must inherit its interface's relationship or relationships with licenses (and with the terms defined by the interface's licenses—although different terms from a different license may prevail for the e-resource).

• An e-resource may inherit its parent e-resource's relationship with an acquisition, administrative information, or access information. Alternatively, the child e-resource may have a separate acquisition, administrative information, and/or access information from its parent.

• An e-resource must inherit its parent e-resource's relationship or relationships with licenses (and with the terms defined by the parent's licenses—although different terms from a different license may prevail for the child e-resource).

Explanation of Complex Relationships or Concepts

Although the overall diagram is large and complex, most of the entities and relationships depicted in the ERD are relatively straightforward, and can be fully understood in consultation with the definitions provided in Appendix D (Data Element Dictionary) and Appendix E (Data Structure).

Several of the relationships depicted merit further explanation.

ELECTRONIC PRODUCT AND ITS SUBTYPES

The *electronic product* entity represents electronic things that may be acquired, licensed, or managed. Electronic product encompasses interfaces, e-resource packages, packages of packages, and individual e-resource titles.

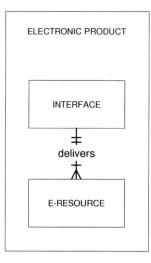

Many attributes and relationships are shared by all electronic products, regardless of whether the electronic product is an interface, package, or individual title. For example, all types of electronic products may be licensed, may be acquired, may undergo a product trial, etc. On the other hand, interfaces and e-resources do have some unique characteristics and in certain cases need to be handled in distinct ways. The electronic product entity and its subtypes accommodate the depiction of these relationships.

E-RESOURCE RECURSIVE RELATIONSHIP

The *e-resource* entity represents e-resource packages, packages of packages, and individual e-resource titles. Any given e-resource title may be a standalone product, or may be a part of an e-resource package. An e-resource package could in turn be part of a larger package. These possible relationships are accommodated with the optional recursive relationship for e-resources:

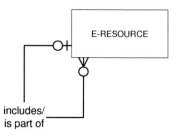

THE ORGANIZATION ENTITY

The *organization* entity represents any business, vendor, provider, publisher, licensor, etc. with which a library does business related to electronic products. Generally, one records the same attributes of an organization, such as name and address, regardless of the role the organization plays. Furthermore, a single organization frequently fills several roles in the e-resource management environment, functioning as vendor, licensor, publisher, and/or provider.

Rather than create separate entities for each role, which may contain duplicate instances of one another, the model contains the single organization entity, with the role or roles of the organization dependent on the relationship or relationships in which the organization participates:

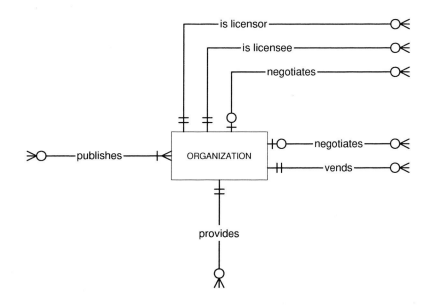

For definitions of the roles indicated by these relationships, see Appendix D (Data Element Dictionary) and Appendix E (Data Structure).

TERMS DEFINED AND PREVAILING TERMS

Each license and each acquisition defines (or may define) a set of associated rights and restrictions on the usage and management of the electronic products covered by the license or acquisition. In some cases, certain terms are defined in licenses, while in other agreements those same term concepts might be defined in the business agreement. To accommodate the uncertainty of where certain rights, responsibilities, and other terms might be defined in any given situation, we have modeled a separate *terms defined* entity:

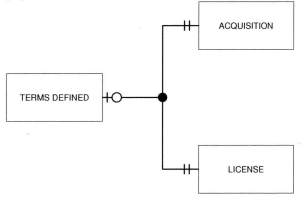

The terms defined entity is able to record all possible rights, responsibilities, and other terms, including terms that are typically defined in licenses (such as "interlibrary loan" or "scholarly sharing" permissions), as well as terms that are typically defined in acquisitions or business terms (such as "number of concurrent users").

Each acquisition may define at most one terms defined instance. Each license may define at most one terms defined instance. Each terms defined instance is defined either by one acquisition or by one license; this relationship is modeled using the exclusive-or relationship.

Use, rights, and restrictions for any given e-resource may be governed by multiple agreements, both legal license terms and negotiated acquisition terms. Each acquisition defines one set of terms, and each license defines one set of terms. Through each electronic product's relationship with an acquisition and its relationship with one or more licenses, one can find all of the terms defined instances that apply to each e-resource.

It may occur that among several terms defined instances that apply to a given electronic product, some of the individual terms are in conflict; this is especially likely in situations where multiple license agreements cover a single electronic product. In such cases it is necessary to determine which of the conflicting terms prevail for the electronic product in question. This is modeled with the *prevailing terms* entity, and its relationships with the terms defined entity:

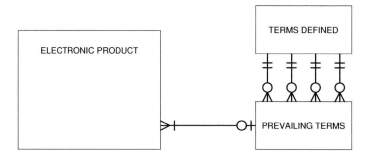

The prevailing terms entity represents all possible terms, just as the terms defined entity does, but for each term merely points to the terms defined entity that prevails. The four relationship lines depicted in the drawing actually represent many relationships: one for each defined term. So while each electronic product may be governed by many different acquisitions and licenses that define terms, each electronic product is governed by at most one complete set of prevailing terms.

Conclusions

This entity relationship diagram depicts the major concepts and relationships needed for managing e-resources. It is neither a complete data model depicting every necessary relational database table, nor is it meant to be a proscriptive design for implementations of ERM systems. Alternate models may capture the necessary attributes and relationships. Hopefully this document, along with the other components of the *Report of the DLF Electronic Resource Management Initiative* will assist developers with envisioning the complexity of the environment that an ERM system must address, and ensure that crucial relationships and features will be included in ERM products.

Appendix D: Data Element Dictionary

Angela Riggio, Ivy Anderson, Adam Chandler, Sharon E. Farb, Timothy Jewell, Kimberly Parker, Nathan D. M. Robertson

Introduction

In the context of the DLF ERMI work, the Data Element Dictionary serves as a basic reference document. It compliments the Data Structure (Appendix E), which expresses the attributes and relationships between the data elements, and the Entity Relationship Diagram (Appendix C), which defines relationships between concepts that exist between groupings of data elements in a system.

The Data Element Dictionary has a very simple structure, consisting of four items. The *data element name* is the full name given to each element in the Dictionary. The *identifier* is the name by which other programs will identify a particular element. For example, the element "E-Product Role" will be called "eprole" when used in an XML schema. The data element *definitions* describe each element. Every effort was made to write the element names and definitions in compliance with ISO 11179, *Specification and Standardization of Data Elements*. The Data Element Dictionary also includes an optional *comments* column, which offers examples for data element values or describes situations in which these data elements might be used. This section also identifies other standards from which a particular data element has taken its definition, or it may recommend that a particular standard be used when entering a value for that element into an ERM system.

DLF Electronic Resource Management Initiative
Data Element Dictionary

Data Element Name	Identifier	Definition	Comments
Access Confirmation Indicator	accessconfirmation	An indication that access to the product was functional when tested	
Access Information Identifier	accessinfoid	The identification number assigned to the Access Information record by the ERM system	
Access Information Note	accessinfonote	Additional information pertaining to access issues and unusual situations	e.g., inaccessible or nonsubscribed portions not marked as such at the site, unusual login/logoff requirements, local vs. remote authentication control, and navigation or accessibility features
Access Tested Date	accesstesteddate	The date on which access to the product was tested	
Accessibility Compliance Indicator	accessibilitycompliance	An agreement that the data is provided in a form compliant with relevant accessibility (disabilities) legislation	For more information, see guidelines set forth by the World Wide Web Consortium at http://www.w3.org/wai/
Account Identifier Assigned to Library	accountidassigned	Identifier assigned by an Organization to a Library's account	
Acquisition Identifier	acqid	The identification number assigned to the Acquisition by the electronic resource management system	
Acquisition Note	acqnote	Additional information about the acquisition	
Administrative Documentation	admindoc	Information about and/or location of documentation available for product administrators	
Administrative Identifier	adminid	The identifier used to access the online administration module	Used if different from account ID
Administrative Information	admininfoid	The identification number assigned to the Administrative Information record by the	

Data Element Name	Identifier	Definition	Comments
Identifier		ERM system	
Administrative Password	adminpassword	The password used to access the online administration module	
Administrative Password Note	adminpasswordnote	Any clarification needed to identify an administrative password or to whom it is assigned	
Administrative Uniform Resource Identifier	adminuri	The Uniform Resource Identifier (URI) of the online administration module	
Administrative Uniform Resource Identifier Type	adminuritype	The type of URI that is used for the online administration module	
All Rights Reserved Indicator	allrightsreserved	A clause stating that all intellectual property rights not explicitly granted to the licensee are retained by the licensor	
Alternate Authorization Method	altauthmethod	Additional authorization methods available for the product	
Alternate Uniform Resource Identifier	alturi	An alternate URI available for access to an identical or alternate version of the resource	To be used when the primary URI is compromised or unavailable. Examples include URLs for mirror sites; URLs that provide access to a resource via a different provider, etc.
Alternate Uniform Resource Identifier Type	alturitype	The type of alternate URI being used	
Amount	amount	The contractually specified price for the Electronic Product	May not be equal to the sum paid as recorded in the price element

Data Element Name	Identifier	Definition	Comments
Amount Note	amountnote	Information relating to the amount quoted for the Electronic Product	
Applicable Copyright Law	applicablecopyrightlaw	A clause that specifies the national copyright law agreed to in the contract	
Archiving Format	archivingformat	The format of the archival content	Values should be site-definable (e.g., remote, CD-ROM)
Archiving Note	archivingnote	Additional information related to archiving rights, product, and format	
Archiving Right	archivingright	The right to permanently retain an electronic copy of the licensed materials	
Authentication Status	authenticationstatus	An indication that provided methods of authentication have been identified and accommodated	
Author	author	The person or body that is identified as the creator of the electronic resource	Usually present on monographs
Available to Location Identifier	availabletolocationid	The identification number assigned to the Available to Location Bridge by the ERM system	
Available to User Identifier	availabletouserid	The identification number assigned to the Available to User Bridge by the ERM system	
Cataloging Priority	catpriority	The level of priority that the product should be assigned in the cataloging workflow	e.g., low, normal, rush
Cataloging Request Date	catrequestdate	The date when a request to catalog the product was made	
Citation Requirement Detail	citationrequirementdetail	A specification of the required or recommended form of citation	

Data Element Name	Identifier	Definition	Comments
Clickwrap Modification Clause Indicator	clickwrapmodification	A clause indicating that the negotiated agreement supersedes any click-through, click-wrap, other user agreement, or terms of use residing on the provider's server that might otherwise function as a contract of adhesion	
Completeness of Content Clause Indicator	completenessofcontent	The presence of a provision in the contract stating that the licensed electronic materials shall include all content found in the print equivalent	
Concurrency with Print Version Clause Indicator	concurrencywithpversion	The presence of a provision in the contract which states that the licensed materials will be available before, or no later than the print equivalent, and/or will be kept current	
Concurrent User	concuser	1. The licensed number of concurrent users for a resource 2. The number of concurrent users if shared across an interface rather than for a specific resource	
Concurrent User Note	concusernote	1. A specific explanation of how users are allocated or shared if pooled or platform-based 2. Additional information about the number of concurrent users	
Confidentiality of Agreement	confidentialityofagreement	The presence or absence of clauses that specify or detail restrictions on the sharing of the terms of the license agreement	The clause may specify terms to be held confidential, or may refer to the entire agreement. This clause may be limited by state law for U.S. public institutions
Confidentiality of Agreement Note	confidentialityofagreementnote	Specific details about what aspects of the license are private	

Data Element Name	Identifier	Definition	Comments
Confidentiality of User Information Indicator	confidentialityofuserinfo	The requirement that user data should not be shared with third parties, reused or resold without permission	
Configurable Session Timeout Indicator	configsessiontimeout	The availability of a configurable inactivity timeout	
Consortial Agreement Indicator	consortialagreement	Indicates whether an acquisition falls under a multiparty agreement that uses the same license for all parties	
Consortial Fund Contribution	consortialfundcontribution	The monetary contribution made by the partner library in a consortial purchase	Can be expressed as a percentage of the total amount or as a dollar figure
Consortial Issues Note	consortialissuesnote	Information relating to or clarifying consortial issues in this agreement	
Consortium Address	consortiumaddress	The mailing address of the consortium	
Consortium Alternate Name	consortiumaltname	Other names by which the consortium may be known	
Consortium Identifier	consortiumid	The identification number assigned to the Consortium by the ERM system	
Consortium Name	consortiumname	The official name of the consortium	
Consortium Note	consortiumnote	Notes which clarify the consortium information	
Consortium Participation Identifier	consortiumparticipationid	The identification number assigned to the bridge record by the ERM system	
Contact Address	contactaddress	The mailing address of the contact	

Data Element Name	Identifier	Definition	Comments
Contact Email Address	contactemail	The email address of the contact	
Contact Fax Number	contactfax	The fax number of the contact	
Contact Identifier	contactid	The identification number assigned to the Contact by the ERM system	
Contact Name	contactname	The name of the contact individual	
Contact Phone Number	contactphone	The phone number of the contact	
Contact Responsibilities Identifier	contactresponsibilitiesid	The identification number assigned to the Bridge record by the ERM system	
Contact Role	contactrole	The responsibility assigned to the contact person in general for electronic products	Roles should be site defined (e.g., Technical Support, Customer Support, Sales, etc.)
Contact Title	contacttitle	The title of the contact individual	
Content Warranty	contentwarranty	A clause that guarantees a remedy to the licensee if the quantity or quality of material contained within the resource is materially diminished	The clause is usually in the form of a pro-rata refund or termination right
Cost Share	costshare	Amount contributed by the Library to an electronic product acquisition	To be used when a library is contributing a flat amount to the acquisition
Cost Share Note	costsharenote	Other agreements regarding cost share	
Cost Share Percentage	costsharepercentage	The proportion of funds contributed by the Library to the cost of an ELECTRONIC Product	To be used when a library is contributing a percentage of the total to the acquisition

Data Element Name	Identifier	Definition	Comments
Course Pack Electronic	coursepacke	The right to use licensed materials in collections or compilations of materials assembled in an electronic format by faculty members for use by students in a class for purposes of instruction	
Course Pack Print	coursepackp	The right to use licensed materials in collections or compilations of materials assembled in a print format by faculty members for use by students in a class for purposes of instruction	e.g., book chapters, journal articles
Course Pack Term Note	coursepacktermnote	Information which qualifies a permissions statement on Course Packs	
Course Reserve Electronic / Cached Copy	coursereserveecopy	The right to make electronic copies of the licensed materials and store them on a secure network	e.g., book chapters, journal articles stored on a secure network, for course reserves and online course websites
Course Reserve Print	coursereservep	The right to make print copies of the licensed materials and place them in a controlled circulation area of the library for reserve reading in conjunction with specific courses of instruction	
Course Reserve Term Note	coursereservetermnote	Information which qualifies a permissions statement on Course Reserves	
Cure Period for Breach	cureperiodforbreach	The cure period for an alleged material breach	
Cure Period for Breach Unit of Measure	cureperiodforbreachmeasure	The time interval that measures the Cure Period for Breach	

Data Element Name	Identifier	Definition	Comments
Database Protection Override Clause Indicator	dbprotectionoverride	A clause that provides fair use protections within the context of assertions of database protection or additional proprietary rights related to database content not currently covered by U.S. copyright law	Applicable for U.S. libraries but may be of interest for other countries when recording terms for products licensed by U.S. businesses
Date IP Address Registered	dateipaddressregistered	The most recent date on which IP addresses were registered with the product provider	
Description	description	An account of the content of the resource	The description may include pointers to other relevant objects (e.g., tables of contents). Source of definition: Dublin Core Metadata Initiative
Digital Object Identifier	doi	A digital identifier for any object of intellectual property	Source of definition: DOI Homepage: http://doi.org/faq/html#1 This element is included under the assumption that the DOI will be assigned to digital objects above the article level
Digitally Copy	digitallycopy	The right of the licensee and authorized users to download and digitally copy a reasonable portion of the licensed materials	
Digitally Copy Term Note	digitallycopytermnote	Information which qualifies a permissions statement on Digitally Copy	
Discount on Price	discount	A discount in price or in pricing formula	
Distance Education	distanceed	The right to use licensed materials in distance education	
Distance Education Term Note	distanceedrestrictionnote	Information which qualifies a permissions statement on distance education	
Domain Name	domainname	Any domain names associated with a given product	Some proxy servers require this information

Data Element Name	Identifier	Definition	Comments
Electronic Holdings	eholdings	The extent of material that is made electronically available	An accepted standard is recommended. The NISO/EDItEUR Joint Working Party for the Exchange of Serials Subscription Information is currently working on an XML-based holdings schema
Electronic International Standard Book Number	eisbn	The ISBN assigned to the electronic resource	If there is no assigned electronic ISBN, institutions may repeat print ISBN or leave element value blank
Electronic International Standard Serial Number	eissn	The ISSN assigned to an electronic resource	If there is no assigned electronic ISSN, institutions may repeat print ISSN or leave element value blank
Electronic Link	elink	The right to link to the licensed material	
Electronic Link Term Note	elinktermnote	Information which qualifies a permissions statement on Electronic Links	
Electronic Product Evaluation History	epevaluationhistory	1. Information regarding evaluations of the product made during the pre-selection process 2. Notes recorded about evaluations made by individuals in the renewal review process	
Electronic Product Local User Identifier	eplocaluserid	An identifier associated with a local institution identity file	e.g., for distribution to end-users and/or for remote access purposes, or other relevant information
Electronic Product Pre-Selection Cost Information	eppreselectioncostinfo	Pricing information for staff review	

Data Element Name	Identifier	Definition	Comments
Electronic Product Pre-Selection Expected Decision Date	eppreselectiondecisiondate	The date by which a decision to acquire the Electronic Product must be made	
Electronic Product Pre-Selection Note	eppreselectionnote	Additional information pertaining to pre-selection actions and decisions	
Electronic Product Renewal Expected Decision Date	eprenewalexpecteddate	The date by which a decision for renewal must be made	
Electronic Product Renewal Review Status	eprenewalreviewstatus	The status of an Electronic Product that is undergoing renewal review	
Electronic Product Renewal Status Note	eprenewalstatusnote	Detail on renewal or termination actions and decisions	
Electronic Product Role	eprole	The role that the Contact is playing in the care of this Electronic Product	
Electronic Product Termination Status	epterminationstatus	The current status in the workflow of the termination of an Electronic Product	
Electronic Product Termination Status Note	epterminationstatusnote	Information regarding a decision to terminate the Electronic Product	
Electronic Product User Identifier	epuserid	The user identifier that provides access to the product	May be independent of primary access method selected for use (as when both IP and user id-based methods are available)

Data Element Name	Identifier	Definition	Comments
Electronic Product User Password	epuserpassword	The password that provides access to the product	May be independent of primary access method selected for use (as when both IP and user id-based methods are available)
Electronic Product User Password Note	epuserpasswordnote	Additional information about user identifiers and passwords	e.g., for distribution to end-users and/or for remote access purposes, or other relevant information
Electronic Resource Alternate Title	eralttitle	A variation in the title proper of the resource, including acronyms, parallel titles, titles in other languages, etc.	
Electronic Resource Contained By	ercontainedby	A collective resource consisting of one or more electronic titles licensed as an entity or group, of which the electronic resource is a constituent part	
Electronic Resource Contains	ercontains	The electronic titles that are components of the collective resource described	
Electronic Resource Identifier	erid	The identification number assigned to the Electronic Resource by the ERM system	
Electronic Resource License Identifier	erlicenseid	The identification number assigned to each Bridge record by the ERM system	
Electronic Resource Package Type	erpackagetype	Indicates whether the electronic resource package is complete (all titles available) or partial (selected titles)	
Electronic Resource Status	erstatus	The current standing, or status in the workflow of the electronic resource	Value examples include "In pre-selection," "on trial," "under review," etc.

Data Element Name	Identifier	Definition	Comments
Electronic Resource Suppression Indicator	ersuppression	Indicates whether the resource has been hidden from public view	
Electronic Resource Title	ertitle	The word or group of words that name an electronic resource	The electronic resource title should be taken from the chief source of information (usually a title screen; the title proper of an electronic resource); if access to the resource is not possible, use the title as given from the supplier of the electronic resource
Electronic Resource Title Continued By	ertitlecontinuedby	The title immediately succeeding the title of the resource	MARC 21 equivalent: field 785
Electronic Resource Title Continues	ertitlecontinues	The title immediately preceding the title of the resource	MARC 21 equivalent: field 780
Embargo Period	embargoperiod	The amount of time by which content is intentionally delayed	Refer to developing standards (e.g., ONIX for Serials) for values
Fair Use Clause Indicator	fairuseclause	A clause that affirms statutory fair use rights under U.S. copyright law (17 USC Section 107), or that the agreement does not restrict or abrogate the rights of the licensee or its user community under copyright law	Fair use rights include, but are not limited to, printing, downloading, and copying Most applicable for U.S. libraries but may be of interest for other countries when recording terms for products licensed by U.S. businesses
Format	format	The form of presentation of a resource	Examples of electronic formats include descriptions of text (e.g., ASCII); images (e.g., JPEG); audio (e.g., "basic")

Data Element Name	Identifier	Definition	Comments
Governing Jurisdiction	governingjurisdiction	The venue or jurisdiction to be used in the event of an alleged breach of the agreement	
Governing Law	governinglaw	A clause specifying the governing law to be used in the event of an alleged breach of the agreement	
Hardware Requirement	hardwarerequirement	Information about hardware requirements	
Holdings Link Activated Indicator	holdingslinkactivated	The activation of a link to library holdings	
Hook to Holdings Indicator	hooktoholdings	The availability of a link to library holdings	
Implemented Authorization Method	implementedauthmethod	The method by which access to the product is controlled	If the provider supports more than one access method, this element records the method(s) selected for use by the subscribing institution
In Process Note	inprocessnote	Additional information regarding in-process actions and decisions	
Inbound Linking Activation Status Indicator	inboundlinkingactivationstatus	The activation of a link to internal stable locations within a product	
Inbound Linking Indicator	inboundlinking	The availability of a link to internal stable locations within a product	
Incident Log	incidentlog	A log of downtime and problem reports and their resolution	An external call tracking system may be used instead
Indemnification by Licensee Clause Indicator	indemnificationbylicensee	A clause by which the licensee agrees to indemnify the licensor against a legal claim, usually for a breach of agreement by the licensee	

Data Element Name	Identifier	Definition	Comments
Indemnification by Licensor Clause	indemnificationbylicensor	A clause by which the licensor agrees to indemnify the licensee against a legal claim	This may specifically include intellectual property claims (third party rights), or may be broader in application
Indemnification Clause Note	indemnificationnote	Additional information providing amplification of any nuances to the indemnification clauses	
Instruction Tools Status	instructiontoolsstatus	The status of instructional tools for the product	
Intellectual Property Warranty Indicator	intellectualpropertywarranty	A clause in which the licensor warrants that making the licensed materials available does not infringe upon the intellectual property rights of any third parties	This clause, in the form of a warranty, may or may not include an indemnification of licensee
Interface Customization Status	interfacecustomizationstatus	The status of customizing the interface for the product	Many products do not offer the capability to customize the Interface
Interface Digital Object Identifier	interfacedoi	The Digital Object Identifier (DOI) assigned to the Interface	This element is included on the assumption that DOIs will be available for objects above the article level
Interface Identifier	interfaceid	The identification number assigned to the Interface by the ERM system	
Interface Language Implemented	interfacelanguage	The activation of one or more interface languages	Refer to three-letter MARC Language Codes, e.g., "eng" for English, "akk" for Akkadian. May derive or point at print version of resource for value. Another standard may be used for these values as long as translation routines are available
Interface Languages Availability Indicator	interfacelanguagesavail	The availability of multiple languages for the interface	

Data Element Name	Identifier	Definition	Comments
Interface Name	interfacename	The word or group of words that name an Interface	If an Interface is unnamed, the value can be assigned locally
Interface Other Identifier Number	interfaceotheridno	A number assigned to an Interface by the locally defined system	This data element allows sites to locally assign and utilize interface identifier numbers
Interface Other Identifier Source	interfaceotheridsource	Identifies a system which supplies an identifier for an Interface	This data element allows sites to locally assign and utilize system identifiers
Interface Provider	interfaceprovider	The service that brings the content to your server or puts it on the Web and provides electronic access	
Interface Public Note	interfacenote	Additional information regarding the Interface that is intended for public use	
Interface Status	interfacestatus	The current standing, or status in the workflow for the Interface	
Interlibrary Loan Electronic	illelectronic	The right to provide the licensed materials via interlibrary loan by way of electronic copies	
Interlibrary Loan Print Or Fax	illprintorfax	The right to provide the licensed materials via interlibrary loan by way of print copies or facsimile transmission	
Interlibrary Loan Record Keeping Required Indicator	illrecordkeepingreq	The requirement to keep records of interlibrary loan activity and provide reports to the licensor at periodic intervals or upon request	
Interlibrary Loan Secure Electronic Transmission	illsecureetransmission	The right to provide the licensed materials via interlibrary loan by way of secure electronic transmission	
Interlibrary Loan Term Note	Illtermnote	Additional information related to interlibrary loan	

Data Element Name	Identifier	Definition	Comments
International Standard Text Code	istc	A voluntary numbering system for the identification of textual works	
IP Address General Note	ipaddressnote	Additional notes pertaining to IP address information	
IP Address Registration Instruction	ipaddressreginstruction	The URI at which IP addresses are registered, the email address or contact role to which updates are sent, or other relevant instructions	
IP Address Registration Method	ipaddressregmethod	The method by which IP addresses are sent to the product provider	e.g., by email, by post
IP Addresses Registered for Access	ipaddressregforaccess	IP addresses registered for use with the product	May contain a list of registered IP addresses, or link to an external file or database where such addresses are maintained. Usage note: a method for automatic update and provider notification when IP addresses are updated may be desirable
Language	language	The predominant language(s) of the resource	Refer to three-letter MARC Language Codes, e.g., "eng" for English, "akk" for Akkadian. May derive or point at print version of resource for value. Another standard may be used for these values as long as translation routines are available
Library Acquisition Identifier	libacqid	The identification number assigned to each Bridge record by the ERM system	
Library Address	libaddress	The mailing address of the library	
Library Alternate Name	libaltname	Other name(s) by which the library is known	

Data Element Name	Identifier	Definition	Comments
Library Identifier	libid	The identification number assigned to the Library by the ERM system	
Library Name	libname	The official name of the library	
Library Note	libnote	Additional information needed to clarify the library data	
License Delivery Instructions	licensedelivery	The required medium in which official communications must be delivered	
License Duration	licenseduration	The period of time covered by the license agreement	
License End Date	licenseenddate	The date on which a license agreement terminates	
License End Date Tickler	licenseenddatetickler	The advance notice interval, in days, desired by the library to warn of an upcoming license end date	
License Execution Date	licenseexecutiondate	The date on which the license was signed or otherwise agreed to by the licensee	e.g., the click-through date for an online license
License Identifier	licenseid	The identification number assigned to the License by the ERM system	
License Name	licensename	The locally-assigned name of the license agreement	

Data Element Name	Identifier	Definition	Comments
License Replaced By	licensereplacedby	The license agreement that succeeds a superseded agreement	
License Replaces	licensereplaces	The license agreement which preceded the current agreement	
License Reviewer	licensereviewer	An individual reviewing the license for the local institution or consortium	
License Reviewer Note	licensereviewernote	Comments recorded by the license reviewer regarding the license	
License Start Date	licensestartdate	The date on which a license agreement goes into effect	
License Status	licensestatus	The current standing, or status in the workflow of the license	
License Type	licensetype	The kind of license that governs access to the product	
License Uniform Resource Identifier	licenseuri	The URI at which the license agreement is made available	
License Uniform Resource Identifier Type	licenseuritype	The type of URI being used to locate the license agreement	

Data Element Name	Identifier	Definition	Comments
Licensee	licensee	1. One to whom a license is granted 2. The legal party who signs or otherwise assents to the license	
Licensee Notice Period for Termination	licenseenoticeperiodforterm	The amount of advance notice required prior to contract termination by the Licensee	
Licensee Notice Period for Termination Unit of Measure	licenseenoticeperiodfortermunit	The time interval in which the Licensee Notice Period for Termination by the library is measured	
Licensee Termination Condition	licenseeterminationcondition	The conditions that would allow a licensee to terminate acquisition during a contract period	
Licensee Termination Right Indicator	licenseeterminationright	The ability of the licensee to terminate an acquisition during a contract period	
Licensing Agent	licensingagent	An organization (such as a subscription agent) or an individual that facilitates a licensing transaction on behalf of one or more parties	The agent may or may not serve in one or more of the following capacities: as negotiating intermediary, with or without a fee for services; as the vendor who accepts payment for the resource; or as the named Licensee for a particular agreement.
Licensing Note	licensingnote	Additional information regarding the license, the negotiation of the license, the product, etc.	

Data Element Name	Identifier	Definition	Comments
Licensor	licensor	1. One who grants a license to another 2. The party who formulates the terms and conditions of use for the product with whom the licensee (purchaser) is bound in contract by signing or otherwise assenting to a license agreement	
Licensor Notice Period for Termination	licensornoticeforterm	The amount of advance notice required prior to contract termination by the licensor	
Licensor Notice Period for Termination Unit of Measure	licensornoticefortermmeasure	The time interval in which the Licensor Notice Period for Termination is measured	
Licensor Termination Condition	licensortermcondition	The conditions that would allow a Licensor to terminate an acquisition during a contract period	
Licensor Termination Right Indicator	licensortermright	The ability of a Licensor to terminate an acquisition during a contract period	
Linking Note	linkingnote	Additional information about linking	e.g., implementation details or other notes
Local Authorized User Definition Indicator	localauthuserdefinition	The inclusion of an institution-specific preferred authorized user definition	
Local Performance Monitoring Note	localmonitoringnote	Information concerning websites or programs that carry out local performance monitoring	
Local Persistent Uniform Resource Identifier	localpuri	A persistent URI that is created locally to access the product	

Data Element Name	Identifier	Definition	Comments
Local Persistent Uniform Resource Identifier Type	localpuritype	The type of locally created URI	e.g., PURL, PID, ARK, etc.
Local Record Number	localrecordno	The record number that is assigned by a local library management system (LMS) to the bibliographic record for the related version	
Local Services Status	localservicesstatus	The status of setting up access to the product in other local services	e.g. OpenURL resolver, broadcast search, etc.
Local System Number	localsystemnumber	The record number that is assigned by a local library management system (LMS) to the bibliographic record for the resource	
Location Identifier	locationid	The identification number assigned to each Location record by the ERM system	
Location IP Subset	locationipsubset	The set of IP addresses associated with a specific location	
Location Name	locationname	The name of a specific location category for the local institution	e.g., organizational units, buildings, campuses, etc.
Location Note	locationnote	Additional information pertaining to this location	
Location Permission Legal Interpretation	locationlegalinterpretation	Designates whether the license or business agreement defining these terms permits or prohibits access from the location in question	
Location Permission Operational Value	locationoperationalvalue	Designates a local decision to further constrain access beyond that required by the license or business agreement	

Data Element Name	Identifier	Definition	Comments
Location Proxy Information	locationproxyinfo	The URI prefix used to direct access through a proxy server for this location or other information needed to establish proxy connections for the location	
Logout Uniform Resource Identifier Indicator	logouturi	Indicates whether the product supports a locally specified URI to which the user is directed upon exiting the Electronic Product	
Logout Uniform Resource Identifier Type	logouturitype	The type of logout URI being used	
Logout Uniform Resource Identifier Value	logouturivalue	The locally specified URI to which the user is directed upon exiting the Electronic Product	
Maintenance Window	maintenancewindow	The recurring period of time reserved by the product provider for technical maintenance activities, during which online access may be unavailable	
Maintenance Window Value	maintenancewindowvalue	The provider's regularly-scheduled downtime window for this product	
MARC Record Availability Indicator	marcrecordavailable	The availability of MARC records for the resource	
MARC Record Note	marcrecordnote	Further information regarding the availability of MARC record sets	e.g., free or purchased, acquisition and implementation status, etc.
Medium	medium	The agent of presentation of the resource	Examples include: online, CD-ROM, DVD-ROM, etc.
Non-Renewal Notice Period	nonrenewalnotice	The amount of advance notice required prior to license renewal if the licensee does not wish to renew the subscription	Use only if renewal type is automatic

Data Element Name	Identifier	Definition	Comments
Non-Renewal Notice Period Unit of Measure	nonrenewalnoticeunitmeasure	The time interval in which the Non-Renewal Notice Period is measured	
Notice Address Licensor	noticeaddresslicensor	The notice address of the licensor	To be used if different than the address listed in licensor role
Number of Consortial Participants	noconsortialparticipants	The number of library participants in a consortial deal	
OCLC Number	oclcno	The unique record number assigned to a bibliographic record by the OCLC cataloging utility	Other system numbers can be locally defined and recorded as needed
Open URL Activation Status Indicator	openurlactivationstatus	The activation of external links from this product	
Open URL Compliance Indicator	openurlcompliance	Indicates whether the Electronic Product and its content is generating OpenURL Standard compliant metadata	For more information on OpenURL see http://www.niso.org/committees/committee_ax.html
Order Request Date	orderrequestdate	The date upon which a request is made for the production of a purchase order for the product	
Order Request Note	orderrequestnote	Additional information about the request for order creation for an Electronic Product	
Organization Address	orgaddress	The mailing address of the organization	
Organization Alternate Name	orgaltname	Other names by which the organization is known	
Organization Identifier	orgid	The identification number assigned to the Organization by the ERM system	

Data Element Name	Identifier	Definition	Comments
Organization Library Bridge Identifier	orglibbridgeid	The identification number assigned to the Bridge by the ERM system	
Organization Name	orgname	The official name of the Organization	
Organization Note	orgnote	Additional information required to clarify the Organization information	
Other Identifier Number	otheridno	A number assigned to the resource by a locally defined source	This data element allows sites to locally assign and utilize system identifier numbers other than those defined by this model
Other Identifier Source	otheridsource	The name of another source which supplies an identifier number for a resource	This data element allows sites to locally assign and utilize system identifiers other than those defined by this model
Other Use Restriction Note	otheruserestriction	Additional information about other use restrictions not adequately described elsewhere	e.g., time of day restrictions on Concurrent Users
Other User Restriction Note	otheruserrestriction	Additional information about other user restrictions not adequately described elsewhere	e.g., users located outside of United States or relevant country of institution
Partner Library Address	partnerlibaddress	The mailing address of the partner library	
Partner Library Alternate Name	partnerlibaltname	Other name(s) by which the partner library is known	
Partner Library Identifier	partnerlibid	The identification number assigned to the Consortium by the ERM system	
Partner Library IP Ranges	partnerlibipranges	The set of IP addresses associated with the partner library	
Partner Library Name	partnerlibname	The official name of the partner library	

Data Element Name	Identifier	Definition	Comments
Partner Library Note	partnerlibnote	Information needed to clarify the partner library or its role in the consortium	
Payment Detail	paymentdetail	Information about the specifics of payment at an institution	e.g., shared funding
Payment Note	paymentnote	Additional information about payment	
Performance Warranty Indicator	performancewarranty	Indicates whether a clause that requires a satisfactory level of online availability and/or response time is present	
Performance Warranty Uptime Guarantee	performanceuptimeguarantee	The specific percentage of up-time guaranteed for the product being licensed, and the context for that percentage	e.g., routine maintenance, excluding routine maintenance, etc.
Perpetual Access Holdings	perpetualaccessholdings	The dates of coverage for which perpetual rights are available and agreed upon in the legal contract	An accepted standard is recommended. The NISO/EDItEUR Joint Working Party for the Exchange of Serials Subscription Information is currently working on an XML-based holdings schema
Perpetual Access Note	perpetualaccessnote	Additional information related to perpetual access	
Perpetual Access Right	perpetualaccessright	The right to permanently access the licensed materials paid for during the period of the license agreement	
Personalization Services Indicator	personalizationservices	The availability of personalization features	e.g., alerts, etc.
Physical License Location	licenselocation	The place where a printed or other tangible instance of the license is stored	e.g., a department, office, file drawer, etc.
Pooled Concurrent Users	pooledconcusers	The number of concurrent users if shared across a consortium rather than within a specific institution	

Data Element Name	Identifier	Definition	Comments
Prevailing Non-Renewal Notice Period Unit of Measure	prevailingnonrenewalmeasure	The time interval in which the Non-Renewal Notice Period is measured	
Prevailing Terms Identifier	prevailingtermsid	The identification number assigned to each Prevailing Term record by the ERM system	
Prevailing Terms Note	prevailingtermsnote	Notes about the prevailing terms as a whole, or any explanations about choices made to set prevailing terms	
Price	price	The amount paid for the product	
Price Cap	pricecap	The maximum percentage of annual increase in a multi-year agreement	The percentage can vary from year to year
Pricing Model	pricingmodel	A description of the fee structure applicable to the product	
Primary Access Uniform Resource Identifier	primaryaccessuri	The method of access, the location, and the file name of an Electronic Product	Usually a URL
Primary Access Uniform Resource Identifier Type	primaryaccessuritype	The type of URI being used to locate and identify the product	e.g., URL, URN, OpenURL, etc.
Print Cancellation Note	pcancellationnote	Additional information about specific cancellation restrictions for print versions of electronic titles covered by the license	
Print Cancellation Restriction Indicator	pcancellationrestriction	Any restriction(s) on canceling print versions of electronic titles covered by a license	

Data Element Name	Identifier	Definition	Comments
Print Copy	pcopy	The right of the licensee and authorized users to print a portion of the licensed materials	
Print Copy Term Note	pcopytermnote	Information which qualifies a permissions statement on Print Copy	
Print International Standard Book Number	pisbn	A unique machine-readable identification number assigned to the print version of a resource	Source of definition: ISBN Home page: http://www.isbn.org/
Print International Standard Serial Number	pissn	A unique identification number assigned to each serial title by centers of the International Standard Serial Number Network	Source of definition: CONSER Editing Guide
Print Price	printprice	The price of the print version of the electronic resource	
Print Subscription Identifier	psubscriptionid	An identifier associated with a print subscription that must be used to register the electronic version for online access	e.g., a subscription number
Process Identifier	processid	The identification number assigned to the Processing Workflow record by the ERM system	
Product Advisory Note	productadvisorynote	A note for public display of temporary information about a product	Used to describe a problem with a product, provide advance notice of anticipated downtime, or convey other temporary information
Product Unavailable Indicator	productunavailable	A flag that indicates that a product is not available	May trigger a particular action
Provider Reference Linking Indicator	providerreferencelinking	The availability of links to external content created by the provider of the product	
Provider System Status Uniform Resource Identifier	providersystemstatusuri	The URI at which the provider posts system status information	

Data Element Name	Identifier	Definition	Comments
Provider System Status Uniform Resource Identifier Type	providersystemstatusuritype	The type of URI used to post system status information	
Proxy Information	proxyinfo	The URI prefix used to direct access through a proxy server or other information needed to establish proxy connections in general	
Proxy Registration Status	proxyregstatus	The status of the registration of access information with the relevant proxy server	
Proxy Server Decision Indicator	proxyserverdecision	The decision to make the product available through a server that operates as an intermediary between the user's computer and the resource to ensure proper authorization	The purpose of this element is not to convey license information (e.g., whether proxy servers are permitted), but to facilitate interoperation with local access management systems
Public Display Release Status	publicdisplayreleasestatus	The status of releasing the product to public display	
Public Note	publicnote	Additional information regarding the resource that is intended for public use	
Publicity Status	publicitystatus	The status of preparing publicity for the product	
Purchase Order Number	ponumber	The number assigned to the purchase order of a product	Probably informed by or linked to an acquisitions system
Purchase Renewal Date	purchaserenewaldate	The date on which the subscription will expire if it is not renewed	For multi-year agreements, the purchase renewal date may differ from the license renewal date

Data Element Name	Identifier	Definition	Comments
Purchase Renewal Tickler	purchaserenewaltickler	The advance notice interval, specified in days, desired by the library to warn of an upcoming purchase renewal date	
Related Version Identifier	relatedversionid	The identification number assigned to the Related Version by the ERM system	
Related Version Title	relatedversiontitle	Title for the print or other tangible version of the resource	
Remote Access	remoteaccess	The right of an authorized user to gain access to an Electronic Product from an offsite location	
Renewal Decision Date	renewaldecisiondate	The date on which the decision to renew a subscription must be made	
Renewal Status	renewalstatus	The status associated with a renewal evaluation or retention process for a product	
Renewal Type	renewaltype	A clause which specifies whether renewal is automatic or explicit	
Resource Type	resourcetype	A categorization of an item according to its physical or intellectual characteristics	Examples include: electronic journals, atlases, book reviews, software, video, government documents, etc. As a real-life example of "types" used in an electronic resource discovery tool, see UCSD's list for SAGE at: http://libraries.ucsd.edu/sage/types.html
Scholarly Sharing	scholarlysharing	The right of authorized users and/or the licensee to transmit hard copy or an electronic copy of a portion of the licensed materials to a third party for personal, scholarly, educational, scientific or professional use	

Data Element Name	Identifier	Definition	Comments
Scholarly Sharing Term Note	scholarlysharingtermnote	Information which qualifies a permissions statement on Scholarly Sharing	
Session Timeout Value	sessiontimeoutvalue	The inactivity timeout used for the resource	The timeout period can be fixed or configurable
Software Requirement	softwarerequirement	Information about software requirements	e.g., browser versions, plug-ins, fonts, and special client software
Statistics Standard Compliance	statisticsstandardcompliance	The official standard to which the usage statistics conform	For more information, see guidelines set forth at http://www.projectcounter.org and http://www.library.yale.edu/consortia/2001webstats.htm
Subject	subject	The topic of the content of a resource, which may be expressed as keywords or terms from accepted classifications or thesauri	Source of definition: Dublin Core Metadata Initiative.
Subscriber Branding Activation Status Indicator	subscriberbrandingstatus	The activation of a branding feature	
Subscriber Branding Indicator	subscriberbranding	The availability of a branding feature	
Subscriber Branding Note	subscriberbrandingnote	Additional information about subscriber branding	
Subscription Identifier	subscriptionid	An identifier assigned to the resource by a publisher or like organization intended to verify the library's subscription to the resource	
Termination Date	terminationdate	The date on which a subscription was terminated	May or may not be the same as a renewal expiration date, since some acquisitions permit early termination by one or more parties

Data Element Name	Identifier	Definition	Comments
Termination Reason	terminationreason	The reason a subscription was terminated	
Termination Requirement	terminationrequirement	The obligation to take certain actions upon termination of the contract	
Termination Requirements Note	terminationrequirementsnote	A clarification of the termination requirements and what certification of the requirement activities is necessary	
Termination Right Note	terminationrightnote	Additional information necessary to amplify any specifications of termination rights	
Terms Defined Identifier	termsdefinedid	The identification number assigned to each Terms Defined record by the ERM system	
Terms Note	termsnote	Notes about the terms in the business agreement of the license as a whole	
Training Information	traininginfo	Information regarding the availability of special training	e.g., instructions on how to bypass simultaneous user restrictions. May also include training contact names and other general information
Trial Available to Public Indicator	trialavailtopublic	An indication of the availability of the trial product to the public	
Trial Expire Date	trialexpiredate	The date on which the trial ends or that the product will no longer be accessible unless acquired	
Trial Identifier	trialid	The identification number assigned to the Trial Record by the ERM system	
Trial License Required Indicator	triallicenserequired	Indicates whether a license is required for the product's trial period	
Trial Note	trialnote	Additional information about the trial access	

Data Element Name	Identifier	Definition	Comments
Trial Password	trialpassword	The password that must be used to access the product on trial	
Trial Start Date	trialstartdate	The date the trial begins or on which the product becomes available	
Trial Uniform Resource Identifier	trialuri	The URI used to access the product during the trial period	
Trial Uniform Resource Identifier Type	trialuritype	The type of URI that is being used for the trial	
Trial Username	trialusername	The user name that must be used to access the product on trial	
UCITA Override Clause Indicator	ucitaoverride	A clause that reflects the licensor's agreement to use U.S. state contract law in the event UCITA is ever passed and implemented in the specified governing law state	UCITA is a state-by-state legislative proposal that would make click-through and shrink wrap licenses binding and enforceable. ARL libraries and consumers groups oppose the legislation
Uniform Title	uniformtitle	A heading consisting of the title by which an item or a series is identified for cataloging purposes when the title is not entered under a personal, corporate, meeting, or jurisdiction name in a name/title heading construction	Source of definition: MARC 21
Update Frequency	updatefrequency	The interval of time at which new data is added to an ongoing electronic resource	The update frequency may or may not be the same as publication frequency

Data Element Name	Identifier	Definition	Comments
URI to Z39.50 Information	uritoz3950	Information to assist Z39.50 access via a web interaction	
Usage Data Setup Status	usagedatasetupstatus	The status of the library's arrangement to receive usage data for the product	
Usage Statistics Addressee	usagestatsaddressee	The local person to whom usage statistics are sent	
Usage Statistics Availability Indicator	usagestatsavail	The availability of usage statistics for the product	
Usage Statistics Delivery Method	usagestatsdelivery	The manner in which usage statistics are made available	
Usage Statistics Format	usagestatsformat	The format(s) in which usage statistics are made available	
Usage Statistics Frequency	usagestatsfrequency	The frequency with which usage statistics are made available	
Usage Statistics Locally Stored	usagestatslocallystored	Information about and/or links to locally-stored usage data	
Usage Statistics Note	usagestatsnote	Additional information regarding usage statistics	
Usage Statistics Online Location	usagestatsonlinelocation	The online location at which usage statistics can be accessed	e.g., URL or file path
Usage Statistics Password	usagestatspassword	The password used for online access to the usage statistics management site or dataset	
Usage Statistics User Identifier	usagestatsuserid	The identifier used for online access to the usage statistics file	

Data Element Name	Identifier	Definition	Comments
User Documentation	userdoc	Information about and/or location of documentation available for end users	
User Group Identifier	usergroupid	The identification number assigned to each User Group record by the ERM system	
User Group Permission Legal Interpretation	usergrouplegalinterpretation	Designates whether the license or business agreement defining these terms permits or prohibits the user group's access to the product	
User Group Permission Operational Value	usergroupoperationalvalue	Designates a local decision to further constrain access beyond that required by the license or business agreement	
User Interface Configuration Indicator	userinterfaceconfig	The ability to control user interface features	
User Note	usernote	Additional information about user categories or special restrictions not covered elsewhere	
User Proxy Information	userproxyinformation	The URI prefix used to direct access through a proxy server for this user group or other information needed to establish proxy connections for the group	
User Status	userstatus	The specific user group categories for the institution	
Walk-In User Term Note	walkinusertermnote	Information which qualifies the status or permitted actions of Walk-In Users	

Data Element Name	Identifier	Definition	Comments
Work Associated with Related Version	workassociated	The work from which the electronic resource has been derived	
Work Identifier	workid	The identification number assigned to the Work by the ERM system	
Z39.50 Access Status	z3950accessstatus	The status of setting up Z39.50 access to the product	
Z39.50 Address	z3950address	Address used to provide Z39.50 access	
Z39.50 Attributes	z3950attributes	Attributes necessary to activate Z39.50 access	
Z39.50 Authentication Information	z3950authinfo	Authentication information necessary to activate Z39.50 access	
Z39.50 Database Name Long	z39050databasenamelong	Long database name necessary to enable Z39.50 access	
Z39.50 Database Name Short	z3950databasenameshort	Short database name necessary to enable Z39.50 access	
Z39.50 Indicator	z3950	Indicates whether the Z39.50 computer-to-computer communication protocol is supported by the Interface	ANSI Standard; element indicates the ability of the Interface of the resource to support this standard
Z39.50 Port	z3950port	Port used to provide Z39.50 access	

Glossary

Bridge (Bridge Entity): The bridge entity allows for the unique expression of each single relationship between two entities when they are linked by a many-to-many relationship. A bridge can also capture unique attributes of each individual relationship (for more information, see Appendix C: Entity Relationship Diagram for Electronic Resource Management)

Consortium: A group embodying two or more libraries or organizations that enter into a cooperative purchasing agreement for a particular electronic product

Electronic Product (Electronic Product): In this model, an electronic product represents a superclass. It is comprised of the Electronic Resource Entity and the Interface Entity (for more information, see Appendix E: Electronic Resources Management System Data Structure)

Electronic Resource(Electronic Resource): Material encoded for manipulation by computer, including texts, sounds, images, numeric data, computer programs, etc. alone or in combination, as well as materials that require the use of peripheral devices directly connected to a computer (e.g. CD-ROM drive or player) or that require a connection to a computer network (e.g. the Internet). –AACR2

Entity: A high-level concept within a data model. An entity can be represented as a table in a relational database (for more information, see Appendix C: Relationship Diagram for Electronic Resource Management)

External Linking: The provision within an electronic product of context-sensitive hyperlinks leading to external resources

Interface: The software platform or website through which a particular e-resource is made available

IP Address: A number that identifies the network, node, server, or individual workstation that transmits or receives information via the Internet

Online Administration Module: An administrative interface supplied by the provider for library staff use wherein the public interface of the electronic product can be modified to local specifications

Platform Simultaneous Users: A limitation on the number of users who may access an interface simultaneously. This number is distinct from the use limit set on individual resources contained within the interface, and may impact access to a particular resource if the simultaneous use of other resources has taken up some or all of the available interface user allowance

Pooled Users: A limited number of simultaneous users which is shared by a group of partner libraries. One institution could exploit all of the available user slots in the pool at any given time. Within this model, pooled users are generally shared within a consortium

Print Version: The paper-based form of an electronic resource, which often serves as the basis for the electronic content

Provider: The organization or service that supplies electronic access to the electronic content

Publisher: The organization responsible for the production of the information contained in the product

Related Version: The print or other tangible form of an electronic resource, which often serves as the basis for the electronic content

Subscriber Branding: The presence of the subscriber name, identifier, logo, or symbol on an electronic resource, which identifies the subscriber as the party responsible for making the resource available at a particular institution or to a specific user group

Uniform Resource Identifier (URI): Identifies the method of access, the location, and the file name of an e-resource

Uniform Resource Locator (URL): A particular kind of URI which locates a file residing on the Internet

Vendor: The organization responsible for accepting payment for the electronic product

Appendix E: Electronic Resources Management System Data Structure

Kimberly Parker, Ivy Anderson, Adam Chandler, Sharon E. Farb, Timothy Jewell, Angela Riggio, and Nathan D. M. Robertson

TABLE OF CONTENTS

Introduction

This document is a data structure and supporting tool for understanding and interpreting the interaction between the Entity Relationship Diagram and the Data Elements Dictionary. The Data Structure maps the elements defined in the Data Elements Dictionary into the entities defined by the Entity Relationship Diagram in a way that supports the functional specifications delineated in the Functional Requirements and the workflow described in the Workflow Flowchart document. As part of a data model, the Data Structure is not intended to be absolutely prescriptive. System designers should feel free to develop their own approach to integrating the elements and entities. However, designers are cautioned from deviating too widely from the concepts of the below approach, as any deviations will need to be transformable for the purposes of data sharing and migration.

The following pieces of information may be helpful in understanding the presentation of the data model in the Electronic Resource Management System Data Structure.

Data **Elements** and **Definitions** are extracted from the Data Element Dictionary with as little variation as possible. However, some elements that are duplicates of others in concept (e.g. elements in the Prevailing Terms entity), or pointers, which are in essence a reference to another entity, may not be listed in the Data Element Dictionary.

Element Types are restricted to text, numeric, logical, date, unique ID, or pointers. Unique IDs are only used for the record identifiers in each entity. Pointers are ID elements from another entity which either supply information from that other entity where needed in the one containing the pointer, or which establish a type of relationship. For example, a one-to-many relationship requires the listing of a pointer to the ID from the "one" side of the equation in the entity of the "many" side of the equation.

System Use / Functionality is used to describe ways the system software may use or need to treat the element or the expected functionality the element is expected to fulfill. References to the outline of the Functional Requirements are made either in the Notes of an entity (for those specifications that the entire entity fulfills) or in the System Use / Functionality area. Functional Requirement outline references are made in the following form: FR#.# and those not recorded in this area are annotated in the Appendix Notes. Not all functional uses of every element are spelled out, but the annotation in the Data Structure is intended to point out the integration of the data model with the Functional Requirements document. Another use of this System Use / Functionality area is to record the binding of paired or grouped elements. Some pairs or groups are simply logical associations, as when the unit of measure should be attached to the element recording the item being measured. Other pairs or groups are functional necessities, as when the pair or group repeats as a pair or group and is actually a surrogate representation of a separate nested table of elements.

Values record the suggested possible entries for an element, or the suggested possible layout of such entries. A few value lists of extensive length are recorded as appendices. System implementers may use alternate terminology as appropriate.

The **Optionality** area records whether an element is required. The key to the abbreviations is:

> R = Required
> RA = Required if Applicable
> O = Optional

The **Repeatability** area supplies information on the unique or repeating nature of the element

The **Notes / Examples** area provides a space to clarify further details about the element or raise issues that are still unresolved.

A number of entities with lengthy lists of elements are separated into Groups for the sake of convenience and clarity. There is no functional purpose to the groupings and they may be ignored for the purpose of system design structures.

The terms *electronic product* and *electronic resource* have been shortened to *e-product* and *e-resource* throughout this document for brevity's sake; refer to the Data Dictionary, Appendix D, for full element names.

ELECTRONIC PRODUCT SET

Definition	Electronic Product is the superclass. It is comprised of both the Electronic Resource entity and the Interface entity.
Notes	Interfaces and Electronic Resources share many characteristics and yet have a number of differences. Thus we use two different entities and one superclass to describe these concepts.

Electronic Resource Entity

Definition	Electronic Resource entity is part of the master set Electronic Product. It is comprised of many elements identifying or associated with an electronic resource. An electronic resource is: "Material encoded for manipulation by computer, including texts, sounds, images, numeric data, computer programs, etc. alone or in combination, as well as materials that require the use of peripheral devices directly connected to a computer (e.g. CD-ROM drive or player) or that require a connection to a computer network (e.g. the Internet)."
Notes	Elements may be derived from other linked entities as appropriate. Electronic Resource is one of two subsets of the Electronic Product set; for some entities an id from either its sibling Interface or from Electronic Resource must be present, but both are not always required. An E-Resource may be the top-level record in a parent-child hierarchy or a child within a hierarchy.

Element	Definition	Element Type	System Use / Functionality	Values	Option-ality	Repeat-ability	Notes / Examples
Electronic Resource ID	The identification number assigned to the E-Resource by the electronic resource management system	unique ID	system generated identifier		R	N	This should be considered a unique local identifier. Links an Electronic Resource record to other data.

Electronic Resource Entity Identifier Group

Definition:	Identifier information about the described object
Elements	*Work Associated With Electronic Resource, Electronic Resource Acquisition, Electronic Resource Prevailing Terms, Electronic Resource Access Information, Electronic Resource Administrative Information, OCLC Number, Electronic International Standard Serial Number, Electronic International Standard Book Number, Digital Object Identifier, Local System Number, Subscription Identifier, Other Identifier Source, Other Identifier Number*
Notes	FR21

Element	Definition	Element Type	System Use / Functionality	Values	Option-ality	Repeat-ability	Notes / Examples
Work Associated With Electronic Resource	The work from which the resource has been derived	pointer	FR8	ID from the Work entity	RA	N	May point to a record in an external system. See the note for the Work entity.
Electronic Resource Acquisition	The business agreement which has made the resource available to the collection	pointer	FR1, FR2	ID from Acquisition entity	RA	N	It can be inherited from a parent e-resource or associated interface

Electronic Resource Entity Identifier Group (continued)

Element	Definition	Element Type	System Use / Functionality	Values	Option-ality	Repeat-ability	Notes / Examples
Electronic Resource Prevailing Terms	The business and legal terms under which the e-resource is licensed and acquired	pointer	FR1, FR2	ID from the Prevailing Terms entity	RA	N	
Electronic Resource Access Information	The access information associated with the electronic resource	pointer	FR14, FR15, FR16, FR17	ID from Access Information entity.	RA	N	
Electronic Resource Administrative Information	The administrative information associated with the e-resource	pointer	FR38, FR39, FR40, FR41	ID from Administrative Information entity	RA	N	
OCLC Number	The unique record number assigned to a bibliographic record by the OCLC cataloging utility	numeric	FR8, FR13		O	N	Other system numbers can be locally defined and recorded in other identifier elements
Electronic International Standard Serial Number	The ISSN assigned to an e-resource	text	FR8, FR13	Layout: ISSN. ISO Standard 3297-1975; ANSI Z39.9-1979.	RA	N	If there is no assigned electronic ISSN, institutions may repeat print ISSN or leave element value blank. The Print ISSN data element resides in the Print Version entity.
Electronic International Standard Book Number	The ISBN assigned to the e-resource	text	FR8, FR13	Layout: ISBN. ISO Standard 2108.	RA	N	If there is no assigned electronic ISBN, institutions may repeat print ISBN or leave element value blank. The Print ISBN data element resides in the Print Version entity.
Digital Object Identifier	A digital identifier for any object of intellectual property	text		Layout: DOI. ANSI/NISO Z39.84-2000 Syntax for the Digital Object	O	N	Source of definition: DOI Home page, at: http://www.doi.org/faq.html#1. This element is included on the assumption that the DOI will be assigned to digital objects above the article level. May be required for particular applications.
Local System Number	The record number that is assigned by a local library management system (LMS) to the bibliographic record	text	FR5, FR8, FR12	Site-defined	O	N	
Subscription Identifier	An identifier assigned to the resource by a publisher or like organization intended to verify the library's subscription to the resource	text	FR38.2		RA	N	For use when a vendor provides a subscriber number or other product-specific account number to enable registration or activation of an Electronic Product.

Electronic Resource Entity Identifier Group (continued)							
Element	Definition	Element Type	System Use / Functionality	Values	Option-ality	Repeat-ability	Notes / Examples
Other Identifier Source	The name of another source which supplies an identifier number for a resource	text	Paired element with Other Identifier Number FR7.3, FR8		O	Y	This data element allows sites to locally assign and utilize system identifiers other than those defined by this model
Other Identifier Number	A number assigned to the resource by a locally defined source	text	Paired element with Other Identifier Source FR7.3, FR8		O	Y	This data element allows sites to locally assign and utilize system identifier numbers other than those defined by this model. e.g., Ebsco title number

Electronic Resource Entity Title Group

Definition:	A name by which the resource is known						
Elements	*Electronic Resource Title, Electronic Resource Alternate Title*						
Note	Descriptive elements may be derived from an external source, e.g. from a MARC record. FR5, FR12, FR19						
Element	Definition	Element Type	System Use / Functionality	Values	Option-ality	Repeat-ability	Notes / Examples
Electronic Resource Title	The word or group of words that name an electronic resource.	text	Used for display and resource discovery. May be derived from an external data source or locally assigned. FR5		R	N	The electronic resource title should be taken from the chief source of information (usually a title screen; the title proper of an e-resource); if access to the resource is not possible, use the title as given from the supplier of the e-resource
Electronic Resource Alternate Title	A variation in the title proper of the resource, including acronyms, parallel titles, titles in other languages, etc.	text	Used for display and resource discovery. May be derived from an external data source or locally assigned. FR5		O	Y	

Electronic Resource Entity Linked Resources Group

Definition:	Relationships between resources						
Elements	*Electronic Resource Interface, Electronic Resource Contained By, Electronic Resource Contains*						
Note	FR1, FR2, FR9						

Element	Definition	Element Type	System Use / Functionality	Values	Option-ality	Repeat-ability	Notes / Examples
Electronic Resource Interface	The interface through which the electronic resource is made available	pointer	FR1, FR2	ID from Interface entity	R	N	All resources are made available through a single interface, even if that interface provides access to only one electronic resource. Otherwise "identical" electronic resources delivered via different interfaces are different e-resources and require separate records.
Electronic Resource Contained By	A collective resource consisting of one or more electronic titles licensed as an entity or group, of which this electronic resource is a constituent part	pointer	FR1, FR2	ID from Electronic Resource entity	RA	N	This element points to another record in the Electronic Resource entity: "a parent"
Electronic Resource Contains	The electronic titles that are components of the collective resource described	pointer	FR1, FR2	ID from Electronic Resource entity	RA	Y	This element points to another record in the Electronic Resource entity: "a child." Some system designers may choose to only point in one direction (to the parent electronic resource from the children but not vice-versa.)

Electronic Resource Entity Other Description Group

Definition:	Other descriptive information about the described resource						
Elements	*Electronic Resource Package Type, Language, Format, Resource Type, Update Frequency, Description, Public Note*						
Notes	FR7						

Element	Definition	Element Type	System Use / Functionality	Values	Option-ality	Repeat-ability	Notes / Examples
Electronic Resource Package Type	Indicates whether the electronic resource package is complete (all titles available) or partial (selected titles)	text	Use when electronic resource is a package	Partial / Complete	RA	N	Permits retrieval of materials where all titles are acquired vs. partial acquisition of offerings from that provider or package or aggregation. Information about whether a resource represents a fixed or selective bundle is necessary for acquisitions and collection development, troubleshooting and support, and interoperation with external data providers or services.

Electronic Resource Entity Other Description Group (continued)							
Element	**Definition**	**Element Type**	**System Use / Functionality**	**Values**	**Option-ality**	**Repeat-ability**	**Notes / Examples**
Language	The predominant language(s) of the resource	text	Value should default to English	code values from ISO 639-2 (three-letter language code)	O	Y	Examples include "eng" for English, "akk" for Akkadian. Derive from print version if print version exists. May use another standard for language code values (e.g. RFC3066) at the preference of the system designer as long as translation routines are available.
Format	The form of presentation of a resource	text		restricted to a canonical list of formats (site-defined)	O	Y	Examples of electronic formats include descriptions of text (e.g., ascii); images (e.g., jpeg); audio (e.g., basic)
Resource Type	A categorization of an item according to its physical or intellectual characteristics	text		restricted to a canonical list of types (site-defined)	O	Y	Examples include: electronic journals, atlases, book reviews, software, video, government documents, etc. As a real-life example of "types" used in an electronic resource discovery tool, see UCSD's list for SAGE at: http://libraries.ucsd.edu/sage/types.html
Update Frequency	The interval of time at which new data is added to an ongoing e-resource	text		MARC Holdings Format codes http://www.loc.g ov/marc/holdings /echdcapt.html	O	N	The update frequency may or may not be the same as publication frequency
Description	An account of the content of the resource	text	Use for public display in online catalogs and portals		O	N	The description may include pointers to other relevant objects (e.g., tables of contents)
Public Note	Additional information regarding the resource that is intended for public use	text	Use for public display in online catalogs and portals FR7.2		O	N	

Electronic Resource Entity Holdings Group

Definition:	Holdings information about the described resource
Elements	*Electronic Holdings, Embargo Period*
Notes	FR13.2, FR13.3

Element	Definition	Element Type	System Use / Functionality	Values	Option-ality	Repeat-ability	Notes / Examples
Electronic Holdings	The extent of material that is made electronically available	text	Actionable information about coverages for use in communicating with other systems (such as OpenURL resolvers, etc.	Layout: ANSI/NISO Z39.71 MARC21 holdings format	R	N	Layout standard is preferred. XML holdings schema produced by Joint Working Party will be substituted here when it is released.
Embargo Period	The amount of time by which content is intentionally delayed	numeric		expressed in days	RA	N	Refer to developing standards, e.g. Onix for serials. This could be implemented with a pre-defined list, e.g. 30, 60, 90, 180, 365, etc.

Electronic Resource Entity Status Group

Definition:	Status information about the described resource
Elements	*Electronic Resource Status, Electronic Resource Suppression Indicator*
Notes	

Element	Definition	Element Type	System Use / Functionality	Values	Option-ality	Repeat-ability	Notes / Examples
Electronic Resource Status	The current standing, or status in the workflow of the electronic resource	text	If value is Rejected or Retired, Electronic Resource should not appear in public lists of available resources FR19, FR24, FR30	New request / Under evaluation / On trial / Recommended / Approved for purchase / Selection rejected / Ordered / Implementation in process / Active / Under review / Retired / Perpetual archive	R	N	Values are examples and can/should be defined and/or expanded by local institutions
Electronic Resource Suppression Indicator	Indicates whether the resource has been hidden from public view	logical	Removing from public view temporarily FR22	Yes / No	R	N	

Interface Entity

Definition	Interface entity is part of the master set Electronic Product. It is comprised of many elements identifying or associated with the interface of an electronic resource. An interface is the software platform or website through which a particular electronic resource is made available.
Elements	*Interface ID, Interface Acquisition, Interface Prevailing Terms, Interface Access Information, Interface Administrative Information, Interface Name, Interface Digital Object Identifier, Interface Other Identifier Source, Interface Other Identifier Number, Interface Provider, Medium, Interface Status, Interface Public Note*
Notes	Elements may be derived from other linked entities as appropriate. Interface is one of two subsets of the Electronic Product set; for some bridge entities an id from either its sibling Electronic Resource or from Interface must be present, but both are not always required. FR19

Element	Definition	Element Type	System Use / Functionality	Values	Option-ality	Repeat-ability	Notes / Examples
Interface ID	The identification number assigned to the interface by the electronic resource management system	unique ID	system generated identifier		R	N	This should be considered a unique local identifier. Links an Interface record to other data.
Interface Acquisition	The acquisition which has made the interface available to the collection	pointer		ID from Acquisition entity	RA	N	
Interface Prevailing Terms	The business and legal terms under which the interface is licensed and acquired	pointer	FR1, FR2	ID from the Prevailing Terms entity	RA	N	
Interface Access Information	The access information associated with the interface	pointer		ID from Access Information entity	RA	N	
Interface Administrative Information	The administrative information associated with the interface	pointer		ID from Administrative Information entity	RA	N	
Interface Name	The word or group of words that name an interface	text	Used for display and resource discovery FR5, FR19		R	N	If an interface is unnamed, a name can be locally assigned
Interface Digital Object Identifier	The Digital Object Identifier (DOI) assigned to the Interface	text		Layout: DOI. ANSI/NISO Z39.84-2000 Syntax for the Digital Object	O	N	This element is included on the assumption that DOIs will be available for objects above the article level

Interface Entity (continued)							
Element	**Definition**	**Element Type**	**System Use / Functionality**	**Values**	**Option-ality**	**Repeat-ability**	**Notes / Examples**
Interface Other Identifier Source	Identifies a system which supplies an identifier for an interface	text	Paired element with Interface Other Identifier FR7.3		O	Y	
Interface Other Identifier Number	A number assigned to an interface by an external system	text	Paired element with Interface Other Identifier Source FR7.3		O	Y	
Interface Provider	The service that brings the content to your server or puts it on the Web and provides electronic access	pointer	FR19	ID from Organization entity	R	N	May be different from the publisher or vendor and may or may not require an additional payment
Medium	The agent of presentation of the interface	text		restricted to a canonical list of media types, (site-defined or taken from an external authoritative list)	O	N	Examples include: Online, CD-ROM, DVD-ROM, etc.
Interface Status	The current standing, or status in the workflow for the interface	text	If value is Rejected or Retired, interface should not appear in public lists of available resources FR24, FR30	New request / Under evaluation / On trial / Recommended / Approved for purchase / Selection rejected / Ordered / Implementation in process / Active / Under review / Retired / Perpetuated archive	R	N	Values are examples and can/should be defined and/or expanded by local institutions
Interface Public Note	Additional information regarding the interface that is intended for public use	text	Use for public display in online catalogs and portals FR7.2, FR8, FR9		O	N	

Acquisition Entity

Definition	Information about the business agreement that has made the Electronic Product available to the collection. An acquisition may be of a product that does not have a cost associated with its purchase.
Notes	Information about Access, Administrative issues, Terms, and Licenses are all recorded in separate entities

Element	Definition	Element Type	System Use / Functionality	Values	Option-ality	Repeat-ability	Notes/Examples
Acquisition ID	The identification number assigned to the Acquisition by the electronic resource management system	unique ID	system generated identifier		R	N	Links an Acquisition record to other data

Acquisition Entity Identifier Group

Definition:	Identifiers associated with the acquisition
Elements	*Acquisition Vendor, Purchase Order Number*
Note	

Element	Definition	Element Type	System Use / Functionality	Values	Option-ality	Repeat-ability	Notes / Examples
Acquisition Vendor	The vendor that is selling or making available the Electronic Product	pointer		ID from the Organization entity	R	N	
Purchase Order Number	The number assigned to the purchase order of a product	text	Link to LMS acquisitions module data FR44.1.2		O	N	Probably informed by or linked to an acquisitions system

Acquisition Entity Consortial Group

Definition:	Information about the consortial aspect of the acquisition, if acquisition is via a consortium						
Elements	*Consortial Agreement Indicator*						
Note	The involved consortium is recorded in the Consortial Participation bridge entity.						

Element	Definition	Element Type	System Use / Functionality	Values	Option-ality	Repeat-ability	Notes / Examples
Consortial Agreement Indicator	Indicates whether an acquisition falls under a multiparty agreement that uses the same license for all parties	logical	May be used to generate reports about consortial agreements or to trigger certain actions, e.g. route messages to a consortial liaison FR19, FR45.1	Yes / No	RA	N	

Acquisition Entity Renewal and Termination Group

Definition:	Used to manage information about the renewal or termination of an acquisition						
Elements	*Purchase Renewal Date, Purchase Renewal Tickler, Renewal Status, Renewal Decision Date, Termination Date, Termination Reason*						
Note	FR46, FR47						

Element	Definition	Element Type	System Use / Functionality	Values	Option-ality	Repeat-ability	Notes / Examples
Purchase Renewal Date	The date on which the subscription will expire if it is not renewed	date	It should be possible to update this date automatically if a renewal payment is made within the system FR46.1		RA	N	For multi-year agreements, the Purchase Renewal Date may differ from the License Renewal date
Purchase Renewal Tickler	The advance notice interval, specified in days, desired by the library to warn of an upcoming purchase renewal date	numeric	Generates a notification to designated library staff FR46.2		O	N	

Acquisition Entity Renewal and Termination Group (continued)

Element	Definition	Element Type	System Use / Functionality	Values	Option-ality	Repeat-ability	Notes / Examples
Renewal Status	The status associated with a renewal evaluation or retention process for a product	text	FR46.5	Under review / On hold / Cancelled / Renewed / Approved for renewal	O	N	
Renewal Decision Date	The date on which the decision to renew a subscription must be made	date	FR46.5		RA	N	
Termination Date	The date on which a subscription was terminated	date	FR47.3		RA	N	May or may not be the same as a renewal expiration date, since some acquisitions permit early termination by one or the other parties
Termination Reason	The reason a subscription was terminated	text	FR47.3, FR47.4		O	N	

Acquisition Entity Price and Payment Group

Definition:	Information about pricing and payments for an acquisition						
Elements Note	*Price, Discount On Print, Pricing Model, Print Cancellation Restriction Indicator, Print Cancellation Note, Price Cap, Payment Detail, Payment Note*						

Element	Definition	Element Type	System Use / Functionality	Values	Option-ality	Repeat-ability	Notes / Examples
Price	The amount paid for the product	numeric			O	N	This should be a hook into LMS acquisitions module if possible
Discount On Price	A discount in price or in pricing formula	numeric	Informational- not intended for system to act upon		O	N	Discounts due to consortial arrangements can be recorded here, as well as other discounts offered from a "list" price
Pricing Model	A description of the fee structure applicable to the product	text	FR43.1		O	N	
Print Cancellation Restriction Indicator	Any restriction(s) on canceling print versions of electronic titles covered by a license	logical	FR43.4	Yes / No	RA	N	
Print Cancellation Note	Additional information about specific cancellation restrictions for print versions of electronic titles covered by the license	text	FR7.2, FR43.4		RA	N	
Price Cap	The maximum percentage of annual increase in a multi-year agreement	text	FR43.5		RA	Y	The actual percentage can vary from year to year

Acquisition Entity Price and Payment Group (continued)

Element	Definition	Element Type	System Use / Functionality	Values	Option-ality	Repeat-ability	Notes / Examples
Payment Detail	Information about the specifics of payment at an institution	text	FR44.1.3		O	N	e.g., shared funding. Could be used for automatic calculation of payment amounts based on percentages.
Payment Note	Additional information about payment	text	FR7.2, FR44.1.3		O	N	

Acquisition Entity Local Group

Definition:	Used to record local information about this acquisition
Elements	*Acquisition Note, Locally Defined Acquisition Fields*
Note	Other elements may be needed to cover more aspects of acquisition information but have not yet been defined in detail

Element	Definition	Element Type	System Use / Functionality	Values	Option-ality	Repeat-ability	Notes / Examples
Acquisition Note	Additional information about the acquisition	text	FR7.2		O	N	
Locally Defined Acquisition Fields	Flexible and locally definable fields for controlling information related to purchase and business activities	text	FR7.1		O	Y	

License Entity

Definition:	Information from the legal document, a contractual agreement, that defines the terms and conditions of use for the product and the relationship between the grantor (licensor) and the licensee
Notes	FR19

Element	Definition	Element Type	System Use / Functionality	Values	Option-ality	Repeat-ability	Notes / Examples
License ID	The identification number assigned to the License by the electronic resource management system	unique ID	system generated identifier		R	N	Links a License record to other data

License Entity Identifier Group

Definition:	Identifier information from the license						
Elements	*License Name, License Type, License Uniform Resource Identifier, License Uniform Resource Identifier Type, Physical License Location*						
Notes							

Element	Definition	Element Type	System Use / Functionality	Values	Option-ality	Repeat-ability	Notes / Examples
License Name	The locally-assigned name of the license agreement	text	Used for display in administrative contexts FR19		O	N	How it is referred to
License Type	The kind of license that governs access to the product	text	FR35	Negotiated / Click-through / Manifest assent / Shrinkwrap	R	N	
License Uniform Resource Identifier	The URI at which the license agreement is made available	text	Hypertext link functionality. Generally used for posting online. Paired element with License Uniform Resource Identifier Type. FR36	Layout: URI. Latest Draft: Uniform Resource Identifiers (URI): Generic Syntax (RFC 2396) (August 1998.)	O	N	e.g., A redacted version of the agreement (minus the business terms)
License Uniform Resource Identifier Type	The type of URI being used to locate the license agreement	text	Paired element with License Uniform Resource Identifier FR36	URL, URN, etc.	O	N	
Physical License Location	The place where a printed or other tangible instance of the license is stored	text	FR35	site-definable list	O	N	

License Entity Review Group

Definition:	Information for managing license review
Elements	*License Status, License Reviewer, License Reviewer Note, Licensing Note*
Notes	

Element	Definition	Element Type	System Use / Functionality	Values	Option-ality	Repeat-ability	Notes / Examples
License Status	The current standing, or status in the workflow of the license	text	FR25, FR26	Awaiting vendor generic license / Under local review / In negotiation / Pending vendor response / Pending local response / Approved locally / Final version awaiting local signature / Final version awaiting licensor signature / Final legal version received / Electronic version created / Redacted version created / Retired	R	N	Values are examples and can/should be defined by the local institution
License Reviewer	An individual reviewing the license for the local institution or consortium	pointer	Paired element with License Reviewer Note FR25, FR26	ID from Contact entity	R	Y	
License Reviewer Note	Comments recorded by the license reviewer regarding the license	text	Paired element with License Reviewer FR25, FR26		O	Y	
Licensing Note	Additional information regarding the license, the negotiation of the license, the product, etc.	text	FR7.2, FR25		O	N	

License Entity Date Group

Definition:	Date and duration information about the described license
Elements	*License Execution Date, License Start Date, License End Date, License End Date Tickler, License Duration*
Notes	

Element	Definition	Element Type	System Use / Functionality	Values	Option-ality	Repeat-ability	Notes / Examples
License Execution Date	The date on which the license was signed or otherwise agreed to by the licensee	date	FR35	Layout: YYYY-MM-DD. ISO 8601 [W3CDTF] http://www.w3.org/TR/NOTE-datetime	R	N	e.g., the date assented to for a click-through license
License Start Date	The date on which a license agreement goes into effect	date	FR35	Layout: YYYY-MM-DD. ISO 8601 [W3CDTF] http://www.w3.org/TR/NOTE-datetime	O	N	If not available or obvious, may be left blank and assumed to be License Execution Date. The license start date does not change when a license is automatically renewed.
License End Date	The date on which a license agreement terminates	date	It should be possible to update this date automatically if a renewal payment is made within the system FR35	Layout: YYYY-MM-DD. ISO 8601 [W3CDTF] http://www.w3.org/TR/NOTE-datetime	RA	N	This may be extended with renewals. For license agreements that automatically renew, the license end date is extended when a renewal invoice for one or more linked e-products is paid.
License End Date Tickler	The advance notice interval, in days, desired by the library to warn of an upcoming license end date	numeric	Used to generate an alert notice before license ends. Can be auto-calculated from the Renewal Notice Period. FR35	expressed in days	O	N	
License Duration	The period of time covered by the license agreement	numeric	FR35	expressed in days	O	N	Permits calculations

License Entity Parties Group

Definition:	Information about the parties to the described license
Elements	*Licensor, Licensee, Licensing Agent, License Delivery Instruction*
Notes	

Element	Definition	Element Type	System Use / Functionality	Values	Option-ality	Repeat-ability	Notes / Examples
Licensor	1. One who grants a license to another. 2. The party who formulates the terms and conditions of use for the product with whom the licensee (purchaser) is bound in contract by signing or otherwise assenting to a license agreement.	pointer	FR19, FR35	ID from Organization entity	R	N	
Licensee	1. One to whom a license is granted. 2. The legal party who signs or otherwise assents to the license.	pointer	FR19, FR35	ID from Organization entity	R	N	Licensee will usually be the local institution or one of its constituent parts, or a consortium of which the institution is a member. Default value should be a defined norm for the local institution.
Licensing Agent	An organization (such as a subscription agent) or an individual that facilitates a licensing transaction on behalf of one or more parties	pointer	FR26	ID from Organization entity	O	N	Although the licensing agent may also be the vendor, the vendor role is not represented here, but is covered in the Acquisitions entity. The agent may or may not serve in one or more of the following capacities: as negotiating intermediary, with or without a fee for services; as the vendor who accepts payment for the product; or as the named licensee for a particular agreement.
License Delivery Instruction	The required medium in which official communications must be delivered	text		Paper / Fax / Email / Certified mail	RA	Y	It may be necessary to more clearly specify when registered / certified / or hard copy is required as a follow-up to other forms of notice

License Entity Linked Licenses Group

Definition:	Relationships between licenses						
Elements	*License Replaced By, License Replaces*						
Notes							

Element	Definition	Element Type	System Use / Functionality	Values	Option-ality	Repeat-ability	Notes / Examples
License Replaced By	The license agreement that succeeds a superseded agreement	pointer	FR37.2, FR47.6	ID from License entity	O	N	A link to a succeeding license agreement may be necessary for auditing purposes
License Replaces	The license agreement which preceded the current agreement	pointer	FR37.2, FR47.6	ID from License entity	O	N	A link to a previous agreement may be needed for auditing purposes

Electronic Product / License Bridge Entity

Definition:	Clarifies license relationships when a single product falls under a different or additional license to that of its parent package						
Elements	*Electronic Resource License ID, Electronic Resource Licensed, Interface Licensed, License For Electronic Product*						
Notes	If a product requires a license for a trial, institutions may later wish to replace the trial license information record with the production license version if they acquire the product. FR1, FR2, FR6, FR19						

Element	Definition	Element Type	System Use / Functionality	Values	Option-ality	Repeat-ability	Notes / Examples
Electronic Resource License ID	The identification number assigned to each bridge record by the electronic resource management system	unique ID	system generated identifier		R	N	
Electronic Resource Licensed	The electronic resource being licensed	pointer		ID from Electronic Resource entity	RA	N	Use either an Electronic Resource ID or an Interface ID but not both in one record
Interface Licensed	The interface being licensed	pointer		ID from Interface entity	RA	N	Use either an Electronic Resource ID or an Interface ID but not both in one record
License For Electronic Product	The license that governs the Electronic Product	pointer		ID from License entity	R	N	

Terms Defined Entity

Definition:	The business or legal terms under which the Electronic Product is licensed or acquired						
Note	Note that the data structure includes both a Terms Defined entity as well as a Prevailing Terms entity. These two entities are very similar but have different functions: Terms Defined are the terms as defined by one license or by one business agreement. It may occur that among several Terms Defined instances that apply to a single Electronic Product, some of the individual terms are in conflict; therefore, it is necessary to determine which terms are in force for the product. The Prevailing Terms consist of pointers to the appropriate Terms Defined elements that actually apply to an Electronic Product. FR6, FR35						

Element	Definition	Element Type	System Use / Functionality	Values	Option-ality	Repeat-ability	Notes / Examples
Terms Defined ID	The identification number assigned to each Terms Defined record by the electronic resource management system	unique ID	system generated identifier		R	N	Links a Terms Defined record to other data

Terms Defined Entity Identifier Group

Definition:	Identification information about this set of terms						
Elements	*Acquisition Creating Terms, License Creating Terms*						
Note	If there are no terms at all for using the product, this entity and the Prevailing Terms entity simply may not have records associated with a particular Electronic Product.						

Element	Definition	Element Type	System Use / Functionality	Values	Option-ality	Repeat-ability	Notes / Examples
Acquisition Creating Terms	Which business agreement created the terms associated with the record	pointer	FR43.2	ID from Acquisition entity	RA	N	Use either Acquisition ID or License ID but not both in one record
License Creating Terms	Which license agreement created the terms associated with this record	pointer		ID from License entity	RA	N	Use either Acquisition ID or License ID but not both in one record

Terms Defined Entity Amount Group

Definition:	Quoted cost information about the Electronic Product defined by this set of terms
Elements	*Amount, Amount Note*
Note	

Element	Definition	Element Type	System Use / Functionality	Values	Option-ality	Repeat-ability	Notes / Examples
Amount	The contractually specified price for the Electronic Product	numeric	Paired element with Amount Note		O	Y	May not be equal to the sum paid as recorded in the price element. Repeating because it may be necessary to differentiate between one-time and ongoing quotes for the same product.
Amount Note	Information relating to the amount quoted for the Electronic Product	text	Paired element with Amount FR7.2		O	Y	

Terms Defined Entity Authorized User Group

Definition:	Authorized user information about the Electronic Product defined by this set of terms
Elements	*Authorized User Definition, Local Authorized User Definition Indicator*
Note	FR33

Element	Definition	Element Type	System Use / Functionality	Values	Option-ality	Repeat-ability	Notes / Examples
Authorized User Definition	The language in the contract that defines the group of users allowed to use the Electronic Product	text	FR33		O	N	For academic libraries, the preferred definition is typically expressed in terms of students, faculty, and staff regardless of location, as well as on-site users of the libraries or other campus facilities. To be consulted by library staff when questions about the precise nature of the authorized user community arise. Inclusion of this may be desirable when authorized user definitions are nuanced or unusual.
Local Authorized User Definition Indicator	The inclusion of an institution-specific preferred authorized user definition	logical	FR33	Yes / No	O	N	A "Yes" would mean the then local authorized user definition was included in the agreement. Used to flag license agreements for possible review should local requirements change (or to attempt to renegotiate local language where lacking.)

Terms Defined Entity Terms of Use Group

Definition:	Terms of use information from the described agreement
Elements	*Fair Use Clause Indicator, All Rights Reserved Indicator, Database Protection Override Clause Indicator, Citation Requirement Detail, Digitally Copy, Digitally Copy Term Note, Print Copy, Print Copy Term Note, Scholarly Sharing, Scholarly Sharing Term Note, Distance Education, Distance Education Term Note, Interlibrary Loan Print Or Fax, Interlibrary Loan Secure Electronic Transmission, Interlibrary Loan Electronic, Interlibrary Loan Record Keeping Required Indicator, Interlibrary Loan Term Note, Course Reserve Print, Course Reserve Electronic / Cached Copy, Course Reserve Term Note, Electronic Link, Electronic Link Term Note, Course Pack Print, Course Pack Electronic, Course Pack Term Note, Remote Access, Walk-In User Term Note, Local Use Permission Term Fields*
Notes	Permitted (interpreted) and Prohibited (interpreted) values for many of these elements refer to situations where the license is silent or ambiguous on the topic of the specific term element and the local institution chooses to interpret that silence or ambiguity as either a permission or a prohibition to engage in the described activity. FR6.2, FR32, FR35

Element	Definition	Element Type	System Use / Functionality	Values	Option-ality	Repeat-ability	Notes / Examples
Fair Use Clause Indicator	A clause that affirms statutory fair use rights under U.S. copyright law (17 USC Section 107), or that the agreement does not restrict or abrogate the rights of the licensee or its user community under copyright law	logical	For staff display	Present / Absent	RA	N	Fair use rights include, but are not limited to, printing, downloading, and copying. Most applicable for U.S. libraries but may be of interest for other countries when recording terms for products licensed by U.S. businesses.
All Rights Reserved Indicator	A clause stating that all intellectual property rights not explicitly granted to the licensee are retained by the licensor	logical	For staff display	Present / Absent	RA	N	
Database Protection Override Clause Indicator	A clause that provides fair use protections within the context of assertions of database protection or additional proprietary rights related to database content not currently covered by U.S. copyright law	logical	For staff display	Present / Absent	RA	N	Most applicable for U.S. libraries but may be of interest for other countries when recording terms for products licensed by U.S. businesses
Citation Requirement Detail	A specification of the required or recommended form of citation	text	FR6.2.3		RA	N	

Terms Defined Entity Terms of Use Group (continued)							
Element	**Definition**	**Element Type**	**System Use / Functionality**	**Values**	**Option-ality**	**Repeat-ability**	**Notes / Examples**
Digitally Copy	The right of the licensee and authorized users to download and digitally copy a portion of the licensed materials	text	May be used to generate staff and user displays	Permitted (explicit) / Permitted (interpreted) / Prohibited (explicit) / Prohibited (interpreted) / Silent (uninterpreted) / Not Applicable	RA	N	
Digitally Copy Term Note	Information which qualifies a permissions statement on Digitally Copy	text	FR7.2		O	N	Can be used to describe local practice for interpretation in instances such as this one
Print Copy	The right of the licensee and authorized users to print a portion of the licensed materials	text	May be used to generate staff and user displays	Permitted (explicit) / Permitted (interpreted) / Prohibited (explicit) / Prohibited (interpreted) / Silent (uninterpreted) / Not Applicable	RA	N	
Print Copy Term Note	Information which qualifies a permissions statement on Print Copy	text	FR7.2		O	N	Can be used to describe local practice for interpretation in instances such as this one
Scholarly Sharing	The right of authorized users and/or the licensee to transmit hard copy or an electronic copy of a portion of the licensed materials to a third party for personal, scholarly, educational, scientific or professional use	text	May be used to generate staff and user displays FR6.2.1	Permitted (explicit) / Permitted (interpreted) / Prohibited (explicit) / Prohibited (interpreted) / Silent (uninterpreted) / Not Applicable	RA	N	

Terms Defined Entity Terms of Use Group (continued)							
Element	**Definition**	**Element Type**	**System Use / Functionality**	**Values**	**Option-ality**	**Repeat-ability**	**Notes / Examples**
Scholarly Sharing Term Note	Information which qualifies a permissions statement on Scholarly Sharing	text	FR6.2.1, FR7.2		O	N	Can be used to describe local practice for interpretation in instances such as this one
Distance Education	The right to use licensed materials in distance education	text	May be used to generate both staff and user displays FR6.2.1	Permitted (explicit) / Permitted (interpreted) / Prohibited (explicit) / Prohibited (interpreted) / Silent (uninterpreted) / Not Applicable	RA	N	
Distance Education Term Note	Information which qualifies a permissions statement on Distance Education	text	FR6.2.1, FR7.2		O	N	Can be used to describe local practice for interpretation in instances such as this one
Interlibrary Loan Print Or Fax	The right to provide the licensed materials via interlibrary loan by way of print copies or facsimile transmission	text	Used to generate staff displays	Permitted (explicit) / Permitted (interpreted) / Prohibited (explicit) / Prohibited (interpreted) / Silent (uninterpreted) / Not Applicable	RA	N	
Interlibrary Loan Secure Electronic Transmission	The right to provide the license materials via interlibrary loan by way of secure electronic transmission	text	Used to generate staff displays	Permitted (explicit) / Permitted (interpreted) / Prohibited (explicit) / Prohibited (interpreted) / Silent (uninterpreted) / Not Applicable	RA	N	

Terms Defined Entity Terms of Use Group (continued)

Element	Definition	Element Type	System Use / Functionality	Values	Option-ality	Repeat-ability	Notes / Examples
Interlibrary Loan Electronic	The right to provide the licensed materials via interlibrary loan by way of electronic copies	text	Used to generate staff displays	Permitted (explicit) / Permitted (interpreted) / Prohibited (explicit) / Prohibited (interpreted) / Silent (uninterpreted) / Not Applicable	RA	N	
Interlibrary Loan Record Keeping Required Indicator	The requirement to keep records of interlibrary loan activity and provide reports to the licensor at periodic intervals or upon request	logical	Used to generate staff displays	Yes / No	O	N	If providing ILL reports to the licensor at periodic intervals is necessary, use Interlibrary Loan Term Note to record the interval required
Interlibrary Loan Term Note	Additional information related to interlibrary loan	text	Used to generate staff displays FR7.2		O	N	Can be used to describe local practice for interpretation in instances such as this one
Course Reserve Print	The right to make print copies of the licensed materials and place them in a controlled circulation area of the library for reserve reading in conjunction with specific courses of instruction	text	Used to generate staff displays FR6.2.1	Permitted (explicit) / Permitted (interpreted) / Prohibited (explicit) / Prohibited (interpreted) / Silent (uninterpreted) / Not Applicable	RA	N	

Terms Defined Entity Terms of Use Group (continued)							
Element	Definition	Element Type	System Use / Functionality	Values	Option-ality	Repeat-ability	Notes / Examples
Course Reserve Electronic / Cached Copy	The right to make electronic copies of the licensed materials and store them on a secure network	text	Used to generate staff displays FR6.2.1	Permitted (explicit) / Permitted (interpreted) / Prohibited (explicit) / Prohibited (interpreted) / Silent (uninterpreted) / Not Applicable	RA	N	e.g., book chapters, journal articles stored on a secure network, for course reserves and online course websites
Course Reserve Term Note	Information which qualifies a permissions statement on Course Reserves	text	FR6.2.1, FR7.2		O	N	Can be used to describe local practice for interpretation in instances such as this one
Electronic Link	The right to link to the licensed material	text	Used to generate staff displays FR6.2.1	Permitted (explicit) / Permitted (interpreted) / Prohibited (explicit) / Prohibited (interpreted) / Silent (uninterpreted) / Not Applicable	O	N	
Electronic Link Term Note	Information which qualifies a permissions statement on Electronic Links	text	FR6.2.1, FR7.2		O	N	Can be used to describe local practice for interpretation in instances such as this one
Course Pack Print	The right to use licensed materials in collections or compilations of materials assembled in a print format by faculty members for use by students in a class for purposes of instruction	text	May be used to generate both staff and public displays FR6.2.1	Permitted (explicit) / Permitted (interpreted) / Prohibited (explicit) / Prohibited (interpreted) / Silent (uninterpreted) / Not Applicable	RA	N	e.g., book chapters, journal articles

Terms Defined Entity Terms of Use Group (continued)

Element	Definition	Element Type	System Use / Functionality	Values	Option-ality	Repeat-ability	Notes / Examples
Course Pack Electronic	The right to use licensed materials in collections or compilations of materials assembled in an electronic format by faculty members for use by students in a class for purposes of instruction	text	May be used to generate both staff and public displays FR6.2.1	Permitted (explicit) / Permitted (interpreted) / Prohibited (explicit) / Prohibited (interpreted) / Silent (uninterpreted) / Not Applicable	O	N	e.g., book chapters, journal articles
Course Pack Term Note	Information which qualifies a permissions statement on Course Packs	text	FR6.2.1, FR7.2		O	N	Can be used to describe local practice for interpretation in instances such as this one
Remote Access	The right of an authorized user to gain access to an E-Product from an offsite location	text	Default to All but Walkins	Yes / No / All but Walkins	R	N	
Walk-In User Term Note	Information which qualifies the status or permitted actions of Walk-In Users	text	FR6.1, FR7.2		O	N	Can be used to describe local practice for interpretation in instances such as this one
Local Use Permission Term Fields	Flexible and locally definable fields for defining new permitted use terms	text	FR7.1, FR32.2		O	Y	It should be possible for each of these fields associated to define actions such as public displays, reports, and alerts

Terms Defined Entity Restrictions Group

Definition:	Restrictions information from the described agreement
Elements	*Concurrent User, Pooled Concurrent Users, Concurrent User Note, Other User Restriction Note, Other Use Restriction Note*
Notes	

Element	Definition	Element Type	System Use / Functionality	Values	Option-ality	Repeat-ability	Notes / Examples
Concurrent User	1. The licensed number of concurrent users for a resource. 2. The number of concurrent users if shared across an interface rather than for a specific resource.	numeric	May be used to generate staff displays FR38.4		RA	N	

Terms Defined Entity Restrictions Group (continued)

Element	Definition	Element Type	System Use / Functionality	Values	Option-ality	Repeat-ability	Notes / Examples
Pooled Concurrent Users	The number of concurrent users if shared across a consortium rather than within a specific institution	numeric	FR38.4		RA	N	
Concurrent User Note	1. A specific explanation of how users are allocated or shared if pooled or platform-based. 2. Additional information about the number of concurrent users.	text	FR7.2, FR38.4		O	N	
Other User Restriction Note	Additional information about other user restrictions not adequately described elsewhere	text	FR7.2, FR33		RA	N	e.g., restrictions on users located outside of United States or relevant country of institution
Other Use Restriction Note	Additional information about other use restrictions not adequately described elsewhere	text	FR6.2.2, FR32		RA	N	e.g., time of day restrictions on Concurrent Users

Terms Defined Entity Perpetual Rights Group

Definition:	Perpetual rights information from the described agreement
Elements	*Perpetual Access Right, Perpetual Access Holdings, Perpetual Access Note, Archiving Right, Archiving Format, Archiving Note*
Notes	FR47.7

Element	Definition	Element Type	System Use / Functionality	Values	Option-ality	Repeat-ability	Notes / Examples
Perpetual Access Right	The right to permanently access the licensed materials paid for during the period of the license agreement	text	For staff display FR37.1, FR47.7	Yes / No / Undetermined	R	N	May be used to trigger action or notification if license is terminated or product is cancelled or withdrawn
Perpetual Access Holdings	The dates of coverage for which perpetual rights are available and agreed upon in the legal contract	text	For staff display FR37.1, FR47.7	Layout: ANSI/NISO Z39.71	RA	N	Used only if Perpetual Access Right is yes. Dates will generally be open while license is current, closed if license terminates or resource intellectual property rights are transferred to another organization. Layout standard is preferred. XML holdings schema produced by Joint Working Party will be substituted here when it is released.
Perpetual Access Note	Additional information related to perpetual access	text	For staff display FR7.2, FR37.1, FR47.7		O	N	

Terms Defined Entity Perpetual Rights Group (continued)

Element	Definition	Element Type	System Use / Functionality	Values	Option-ality	Repeat-ability	Notes / Examples
Archiving Right	The right to permanently retain an electronic copy of the licensed materials	text	FR37.1, FR47.7	Yes / No / Undetermined	RA	N	
Archiving Format	The format of the archival content	text	Multiple values permitted FR37.1, FR47.7	Remote / CDROM / Tape / Unspecified tangible format	RA	N	Archiving Format values should be site-definable by the local institution
Archiving Note	Additional information related to archiving rights, product and format	text	FR7.2, FR37.1, FR47.7		RA	N	

Terms Defined Entity Obligations Group

Definition:	General obligations described in the license or business agreement
Elements	*Accessibility Compliance Indicator, Completeness Of Content Clause Indicator, Concurrency With Print Version Clause Indicator, Intellectual Property Warranty Indicator, Confidentiality Of User Information Indicator, UCITA Override Clause Indicator, Clickwrap Modification Clause Indicator, Indemnification By Licensor Clause, Indemnification By Licensee Clause Indicator, Indemnification Clause Note, Confidentiality Of Agreement, Confidentiality Of Agreement Note, Governing Law, Governing Jurisdiction, Applicable Copyright Law, Cure Period For Breach, Cure Period For Breach Unit Of Measure, Content Warranty, Performance Warranty Indicator, Performance Warranty Uptime Guarantee, Maintenance Window, Renewal Type, Non-Renewal Notice Period, Non-Renewal Notice Period Unit Of Measure*
Notes	FR35

Element	Definition	Element Type	System Use / Functionality	Values	Option-ality	Repeat-ability	Notes / Examples
Accessibility Compliance Indicator	An agreement that the data is provided in a form compliant with relevant accessibility (disabilities) legislation	logical	FR35	Yes / No	RA	N	For more information, see guidelines set forth by the World Wide Web Consortium at http://www.w3.org/wai
Completeness Of Content Clause Indicator	The presence of a provision in the contract stating that the licensed electronic materials shall include all content found in the print equivalent	logical	FR35	Present / Absent	RA	N	
Concurrency With Print Version Clause Indicator	The presence of a provision in the contract which states that the licensed materials will be available before, or no later than the print equivalent, and/or will be kept current	logical	FR35	Present / Absent	RA	N	

Terms Defined Entity Obligations Group (continued)							
Element	Definition	Element Type	System Use / Functionality	Values	Option-ality	Repeat-ability	Notes / Examples
Intellectual Property Warranty Indicator	A clause in which the licensor warrants that making the licensed materials available does not infringe upon the intellectual property rights of any third parties	logical	FR35	Yes / No	RA	N	This clause, in the form of a warranty, may or may not include an indemnification of licensee
Confidentiality Of User Information Indicator	The requirement that user data should not be shared with third parties, reused or resold without permission	logical	FR35	Yes / No	RA	N	
UCITA Override Clause Indicator	A clause that reflects the licensor's agreement to use U.S. state contract law in the event UCITA is ever passed and implemented in the specified governing law state	logical	FR35	Yes / No	RA	N	UCITA is a state by state legislative proposal that would make click-through and shrink wrap licenses binding and enforceable. ARL libraries and consumers groups oppose the legislation. This may be irrelevant for institutions outside the United States, although possibly of interest when they license products from U.S. companies.
Clickwrap Modification Clause Indicator	A clause indicating that the negotiated agreement supersedes any click-through, click-wrap, other user agreement, or terms of use residing on the provider's server that might otherwise function as a contract of adhesion	logical	For staff display FR35	Yes / No	RA	N	
Indemnification By Licensor Clause	A clause by which the licensor agrees to indemnify the licensee against a legal claim	text	FR35	General / Intellectual property only / Other	RA	N	
Indemnification By Licensee Clause Indicator	A clause by which the licensee agrees to indemnify the licensor against a legal claim, usually for a breach of agreement by the licensee	logical	FR35	Yes / No	RA	N	
Indemnification Clause Note	Additional information providing amplification of any nuances to the indemnification clauses	text	FR35		O	N	
Confidentiality Of Agreement	Presence or absence of clauses that specify or detail restrictions on the sharing of the of terms of the license agreement	text	FR35	No / Financial only / All / All but user terms	RA	N	The clause may specify terms to be held confidential, or may refer to the entire agreement. This clause may be limited by state law for U.S. public institutions.
Confidentiality Of Agreement Note	Specific details of what aspects of the license are private	text	FR7.2, FR35		O	N	

Terms Defined Entity Obligations Group (continued)

Element	Definition	Element Type	System Use / Functionality	Values	Option-ality	Repeat-ability	Notes / Examples
Governing Law	A clause specifying the governing law to be used in the event of an alleged breach of the agreement	text	FR35		RA	N	
Governing Jurisdiction	The venue or jurisdiction to be used in the event of an alleged breach of the agreement	text	FR35		RA	N	
Applicable Copyright Law	A clause that specifies the national copyright law that is agreed to in the contract	text	Default to country of institution FR35		RA	N	If contracting parties and governing law are U.S., assume U.S.; if not, specify. This default should be adjusted for the country of each local installation.
Cure Period For Breach	The cure period for an alleged material breach	numeric	Paired element with Cure Period For Breach Unit Of Measure FR34.1		RA	N	As measured by the Cure Period For Breach Unit Of Measure
Cure Period For Breach Unit Of Measure	The time interval that measures the Cure Period for Breach	text	Paired element with Cure Period For Breach FR34.1	Calendar day / Business day / Week	RA	N	
Content Warranty	A clause that guarantees a remedy to the licensee if the quantity or quality of material contained within the product is materially diminished	text			RA	N	The clause is usually in the form of a pro-rata refund or termination right
Performance Warranty Indicator	Indicates whether a clause that requires a satisfactory level of online availability and/or response time is present	logical	FR41.1	Yes / No	RA	N	
Performance Warranty Uptime Guarantee	The specific percentage of up-time guaranteed for the product being licensed, and the context for that percentage	text	FR41.1		RA	N	e.g., routine maintenance, excluding routine maintenance, etc.
Maintenance Window	The recurring period of time reserved by the product provider for technical maintenance activities, during which online access may be unavailable	text	Used to generate staff and user displays FR41.2		RA	N	
Renewal Type	A clause which specifies whether renewal is automatic or explicit	text	FR46.4	Automatic/ Explicit/ Perpetual	RA	N	

Terms Defined Entity Obligations Group (continued)

Element	Definition	Element Type	System Use / Functionality	Values	Option-ality	Repeat-ability	Notes / Examples
Non-Renewal Notice Period	The amount of advance notice required prior to license renewal if the licensee does not wish to renew the subscription	numeric	Paired element with Non-Renewal Notice Period Unit Of Measure FR46.2		RA	N	Use only if renewal type is automatic
Non-Renewal Notice Period Unit Of Measure	The time interval in which the Non-Renewal Notice Period is measured	text	Paired element with Non-Renewal Notice Period FR46.2		RA	N	

Terms Defined Entity Termination Obligations Group

Definition:	Termination rights and obligations in the described agreement
Elements	*Licensee Termination Right Indicator, Licensee Termination Condition, Licensee Notice Period For Termination, Licensee Notice Period For Termination Unit Of Measure, Licensor Termination Right Indicator, Licensor Termination Condition, Licensor Notice Period For Termination, Licensor Notice Period For Termination Unit Of Measure, Termination Right Note, Termination Requirements, Termination Requirements Note*
Notes	

Element	Definition	Element Type	System Use / Functionality	Values	Option-ality	Repeat-ability	Notes / Examples
Licensee Termination Right Indicator	The ability of the licensee to terminate an acquisition during a contract period	logical	FR47.1	Yes / No	RA	N	
Licensee Termination Condition	The conditions that would allow a licensee to terminate an acquisition during a contract period	text	FR47.1	At will / Breach by licensor / Other	RA	N	It should be possible to insert other values
Licensee Notice Period For Termination	The amount of advance notice required prior to contract termination by the licensee	numeric	Paired element with Licensee Notice Period For Termination Unit Of Measure FR47.1		RA	N	

Terms Defined Entity Termination Obligations Group (continued)

Element	Definition	Element Type	System Use / Functionality	Values	Option-ality	Repeat-ability	Notes / Examples
Licensee Notice Period For Termination Unit Of Measure	The time interval in which the Licensee Notice Period for Termination is measured	text	Paired element with Licensee Notice Period For Termination FR47.1		RA	N	
Licensor Termination Right Indicator	The ability of a licensor to terminate an acquisition during a contract period	logical	FR47.2	Yes / No	RA	N	
Licensor Termination Condition	The conditions that would allow a licensor to terminate an acquisition during a contract period	text	FR47.2	At will / Breach by licensee / Other	RA	N	It should be possible to insert other values
Licensor Notice Period For Termination	The amount of advance notice required prior to contract termination by the licensor	numeric	Paired element with Licensor Notice Period For Termination Unit Of Measure FR47.2		RA	N	
Licensor Notice Period For Termination Unit Of Measure	The time interval in which the Licensor Notice Period for Termination is measured	text	Paired element with Licensor Notice Period For Termination FR47.2		RA	N	
Termination Right Note	Additional information necessary to amplify any specifications of termination rights	text			O	N	
Termination Requirements	The obligation to take certain actions upon termination of the contract	text	FR47.5		RA	N	Presence of text could be used to trigger action or notification if license is terminated or product is cancelled or withdrawn. e.g., requirement to destroy any copies of content.
Termination Requirements Note	A clarification of the termination requirements and what certification of the requirement activities is necessary	text	FR47.5		RA	N	

Terms Defined Entity Notes Group

Definition:	Additional information about the Electronic Product defined by this set of terms							
Elements	*Terms Note, Local Use Terms Fields*							
Note								

Element	Definition	Element Type	System Use / Functionality	Values	Option-ality	Repeat-ability	Notes / Examples
Terms Note	Notes about the terms as a whole	text	FR7.2		O	N	
Local Use Terms Fields	Flexible and locally definable fields for controlling information related to terms	text	FR7.1, FR32.2, FR34.3		O	Y	

Prevailing Terms Entity

Definition:	Defines what information from alternative terms of an acquisition business agreement or a license will prevail locally when applied to an Electronic Product							
Note	Note that the data structure includes both a Terms Defined entity as well as a Prevailing Terms entity. These two entities are very similar but have different functions: Terms Defined are the terms as defined by one license or by one business agreement. It may occur that among several Terms Defined instances that apply to a single Electronic Product, some of the individual terms are in conflict; therefore, it is necessary to determine which terms are in force for the product. The Prevailing Terms consist of pointers to the appropriate Terms Defined elements that actually apply to an Electronic Product. It should be functionally possible to enter a Terms Defined ID and specify that ALL of the Terms associated with that record prevail. FR6, FR35							

Element	Definition	Element Type	System Use / Functionality	Values	Option-ality	Repeat-ability	Notes / Examples
Prevailing Terms ID	The identification number assigned to each Prevailing Term record by the electronic resource management system	unique ID	system generated identifier		R	N	Links a Prevailing Terms record to other data

Prevailing Terms Entity Amount Group

Definition:	Quoted cost information about the Electronic Product defined by this set of terms						
Elements	*Prevailing Amount, Prevailing Amount Note*						
Note							

Element	Definition	Element Type	System Use / Functionality	Values	Option-ality	Repeat-ability	Notes / Examples
Prevailing Amount	The contractually specified price for the Electronic Product	pointer	Paired element with Prevailing Amount Note	ID from Terms Defined entity	RA	Y	May not be equal to the sum paid as recorded in the price element. Repeating because it may be necessary to differentiate between one-time and ongoing quotes for the same product.
Prevailing Amount Note	Information relating to the amount quoted for the Electronic Product	pointer	Paired element with Prevailing Amount FR7.2	ID from Terms Defined entity	RA	Y	

Prevailing Terms Entity Authorized User Group

Definition:	Authorized user information about the Electronic Product defined by this set of terms						
Elements	*Prevailing Authorized User Definition, Prevailing Local Authorized User Definition Indicator*						
Note	FR33						

Element	Definition	Element Type	System Use / Functionality	Values	Option-ality	Repeat-ability	Notes / Examples
Prevailing Authorized User Definition	The language in the contract that defines the group of users allowed to use the Electronic Product	pointer	FR33	ID from Terms Defined entity	RA	N	For academic libraries, the preferred definition is typically expressed in terms of students, faculty, and staff regardless of location, as well as on-site users of the libraries or other campus facilities. To be consulted by library staff when questions about the precise nature of the authorized user community arise. Inclusion of this may be desirable when authorized user definitions are nuanced or unusual.
Prevailing Local Authorized User Definition Indicator	The inclusion of an institution-specific preferred authorized user definition	pointer	FR33	ID from Terms Defined entity	RA	N	Used to flag license agreements for possible review should local requirements change (or to attempt to renegotiate local language where lacking)

Prevailing Terms Entity Terms of Use Group

Definition:	Terms of use information from the described agreement
Elements	*Prevailing Fair Use Clause Indicator, Prevailing All Rights Reserved Indicator, Prevailing Database Protection Override Clause Indicator, Prevailing Citation Requirement Detail, Prevailing Digitally Copy, Prevailing Digitally Copy Term Note, Prevailing Print Copy, Prevailing Print Copy Term Note, Prevailing Scholarly Sharing, Prevailing Scholarly Sharing Term Note, Prevailing Distance Education, Prevailing Distance Education Term Note, Prevailing Interlibrary Loan Print Or Fax, Prevailing Interlibrary Loan Secure Electronic Transmission, Prevailing Interlibrary Loan Electronic, Prevailing Interlibrary Loan Record Keeping Required Indicator, Prevailing Interlibrary Loan Term Note, Prevailing Course Reserve Print, Prevailing Course Reserve Electronic / Cached Copy, Prevailing Course Reserve Term Note, Prevailing Electronic Link, Prevailing Electronic Link Term Note, Prevailing Course Pack Print, Prevailing Course Pack Electronic, Prevailing Course Pack Term Note, Prevailing Remote Access, Prevailing Walk-In User Term Note, Prevailing Local Use Permission Term Fields*
Notes	FR6.2, FR32, FR35

Element	Definition	Element Type	System Use / Functionality	Values	Option-ality	Repeat-ability	Notes / Examples
Prevailing Fair Use Clause Indicator	A clause that affirms statutory fair use rights under U.S. copyright law (17 USC Section 107), or that the agreement does not restrict or abrogate the rights of the licensee or its user community under copyright law	pointer	For staff display	ID from Terms Defined entity	RA	N	Fair use rights include, but are not limited to, printing, downloading, and copying. Most applicable for U.S. libraries but may be of interest for other countries when recording terms for products licensed by U.S. businesses.
Prevailing All Rights Reserved Indicator	A clause stating that all intellectual property rights not explicitly granted to the licensee are retained by the licensor	pointer	For staff display	ID from Terms Defined entity	RA	N	
Prevailing Database Protection Override Clause Indicator	A clause that provides fair use protections within the context of assertions of database protection or additional proprietary rights related to database content not currently covered by U.S. copyright law	pointer	For staff display	ID from Terms Defined entity	RA	N	Most applicable for U.S. libraries but may be of interest for other countries when recording terms for products licensed by U.S. businesses
Prevailing Citation Requirement Detail	A specification of the required or recommended form of citation	pointer	FR6.2.3	ID from Terms Defined entity	RA	N	
Prevailing Digitally Copy	The right of the licensee and authorized users to download and digitally copy a portion of the licensed materials	pointer	May be used to generate staff and user displays	ID from Terms Defined entity	RA	N	
Prevailing Digitally Copy Term Note	Information which qualifies a permissions statement on Digitally Copy	pointer	FR7.2	ID from Terms Defined entity	RA	N	

Prevailing Terms Entity Terms of Use Group (continued)

Element	Definition	Element Type	System Use / Functionality	Values	Option-ality	Repeat-ability	Notes / Examples
Prevailing Print Copy	The right of the licensee and authorized users to print a portion of the licensed materials	pointer	May be used to generate staff and user displays	ID from Terms Defined entity	RA	N	
Prevailing Print Copy Term Note	Information which qualifies a permissions statement on Print Copy	pointer	FR7.2	ID from Terms Defined entity	RA	N	
Prevailing Scholarly Sharing	The right of authorized users and/or the licensee to transmit hard copy or an electronic copy of a portion of the licensed materials to a third party for personal, scholarly, educational, scientific or professional use	pointer	May be used to generate staff and user displays FR6.2.1	ID from Terms Defined entity	RA	N	
Prevailing Scholarly Sharing Term Note	Information which qualifies a permissions statement on Scholarly Sharing	pointer	FR6.2.1, FR7.2	ID from Terms Defined entity	RA	N	
Prevailing Distance Education	The right to use licensed materials in distance education	pointer	May be used to generate both staff and user displays FR6.2.1	ID from Terms Defined entity	RA	N	
Prevailing Distance Education Term Note	Information which qualifies a permissions statement on Distance Education	pointer	FR6.2.1, FR7.2	ID from Terms Defined entity	RA	N	
Prevailing Interlibrary Loan Print Or Fax	The right to provide the licensed materials via interlibrary loan by way of print copies or facsimile transmission	pointer	Used to generate staff displays	ID from Terms Defined entity	RA	N	
Prevailing Interlibrary Loan Secure Electronic Transmission	The right to provide the license materials via interlibrary loan by way of secure electronic transmission	pointer	Used to generate staff displays	ID from Terms Defined entity	RA	N	
Prevailing Interlibrary Loan Electronic	The right to provide the licensed materials via interlibrary loan by way of electronic copies	pointer	Used to generate staff displays	ID from Terms Defined entity	RA	N	

Prevailing Terms Entity Terms of Use Group (continued)							
Element	Definition	Element Type	System Use / Functionality	Values	Option-ality	Repeat-ability	Notes / Examples
Prevailing Interlibrary Loan Record Keeping Required Indicator	The requirement to keep records of interlibrary loan activity and provide reports to the licensor at periodic intervals or upon request	pointer	Used to generate staff displays	ID from Terms Defined entity	RA	N	
Prevailing Interlibrary Loan Term Note	Additional information related to interlibrary loan	pointer	Used to generate staff displays FR7.2	ID from Terms Defined entity	RA	N	
Prevailing Course Reserve Print	The right to make print copies of the licensed materials and place them in a controlled circulation area of the library for reserve reading in conjunction with specific courses of instruction	pointer	Used to generate staff displays FR6.2.1	ID from Terms Defined entity	RA	N	
Prevailing Course Reserve Electronic / Cached Copy	The right to make electronic copies of the licensed materials and store them on a secure network	pointer	Used to generate staff displays FR6.2.1	ID from Terms Defined entity	RA	N	e.g., book chapters, journal articles stored on a secure network, for course reserves and online course websites
Prevailing Course Reserve Term Note	Information which qualifies a permissions statement on Course Reserves	pointer	FR6.2.1, FR7.2	ID from Terms Defined entity	RA	N	
Prevailing Electronic Link	The right to link to the licensed material	pointer	Used to generate staff displays FR6.2.1	ID from Terms Defined entity	RA	N	
Prevailing Electronic Link Term Note	Information which qualifies a permissions statement on Electronic Links	pointer	FR6.2.1, FR7.2	ID from Terms Defined entity	RA	N	
Prevailing Course Pack Print	The right to use licensed materials in collections or compilations of materials assembled in a print format by faculty members for use by students in a class for purposes of instruction	pointer	May be used to generate both staff and public displays FR6.2.1	ID from Terms Defined entity	RA	N	e.g., book chapters, journal articles
Prevailing Course Pack Electronic	The right to use licensed materials in collections or compilations of materials assembled in an electronic format by faculty members for use by students in a class for purposes of instruction	pointer	May be used to generate both staff and public displays FR6.2.1	ID from Terms Defined entity	RA	N	e.g., book chapters, journal articles

Prevailing Terms Entity Terms of Use Group (continued)

Element	Definition	Element Type	System Use / Functionality	Values	Option-ality	Repeat-ability	Notes / Examples
Prevailing Course Pack Term Note	Information which qualifies a permissions statement on Course Packs	pointer	FR6.2.1, FR7.2	ID from Terms Defined entity	RA	N	
Prevailing Remote Access	The right of an authorized user to gain access to an E-Product from an offsite location	pointer		ID from Terms Defined entity	RA	N	
Prevailing Walk-In User Term Note	Information which qualifies the status or permitted actions of Walk-In Users	pointer	FR6.1, FR7.2	ID from Terms Defined entity	RA	N	
Prevailing Local Use Permission Term Fields	Flexible and locally definable fields for defining new permitted use terms	pointer	FR7.1, FR32.2	ID from Terms Defined entity	RA	Y	It should be possible for each of these fields associated to define actions such as public displays, reports, and alerts

Prevailing Terms Entity Restrictions Group

Definition:	Restrictions information from the described agreement
Elements	*Prevailing Concurrent User, Prevailing Pooled Concurrent Users, Prevailing Concurrent User Note, Prevailing Other User Restriction Note, Prevailing Other Use Restriction Note*
Notes	

Element	Definition	Element Type	System Use / Functionality	Values	Option-ality	Repeat-ability	Notes / Examples
Prevailing Concurrent User	1. The licensed number of concurrent users for a resource. 2. The number of concurrent users if shared across an interface rather than for a specific resource.	pointer	May be used to generate staff displays FR38.4	ID from Terms Defined entity	RA	N	
Prevailing Pooled Concurrent Users	The number of concurrent users if shared across a consortium rather than within a specific institution	pointer	FR38.4	ID from Terms Defined entity	RA	N	
Prevailing Concurrent User Note	1. A specific explanation of how users are allocated or shared if pooled or platform-based. 2. Additional information about the number of concurrent users.	pointer	FR7.2, FR38.4	ID from Terms Defined entity	RA	N	
Prevailing Other User Restriction Note	Additional information about other user restrictions not adequately described elsewhere	pointer	FR7.2, FR33	ID from Terms Defined entity	RA	N	e.g., restrictions on users located outside of United States or relevant country of institution

Prevailing Terms Entity Restrictions Group (continued)							
Element	**Definition**	**Element Type**	**System Use / Functionality**	**Values**	**Option-ality**	**Repeat-ability**	**Notes / Examples**
Prevailing Other Use Restriction Note	Additional information about other use restrictions not adequately described elsewhere	pointer	FR6.2.2, FR32	ID from Terms Defined entity	RA	N	e.g., time of day restrictions on Concurrent Users

Prevailing Terms Entity Perpetual Rights Group

Definition:	Perpetual rights information from the described agreement
Elements	*Prevailing Perpetual Access Right, Prevailing Perpetual Access Holdings, Prevailing Perpetual Access Note, Prevailing Archiving Right, Prevailing Archiving Format, Prevailing Archiving Note*
Notes	FR47.7

Element	**Definition**	**Element Type**	**System Use / Functionality**	**Values**	**Option-ality**	**Repeat-ability**	**Notes / Examples**
Prevailing Perpetual Access Right	The right to permanently access the licensed materials paid for during the period of the license agreement	pointer	For staff display FR37.1, FR47.7	ID from Terms Defined entity	RA	N	May be used to trigger action or notification if license is terminated or product is cancelled or withdrawn
Prevailing Perpetual Access Holdings	The dates of coverage for which perpetual rights are available and agreed upon in the legal contract	pointer	For staff display FR37.1, FR47.7	ID from Terms Defined entity	RA	N	
Prevailing Perpetual Access Note	Additional information related to perpetual access	pointer	For staff display FR7.2, FR37.1, FR47.7	ID from Terms Defined entity	RA	N	
Prevailing Archiving Right	The right to permanently retain an electronic copy of the licensed materials	pointer	FR37.1, FR47.7	ID from Terms Defined entity	RA	N	
Prevailing Archiving Format	The format of the archival content	pointer	FR37.1, FR47.7	ID from Terms Defined entity	RA	N	
Prevailing Archiving Note	Additional information related to archiving rights, product and format	pointer	FR7.2, FR37.1, FR47.7	ID from Terms Defined entity	RA	N	

Prevailing Terms Entity Obligations Group

Definition:	General obligations described in the license or business agreement
Elements	*Prevailing Accessibility Compliance Indicator, Prevailing Completeness Of Content Clause Indicator, Prevailing Concurrency With Print Version Clause Indicator, Prevailing Intellectual Property Warranty Indicator, Prevailing Confidentiality Of User Information Indicator, Prevailing UCITA Override Clause Indicator, Prevailing Clickwrap Modification Clause Indicator, Prevailing Indemnification By Licensor Clause, Prevailing Indemnification By Licensee Clause Indicator, Prevailing Indemnification Clause Note, Prevailing Confidentiality Of Agreement, Prevailing Confidentiality Of Agreement Note, Prevailing Governing Law, Prevailing Governing Jurisdiction, Prevailing Applicable Copyright Law, Prevailing Cure Period For Breach, Prevailing Cure Period For Breach Unit Of Measure, Prevailing Content Warranty, Prevailing Performance Warranty Indicator, Prevailing Performance Warranty Uptime Guarantee, Prevailing Maintenance Window, Prevailing Renewal Type, Prevailing Non-Renewal Notice Period, Prevailing Non-Renewal Notice Period Unit Of Measure*
Notes	FR35

Element	Definition	Element Type	System Use / Functionality	Values	Option-ality	Repeat-ability	Notes / Examples
Prevailing Accessibility Compliance Indicator	An agreement that the data is provided in a form compliant with relevant accessibility (disabilities) legislation	pointer	FR35	ID from Terms Defined entity	RA	N	For more information, see guidelines set forth by the World Wide Web Consortium at http://www.w3.org/wai
Prevailing Completeness Of Content Clause Indicator	The presence of a provision in the contract stating that the licensed electronic materials shall include all content found in the print equivalent	pointer	FR35	ID from Terms Defined entity	RA	N	
Prevailing Concurrency With Print Version Clause Indicator	The presence of a provision in the contract which states that the licensed materials will be available before, or no later than the print equivalent, and/or will be kept current	pointer	FR35	ID from Terms Defined entity	RA	N	
Prevailing Intellectual Property Warranty Indicator	A clause in which the licensor warrants that making the licensed materials available does not infringe upon the intellectual property rights of any third parties	pointer	FR35	ID from Terms Defined entity	RA	N	This clause, in the form of a warranty, may or may not include an indemnification of licensee
Prevailing Confidentiality Of User Information Indicator	The requirement that user data should not be shared with third parties, reused or resold without permission	pointer	FR35	ID from Terms Defined entity	RA	N	

Prevailing Terms Entity Obligations Group (continued)							
Element	Definition	Element Type	System Use / Functionality	Values	Option-ality	Repeat-ability	Notes / Examples
Prevailing UCITA Override Clause Indicator	A clause that reflects the licensor's agreement to use U.S. state contract law in the event UCITA is ever passed and implemented in the specified governing law state	pointer	FR35	ID from Terms Defined entity	RA	N	UCITA is a state by state legislative proposal that would make click-through and shrink wrap licenses binding and enforceable. ARL libraries and consumers groups oppose the legislation. This may be irrelevant for institutions outside the United States, although possibly of interest when they license products from U.S. companies.
Prevailing Clickwrap Modification Clause Indicator	A clause indicating that the negotiated agreement supersedes any click-through, click-wrap, other user agreement, or terms of use residing on the provider's server that might otherwise function as a contract of adhesion	pointer	For staff display FR35	ID from Terms Defined entity	RA	N	
Prevailing Indemnification By Licensor Clause	A clause by which the licensor agrees to indemnify the licensee against a legal claim	pointer	FR35	ID from Terms Defined entity	RA	N	
Prevailing Indemnification By Licensee Clause Indicator	A clause by which the licensee agrees to indemnify the licensor against a legal claim, usually for a breach of agreement by the licensee	pointer	FR35	ID from Terms Defined entity	RA	N	
Prevailing Indemnification Clause Note	Additional information providing amplification of any nuances to the indemnification clauses	pointer	FR35	ID from Terms Defined entity	RA	N	
Prevailing Confidentiality Of Agreement	Presence or absence of clauses that specify or detail restrictions on the sharing of the of terms of the license agreement	pointer	FR35	ID from Terms Defined entity	RA	N	The clause may specify terms to be held confidential, or may refer to the entire agreement. This clause may be limited by state law for U.S. public institutions.
Prevailing Confidentiality Of Agreement Note	Specific details of what aspects of the license are private	pointer	FR7.2, FR35	ID from Terms Defined entity	RA	N	
Prevailing Governing Law	A clause specifying the governing law to be used in the event of an alleged breach of the agreement	pointer	FR35	ID from Terms Defined entity	RA	N	
Prevailing Governing Jurisdiction	The venue or jurisdiction to be used in the event of an alleged breach of the agreement	pointer	FR35	ID from Terms Defined entity	RA	N	

Prevailing Terms Entity Obligations Group (continued)							
Element	Definition	Element Type	System Use / Functionality	Values	Option-ality	Repeat-ability	Notes / Examples
Prevailing Applicable Copyright Law	A clause that specifies the national copyright law that is agreed to in the contract	pointer	FR35	ID from Terms Defined entity	RA	N	
Prevailing Cure Period For Breach	The cure period for an alleged material breach	pointer	Paired element with Prevailing Cure Period For Breach Unit Of Measure FR34.1	ID from Terms Defined entity	RA	N	As measured by the Prevailing Cure Period For Breach Unit Of Measure
Prevailing Cure Period For Breach Unit Of Measure	The time interval that measures the Cure Period for Breach	pointer	Paired element with Prevailing Cure Period For Breach FR34.1	ID from Terms Defined entity	RA	N	
Prevailing Content Warranty	A clause that guarantees a remedy to the licensee if the quantity or quality of material contained within the product is materially diminished	pointer		ID from Terms Defined entity	RA	N	The clause is usually in the form of a pro-rata refund or termination right
Prevailing Performance Warranty Indicator	Indicates whether a clause that requires a satisfactory level of online availability and/or response time is present	pointer	FR41.1	ID from Terms Defined entity	RA	N	
Prevailing Performance Warranty Uptime Guarantee	The specific percentage of up-time guaranteed for the product being licensed, and the context for that percentage	pointer	FR41.1	ID from Terms Defined entity	RA	N	e.g., routine maintenance, excluding routine maintenance, etc.
Prevailing Maintenance Window	The recurring period of time reserved by the product provider for technical maintenance activities, during which online access may be unavailable	pointer	Used to generate staff and user displays FR41.2	ID from Terms Defined entity	RA	N	
Prevailing Renewal Type	A clause which specifies whether renewal is automatic or explicit	pointer	FR46.4	ID from Terms Defined entity	RA	N	

Prevailing Terms Entity Obligations Group (continued)

Element	Definition	Element Type	System Use / Functionality	Values	Option-ality	Repeat-ability	Notes / Examples
Prevailing Non-Renewal Notice Period	The amount of advance notice required prior to license renewal if the licensee does not wish to renew the subscription	pointer	Paired element with Prevailing Non-Renewal Notice Period Unit Of Measure FR46.2	ID from Terms Defined entity	RA	N	
Prevailing Non-Renewal Notice Period Unit Of Measure	The time interval in which the Non-Renewal Notice Period is measured	text	Paired element with Prevailing Non-Renewal Notice Period FR46.2	ID from Terms Defined entity	RA	N	

Prevailing Terms Entity Termination Obligations Group

Definition:	Termination rights and obligations in the described agreement
Elements	*Prevailing Licensee Termination Right Indicator, Prevailing Licensee Termination Condition, Prevailing Licensee Notice Period For Termination, Prevailing Licensee Notice Period For Termination Unit Of Measure, Prevailing Licensor Termination Right Indicator, Prevailing Licensor Termination Condition, Prevailing Licensor Notice Period For Termination, Prevailing Licensor Notice Period For Termination Unit Of Measure, Prevailing Termination Right Note, Prevailing Termination Requirements, Prevailing Termination Requirements Note*
Notes	

Element	Definition	Element Type	System Use / Functionality	Values	Option-ality	Repeat-ability	Notes / Examples
Prevailing Licensee Termination Right Indicator	The ability of the licensee to terminate an acquisition during a contract period	pointer	FR47.1	ID from Terms Defined entity	RA	N	
Prevailing Licensee Termination Condition	The conditions that would allow a licensee to terminate an acquisition during a contract period	pointer	FR47.1	ID from Terms Defined entity	RA	N	

Prevailing Terms Entity Termination Obligations Group (continued)

Element	Definition	Element Type	System Use / Functionality	Values	Option-ality	Repeat-ability	Notes / Examples
Prevailing Licensee Notice Period For Termination	The amount of advance notice required prior to contract termination by the licensee	pointer	Paired element with Prevailing Licensee Notice Period For Termination Unit Of Measure FR47.1	ID from Terms Defined entity	RA	N	
Prevailing Licensee Notice Period For Termination Unit Of Measure	The time interval in which the Licensee Notice Period for Termination is measured	pointer	Paired element with Prevailing Licensee Notice Period For Termination FR47.1	ID from Terms Defined entity	RA	N	
Prevailing Licensor Termination Right Indicator	The ability of a licensor to terminate an acquisition during a contract period	pointer	FR47.2	ID from Terms Defined entity	RA	N	
Prevailing Licensor Termination Condition	The conditions that would allow a licensor to terminate an acquisition during a contract period	pointer	FR47.2	ID from Terms Defined entity	RA	N	
Prevailing Licensor Notice Period For Termination	The amount of advance notice required prior to contract termination by the licensor	pointer	Paired element with Prevailing Licensor Notice Period For Termination Unit Of Measure FR47.2	ID from Terms Defined entity	RA	N	
Prevailing Licensor Notice Period For Termination Unit Of Measure	The time interval in which the Licensor Notice Period for Termination is measured	pointer	Paired element with Prevailing Licensor Notice Period For Termination FR47.2	ID from Terms Defined entity	RA	N	
Prevailing Termination Right Note	Additional information necessary to amplify any specifications of termination rights	pointer			RA	N	

Prevailing Terms Entity Termination Obligations Group (continued)

Element	Definition	Element Type	System Use / Functionality	Values	Option-ality	Repeat-ability	Notes / Examples
Prevailing Termination Requirements	The obligation to take certain actions upon termination of the contract	pointer	FR47.5	ID from Terms Defined entity	RA	N	Presence of text could be used to trigger action or notification if license is terminated or product is cancelled or withdrawn. e.g., requirement to destroy any copies of content.
Prevailing Termination Requirements Note	A clarification of the termination requirements and what certification of the requirement activities is necessary	pointer	FR47.5	ID from Terms Defined entity	RA	N	

Prevailing Terms Entity Notes Group

Definition:	Used to record additional information about the E-Product defined by this set of terms or the choices of Prevailing Terms made amongst conflicting Terms Defined
Elements	*Prevailing Terms Note, Prevailing Local Use Terms Fields*
Note	

Element	Definition	Element Type	System Use / Functionality	Values	Option-ality	Repeat-ability	Notes / Examples
Prevailing Terms Note	Notes about the prevailing terms as a whole or any explanations about choices made to set prevailing terms	text	FR7.2		O	N	
Prevailing Local Use Terms Fields	Flexible and locally definable fields for controlling information related to terms	pointer	FR7.1, FR32.2, FR34.3	ID from Terms Defined entity	RA	Y	

User Group Entity

Definition:	Lists categories of persons who, by virtue of an affiliation or some other attribute, may be permitted by contract to access the product
Elements	*User Group ID, User Status, User Proxy Information, User Note*
Note	May be used to inter-operate with a local or vendor-based access management system or proxy server (e.g. by mapping to appropriate authentication credentials) FR6.1, FR7.3, FR15.1, FR18, FR33

Element	Definition	Element Type	System Use / Functionality	Values	Option-ality	Repeat-ability	Notes / Examples
User Group ID	The identification number assigned to each User Group record by the electronic resource management system	unique ID	system generated identifier		R	N	Links a User Group record to other data

User Group Entity (continued)

Element	Definition	Element Type	System Use / Functionality	Values	Option-ality	Repeat-ability	Notes / Examples
User Status	The specific user group categories for the institution	text	FR7.3	Pre-populated options listed in Appendix B	R	N	Values not present in Appendix B can be created to identify user status of additional user categories
User Proxy Information	The URI prefix used to direct access through a proxy server for this user group or other information needed to establish proxy connections for the group	text	FR14.3		O	N	To be used when a proxy setup permits distinguishing accessibility permissions on the basis of user groups and when the license specifies that this particular user group is permitted or prohibited. Otherwise, general library proxy information should be recorded in the Library entity.
User Note	Additional information about user categories or special restrictions not covered elsewhere	text	FR7.2		O	N	

Available To User Bridge Entity

Definition:	Concatenates information from Prevailing Terms entity and User Group entity. Identifies on a case-by-case basis whether a designated user group is permitted access to the product or products governed by the associated terms.
Elements	*Available To User ID, Terms Record Associated With User Group, User Group Associated With Term, User Group Permission Legal Interpretation, User Group Permission Operational Value*
Notes	FR6.1, FR18

Element	Definition	Element Type	System Use / Functionality	Values	Option-ality	Repeat-ability	Notes / Examples
Available To User ID	The identification number assigned to the Available To User Bridge by the electronic resource management system	unique ID	system generated identifier		R	N	
Terms Record Associated With User Group	The Prevailing Terms record for which the user group permissions are defined	pointer		ID from the Prevailing Terms entity	R	N	

Available To User Bridge Entity (continued)							
Element	Definition	Element Type	System Use / Functionality	Values	Option-ality	Repeat-ability	Notes / Examples
User Group Associated With Term	Identifies the user group which, by virtue of an affiliation or some other attribute, is permitted or prohibited by contract to access the product	pointer	May be used to interoperate with a local or vendor-based access management system (e.g. by mapping to appropriate authentication credentials)	ID from the User Group entity	RA	N	
User Group Permission Legal Interpretation	Designates whether the license or business agreement defining these terms permits or prohibits the user group's access to the product	text	Used for public and staff displays	Permitted (explicit) / Permitted (interpreted) / Prohibited (explicit) / Prohibited (interpreted) / Silent (uninterpreted) / Not Applicable	R	N	Used to define those who the license permits or restricts
User Group Permission Operational Value	Designates a local decision to further constrain access beyond that required by the license or business agreement	text	Defaults to User Group Permission Legal Interpretation, but can be overridden	Permitted / Prohibited	RA	N	e.g., a choice to constrain access to the faculty of a particular department to reduce lockouts. If present, this over-rides User Group Permission Legal Interpretation for public displays.

Location Entity

Definition:	Lists those locations that may be permitted by contract to access the product
Elements	*Location ID, Location Name, Location IP Subset, Location Proxy Information, Location Note*
Types	
Note	May be used to interoperate with a local or vendor-based access management system (e.g. by mapping to appropriate IP addresses). In a consortium, the individual libraries participating in the contract could be recorded here for actual authentication management in addition to their record in the Participating Library entity. FR6.1, FR7.3, FR18

Element	Definition	Element Type	System Use / Functionality	Values	Option-ality	Repeat-ability	Notes / Examples
Location ID	The identification number assigned to each Location record by the electronic resource management system	unique ID	system generated identifier		R	N	Links a Location record to other data
Location Name	The name of a specific location category for the local institution	text	May be used to interoperate with a local or vendor-based access management system (e.g. by mapping to appropriate IP addresses)		R	Y	e.g., organizational units, buildings, campuses, etc.
Location IP Subset	The set of IP addresses associated with a specific location	text	FR16.1		RA	N	
Location Proxy Information	The URI prefix used to direct access through a proxy server for this location or other information needed to establish proxy connections for the location	text			O	N	To be used when a proxy setup permits distinguishing accessibility permissions on the basis of locations and when the license specifies that this particular location is permitted or prohibited. Otherwise, general library proxy information should be recorded in the Library entity.
Location Note	Additional information pertaining to this location	text	FR7.2		O	N	

Available To Location Bridge Entity

Definition:	Concatenates information from Terms entity and Location entity. Identifies on a case-by-case basis whether a designated location is permitted access to the product or products governed by the associated terms.
Elements	*Available To Location ID, Terms Available To Location, Location Assigned To Term, Location Permission Legal Interpretation, Location Permission Operational Value*
Notes	In a consortium, the individual libraries participating in the contract could be recorded here. FR6.1, FR18

Element	Definition	Element Type	System Use / Functionality	Values	Option-ality	Repeat-ability	Notes / Examples
Available To Location ID	The identification number assigned to the Available To Location Bridge by the electronic resource management system	unique ID	system generated identifier		R	N	
Terms Available To Location	The Prevailing Terms record for which the location permissions are defined	pointer		ID from the Prevailing Terms entity	R	N	
Location Assigned To Term	Lists the location which is permitted or prohibited by contract to access the product	pointer	May be used to interoperate with a local or vendor-based access management system (e.g. by mapping to appropriate IP addresses)	ID from the Location entity	RA	N	In a consortium, this might be the individual libraries participating in the contract
Location Permission Legal Interpretation	Designates whether the license or business agreement defining these terms permits or prohibits access from the location in question	text	Used for public and staff displays	Permitted (explicit) / Permitted (interpreted) / Prohibited (explicit) / Prohibited (interpreted) / Silent (uninterpreted) / Not Applicable	R	N	Used to define those locations the license permits or restricts. In a consortium, this might be the individual libraries participating in the contract.

Available To Location Bridge Entity (continued)

Element	Definition	Element Type	System Use / Functionality	Values	Option-ality	Repeat-ability	Notes / Examples
Location Permission Operational Value	Designates a local decision to further constrain access beyond that required by the license or business agreement	text	Defaults to Location Permission Legal Interpretation, but can be overridden. May be used to interoperate with a local or vendor-based access management system (e.g. by mapping to appropriate IP addresses.)	Permitted / Prohibited	RA	N	e.g., restricting to an IP subset for a part of a building when the whole building is permitted, because the IP set for the entire building would also include non-licensed locations. In a consortium, this might be the individual libraries participating in the contract. If present, this over-rides Location Permission Legal Interpretation for public displays.

Access Information Entity

Definition:	Information about access points and access requirements needed to make an Electronic Product available						
Notes							

Element	Definition	Element Type	System Use / Functionality	Values	Option-ality	Repeat-ability	Notes / Examples
Access Information ID	The identification number assigned to the Access Information record by the electronic resource management system	unique ID	system generated identifier		R	N	Links an Access Information record to other data

Access Information Entity Identifier Group

Definition:	Identifier information from access data associated with a particular Electronic Product						
Elements	*Primary Access Uniform Resource Identifier, Primary Access Uniform Resource Identifier Type, Alternate Uniform Resource Identifier, Alternate Uniform Resource Identifier Type, Local Persistent Uniform Resource Identifier, Local Persistent Uniform Resource Identifier Type*						
Notes							

Element	Definition	Element Type	System Use / Functionality	Values	Option-ality	Repeat-ability	Notes / Examples
Primary Access Uniform Resource Identifier	The method of access, the location, and the file name of an Electronic Product	text	Hypertext link functionality. Paired element with Primary Uniform Resource Identifier Type FR14.1, FR14.4	Layout: URI. Latest Draft: Uniform Resource Identifiers (URI): Generic Syntax (RFC 2396) (August 1998.)	RA	N	Usually the URL, which is a subset of the URI. A local choice for use of this element might be to use it for a local persistent identifier. In which case, there is no need to repeat information in the local persistent identifier element.
Primary Access Uniform Resource Identifier Type	The type of URI being used to locate and identify the product	text	Paired element with Primary Uniform Resource Identifier FR14.1, FR14.4	URL / URN, etc.	O	N	
Alternate Uniform Resource Identifier	An alternate URI available for access to an identical or alternate version of the product	text	Hypertext link functionality. Paired element with Alternate Uniform Resource Identifier Type FR14.1, FR14.4	Layout: URI. Latest Draft: Uniform Resource Identifiers (URI): Generic Syntax (RFC 2396) (August 1998.)	O	Y	This may be set up to be actionable in specific events. Examples include URLs for mirror sites, URLs that provide access to a resource via a different provider, etc.
Alternate Uniform Resource Identifier Type	The type of alternate URI being used	text	Paired element with Alternate Uniform Resource Identifier FR14.1, FR14.4	URL, URN, etc.	O	Y	

Access Information Entity Identifier Group (continued)

Element	Definition	Element Type	System Use / Functionality	Values	Option-ality	Repeat-ability	Notes / Examples
Local Persistent Uniform Resource Identifier	A persistent URI that is created locally to access the product	text	Hypertext link functionality Paired element with Local Persistent Uniform Resource Identifier Type FR14.1, FR14.2, FR14.4	Layout: URI. Latest Draft: Uniform Resource Identifiers (URI): Generic Syntax (RFC 2396) (August 1998.)	O	Y	
Local Persistent Uniform Resource Identifier Type	The type of locally created URI	text	Paired element with Local Persistent Uniform Resource Identifier FR14.1, FR14.2, FR14.4	URL, URN, etc.	O	Y	

Access Information Entity Authentication Group

Definition:	Authentication information from access data associated with a particular Electronic Product
Elements	*Implemented Authorization Method, Alternate Authorization Method, Electronic Product User Identifier, Electronic Product User Password, Electronic Product Local User Identifier, Electronic Product User Password Note, IP Address Registration Method, IP Address Registration Instruction, IP Addresses Registered For Access, Date IP Addresses Registered, IP Address General Note, Access Information Note*
Notes	

Element	Definition	Element Type	System Use / Functionality	Values	Option-ality	Repeat-ability	Notes / Examples
Implemented Authorization Method	The method by which access to the product is controlled	text	FR14.3	IP address / Password / IP address + Password / Script / Certificate / Unrestricted / Other	R	Y	If the provider supports more than one access method, this element records the method(s) selected for use by the subscribing institution

Access Information Entity Authentication Group (continued)							
Element	Definition	Element Type	System Use / Functionality	Values	Option-ality	Repeat-ability	Notes / Examples
Alternate Authorization Method	Additional authorization methods available for the product	text	FR14.3	IP address / Password / IP address + Password / Script / Certificate / Unrestricted / Other	O	Y	Alternate authorization means available but not in use at local institution
Electronic Product User Identifier	The user identifier that provides access to the product	text	Grouped element with Electronic Product User Password and Electronic Product Local User Identifier FR17		RA	Y	May be independent of primary access method selected for use (as when both IP and User ID-based methods are available)
Electronic Product User Password	The password that provides access to the product	text	Grouped element with Electronic Product User Identifier and Electronic Product Local User Identifier FR17		RA	Y	May be independent of primary access method selected for use (as when both IP and User ID-based methods are available)
Electronic Product Local User Identifier	An identifier associated with a local institution identity file	text	Grouped element with Electronic Product User Identifier and Electronic Product User Password. Linked to institution identity file FR16, FR17		O	Y	e.g., for distribution to end-users and/or for remote access purposes, or other relevant information

Access Information Entity Authentication Group (continued)

Element	Definition	Element Type	System Use / Functionality	Values	Option-ality	Repeat-ability	Notes / Examples
Electronic Product User Password Note	Additional information about user identifiers and passwords	text	FR7.2, FR17		O	N	Can be used to record additional user identifiers and/or passwords available for access to the product (e.g. for distribution to end-users and/or for remote access purposes)
IP Address Registration Method	The method by which IP addresses are sent to the product provider	text	FR16.2	Online / Send to provider	RA	N	
IP Address Registration Instruction	The URI at which IP addresses are registered, the email address or contact role to which updates are sent, or other relevant instructions	text	FR16.2		O	N	
IP Addresses Registered For Access	IP addresses registered for use with the product	text	Text or link to external source FR16.1		RA	N	If a location subset IP address is used, this might simply be a pointer to an Available To Location ID. May contain a list of registered IP addresses, or link to an external file or database where such addresses are maintained. Usage note: a method for automatic update and provider notification when IP addresses are updated may be desirable.
Date IP Addresses Registered	The most recent date on which IP addresses were registered with the product provider	date	This field should be updated automatically if the system supports automatic sending of IP addresses FR16.3		RA	N	
IP Address General Note	Additional notes pertaining to IP address information	text	FR7.2, FR16		O	N	
Access Information Note	Additional information pertaining to access issues and unusual situations	text	FR9, FR16		O	N	e.g., inaccessible or nonsubscribed portions not marked as such at the site, unusual login/logoff requirements, local vs. remote authentication control, or navigation or accessibility features

Access Information Entity Proxy Group

Definition:	Information necessary to enable proxy access to a particular Electronic Product						
Elements	*Proxy Server Decision Indicator, Proxy Registration Status, Domain Name*						
Notes	Those institutions without proxies, or whose proxies do not require any setup for individual resources, would set the Decision Indicator to default to "Yes" and the Status to default to "Not applicable"						

Element	Definition	Element Type	System Use / Functionality	Values	Option-ality	Repeat-ability	Notes / Examples
Proxy Server Decision Indicator	The decision to make the product available through a server that operates as an intermediary between the user's computer and the product to ensure proper authorization	logical	FR15	Yes / No	R	N	The purpose of this element is not to convey license information (e.g. whether proxy servers are permitted) but to facilitate interoperation with local access management systems
Proxy Registration Status	The status of registration of access information with the relevant proxy server	text	FR15	To be registered / Registration in process / Registered / Not applicable	RA	N	
Domain Name	Any domain names associated with a given product	text	FR15		O	Y	Some proxy servers require this information

Access Information Entity Z39.50 Group

Definition:	Information about Z39.50 access data associated with a particular Electronic Product						
Elements	*Z39.50 Address, Z39.50 Port, Z39.50 Attributes, URI To Z39.50 Information, Z39.50 Database Name Long, Z39.50 Database Name Short, Z39.50 Authentication Information*						
Notes	This group probably needs more detail. The authors also recognize that access protocols other than Z39.50 exist and might need similar elements available for information records.						

Element	Definition	Element Type	System Use / Functionality	Values	Option-ality	Repeat-ability	Notes / Examples
Z39.50 Address	Address used to provide Z39.50 access	text	FR38.3		O	N	
Z39.50 Port	Port used to provide Z39.50 access	numeric	FR38.3		O	N	
Z39.50 Attributes	Attributes necessary to activate Z39.50 access	text	FR38.3		O	N	
URI To Z39.50 Information	Information to assist Z39.50 access via a web interaction	text	FR38.3		O	N	
Z39.50 Database Name Long	Long database name necessary to enable Z39.50 access	text	FR38.3		O	N	

Access Information Entity Z39.50 Group (continued)

Element	Definition	Element Type	System Use / Functionality	Values	Option-ality	Repeat-ability	Notes / Examples
Z39.50 Database Name Short	Short database name necessary to enable Z39.50 access	text	FR38.3		O	N	
Z39.50 Authentication Information	Authentication information necessary to activate Z39.50 access	text	FR38.3		O	N	

Administrative Information Entity

Definition:	Information used to manage the life cycle of the Electronic Product						
Note							

Element	Definition	Element Type	System Use / Functionality	Values	Option-ality	Repeat-ability	Notes / Examples
Administrative Information ID	The identification number assigned to the Administrative Information record by the electronic resource management system	unique ID	system generated identifier		R	N	Links an Administrative Information record to other data

Administrative Information Entity Identifier Group

Definition:	Identifier information from administrative data associated with a particular Electronic Product						
Elements	*Administrative Uniform Resource Identifier, Administrative Uniform Resource Identifier Type, Administrative Identifier, Administrative Password, Administrative Password Note*						
Notes							

Element	Definition	Element Type	System Use / Functionality	Values	Option-ality	Repeat-ability	Notes / Examples
Administrative Uniform Resource Identifier	The URI of the online administration module	text	Hypertext link functionality. Paired element with Administrative Uniform Resource Identifier Type FR38.1	Layout: URI. Latest Draft: Uniform Resource Identifiers (URI): Generic Syntax (RFC 2396) (August 1998.)	RA	N	

Administrative Information Entity Identifier Group (continued)							
Element	Definition	Element Type	System Use / Functionality	Values	Option- ality	Repeat- ability	Notes / Examples
Administrative Uniform Resource Identifier Type	The type of URI that is used for the online administration module	text	Paired element with Administrative Uniform Resource Identifier FR38.1	URL, URN, etc	O	N	
Administrative Identifier	The identifier used to access the online administration module	text	Grouped element with Administrative Password and Administrative Password Note FR38.1		RA	Y	Used if different from account ID
Administrative Password	The password used to access the online administration module	text	Grouped element with Administrative Identifier and Administrative Password Note FR38.1		RA	Y	
Administrative Password Note	Any clarification needed to identify an administrative password or to whom it is assigned	text	Grouped element with Administrative Identifier and Administrative Password FR7.2, FR38.1		O	Y	

Administrative Information Entity Configuration Group

Definition:	Describes which features of a product are configurable either online or by the provider, and their values where applicable
Elements	*Configurable Session Timeout Indicator, Session Timeout Value, Logout Uniform Resource Identifier Indicator, Logout Uniform Resource Identifier Value, Logout Uniform Resource Identifier Type, User Interface Configuration Indicator, Subscriber Branding Indicator, Subscriber Branding Activation Status Indicator, Subscriber Branding Note, Personalization Services Indicator, Z39.50 Indicator, Hook To Holdings Indicator, Holdings Link Activated Indicator, Provider Reference Linking Indicator, Inbound Linking Indicator, Inbound Linking Activation Status Indicator, OpenURL Compliance Indicator, OpenURL Activation Status Indicator, Linking Note, MARC Record Availability Indicator, MARC Record Note, Interface Languages Availability Indicator, Interface Language Implemented, Local Use Administrative Fields*
Notes	

Element	Definition	Element Type	System Use / Functionality	Values	Option-ality	Repeat-ability	Notes / Examples
Configurable Session Timeout Indicator	The availability of a configurable inactivity timeout	logical	FR38.3	Yes / No	O	N	
Session Timeout Value	The inactivity timeout used for the product	numeric	FR38.3		RA	N	The timeout period can be fixed or configurable
Logout Uniform Resource Identifier Indicator	Indicates whether the product supports a locally specified URI to which the user is directed upon exiting the Electronic Product	logical	FR38.3	Yes / No	O	N	
Logout Uniform Resource Identifier Value	The locally specified URI to which the user is directed upon exiting the Electronic Product	text	Paired element with Logout Uniform Resource Identifier Type FR38.3		RA	N	
Logout Uniform Resource Identifier Type	The type of Logout URI being used	text	Paired element with Logout Uniform Resource Identifier Value FR38.3	URL, URN, etc	O	N	
User Interface Configuration Indicator	The ability to control user interface features	logical	FR38.3	Yes / No	O	N	
Subscriber Branding Indicator	The availability of a branding feature	logical	FR38.3	Yes / No	O	N	Used to highlight the local institution's role in making the product available to its user community

Administrative Information Entity Configuration Group (continued)

Element	Definition	Element Type	System Use / Functionality	Values	Option-ality	Repeat-ability	Notes / Examples
Subscriber Branding Activation Status Indicator	The activation of a branding feature	logical	FR38.3	Yes/No	RA	N	
Subscriber Branding Note	Additional information about subscriber branding	text	FR38.3		O	N	
Personalization Services Indicator	The availability of personalized features	logical	FR38.3	Yes / No	O	N	e.g. an alerting service, etc.
Z39.50 Indicator	Indicates whether the Z39.50 computer-to-computer communication protocol is supported by the interface	logical	FR38.3	Yes / No	O	N	ANSI Standard
Hook to Holdings Indicator	The availability of a link to library holdings	logical	FR38.3	Yes / No	O	N	
Holdings Link Activated Indicator	The activation of a link to library holdings	logical	FR38.3	Yes / No	RA	N	
Provider Reference Linking Indicator	The availability of links to external content created by the provider of the product	logical	FR38.3	Yes / No	O	N	
Inbound Linking Indicator	The availability of a link to internal stable locations within a product	logical	FR38.3	Yes / No	O	N	Often used for individual journals or books, links can be based on some standard algorithm
Inbound Linking Activation Status Indicator	The activation of a link to internal stable locations within a product	logical	FR38.3	Yes / No	RA	N	
OpenURL Compliance Indicator	Indicates whether the Electronic Product and its content is generating OpenURL Standard compliant metadata	logical	FR38.3	Yes / No	O	N	For more information on OpenURL, see http://www.niso.org/committees/committee_ax.html
OpenURL Activation Status Indicator	The activation of external links from this product	logical	FR38.3	Yes/No	RA	N	
Linking Note	Additional information about linking	text	FR7.2, FR38.3		O	N	e.g., implementation details or other notes
MARC Record Availability Indicator	The availability of MARC records for the resource	logical	FR38.5	Yes / No	O	N	
MARC Record Note	Further information regarding the availability of MARC record sets	text	FR7.2, FR38.5		O	N	e.g., free or purchased, acquisition and implementation status, etc.
Interface Languages Availability Indicator	The availability of multiple languages for the Interface	logical	FR38.3	Yes / No	O	N	

Administrative Information Entity Configuration Group (continued)							
Element	**Definition**	**Element Type**	**System Use / Functionality**	**Values**	**Option-ality**	**Repeat-ability**	**Notes / Examples**
Interface Language Implemented	The activation of one or more interface languages	text	FR38.3	Code values from ISO 639-2 (three-letter language code)	RA	Y	Examples include "eng" for English, "akk" for Akkadian. Derive from print version if print version exists (or point at). May use another standard for language code values (e.g. RFC3066) at the preference of the system designer as long as translation routines are available.
Local Use Administrative Fields	Flexible and locally definable fields for defining new configuration options	text	FR7.1, FR38.3		O	Y	

Administrative Information Entity Usage Statistics Group	
Definition:	Used to record information about usage statistics for the Electronic Product
Elements	*Usage Statistics Availability Indicator, Statistics Standard Compliance, Usage Statistics Delivery Method, Usage Statistics Format, Usage Statistics Frequency, Usage Statistics Online Location, Usage Statistics User Identifier, Usage Statistics Password, Usage Statistics Addressee, Usage Statistics Note, Usage Statistics Locally Stored*
Notes	Most of these elements are relevant for vendor provided statistics on the assumption that locally produced statistics will be housed and managed in a separate system and the ERMS will simply need linkages to that system. FR40

Element	**Definition**	**Element Type**	**System Use / Functionality**	**Values**	**Option-ality**	**Repeat-ability**	**Notes / Examples**
Usage Statistics Availability Indicator	The availability of usage statistics for the product	logical	FR40.1	Yes/No	O	N	
Statistics Standard Compliance	The official standard to which the statistics conform	text	FR40.1	COUNTER version # / ICOLC 1998`	O	N	For more information, see guidelines set forth at http://www.projectcounter.org and http://www.library.yale.edu/consortia/2001webstats.htm
Usage Statistics Delivery Method	The manner in which statistics are made available	text	FR40.1	Online / Email / Paper	RA	N	
Usage Statistics Format	The format(s) in which statistics are made available	text	(Multiple values permitted) FR40.1	HTML / Delimited / Excel / PDF / CSV / ASCII / Other	RA	Y	

Administrative Information Entity Usage Statistics Group (continued)

Element	Definition	Element Type	System Use / Functionality	Values	Option-ality	Repeat-ability	Notes / Examples
Usage Statistics Frequency	The frequency with which statistics are made available	text	FR40.1, FR40.7	Monthly / Quarterly / Bi-Annual / User-selectable	RA	N	
Usage Statistics Online Location	The online location at which statistics can be accessed	text	FR40.2		RA	N	e.g., URL or file path
Usage Statistics User Identifier	The identifier used for online access to the statistics management site or dataset	text	FR40.2	None / Same as Admin ID / Other (free text)	RA	N	May be same as administrative identifier
Usage Statistics Password	The password used for online access to the statistics management site or dataset	text	FR40.2	None / Same as Admin / Other (free text)	RA	N	May be same as administrative password
Usage Statistics Addressee	The local person to whom statistics are sent	pointer	FR26, FR40.1	ID from Contact entity.	RA	N	
Usage Statistics Note	Additional information regarding usage statistics	text	FR40.6		O	N	e.g. missing time periods
Usage Statistics Locally Stored	Information about and/or links to locally-stored data	text	FR40.3		O	N	

Administrative Information Entity Support Group

Definition:	Information necessary to support use of the Electronic Product
Elements	*Hardware Requirement, Software Requirement, Maintenance Window Value, Provider System Status Uniform Resource Indicator, Provider System Status Uniform Resource Indicator Type, Product Unavailable Indicator, Product Advisory Note, Local Performance Monitoring Note, Incident Log, Training Information, Administrative Documentation, User Documentation*
Notes	FR39, FR41

Element	Definition	Element Type	System Use / Functionality	Values	Option-ality	Repeat-ability	Notes / Examples
Hardware Requirement	Information about hardware requirements	text	FR9, FR41.5		RA	N	
Software Requirement	Information about software requirements	text	FR9, FR41.5		RA	N	e.g., browser versions, plug-ins, fonts, or special client software
Maintenance Window Value	The provider's regularly-scheduled downtime window for this product	text	FR11, FR41.2		RA	N	

Administrative Information Entity Support Group (continued)							
Element	**Definition**	**Element Type**	**System Use / Functionality**	**Values**	**Option-ality**	**Repeat-ability**	**Notes / Examples**
Provider System Status Uniform Resource Indicator	The URI at which the provider posts system status information	text	Hypertext link functionality. Paired element with Provider System Status Uniform Resource Indicator Type FR41.4	Layout: URI. Latest Draft: Uniform Resource Identifiers (URI): Generic Syntax (RFC 2396) (August 1998.)	RA	N	
Provider System Status Uniform Resource Indicator Type	The type of URI used to post system status information	text	Paired element with Provider System Status Uniform Resource Indicator FR41.4	URL, URN, etc	O	N	
Product Unavailable Indicator	A flag that indicates that a product is not available	logical	For public display FR10, FR41.6	Available / Unavailable	O	N	May trigger a particular action
Product Advisory Note	A note for public display of temporary information about a product	text	May be used for public display FR7.2, FR10, FR11, FR41.6		RA	N	Used to describe a problem with a product, provide advance notice of anticipated downtime, or convey other temporary information
Local Performance Monitoring Note	Information concerning web sites or programs that carry out local performance monitoring	text	FR41.3		O	N	
Incident Log	A log of downtime and problem reports and their resolution	text	FR41.7, FR42.4		O	N	An external call tracking system may be used instead
Training Information	Information regarding the availability of special training	text	FR39.1, FR39.3		O	N	e.g., instructions on how to bypass simultaneous user restrictions. May also include training contact names and other general information.
Administrative Documentation	Information about and/or location of documentation available for product administrators	text	FR39.2		O	N	
User Documentation	Information about and/or location of documentation available for end users	text	FR39.2		O	N	Value might be a URI pointing to training documentation or interactive tutorials

Processing Workflow Entity

Definition:	The status of various aspects of the lifecycle of an Electronic Product						
Note	This entity is intended as a sample model for a local workflow process but should be highly customizable to closely adhere to each institution's functional needs						

Element	Definition	Element Type	System Use / Functionality	Values	Option-ality	Repeat-ability	Notes / Examples
Process ID	The identification number assigned to the Processing Workflow record by the electronic resource management system	unique ID	system generated identifier		R	N	Links a Processing Workflow record to other data

Processing Workflow Entity Identifier Group

Definition:	Used to identify which Electronic Product is being controlled						
Elements	*Interface In Process, Electronic Resource In Process*						
Notes							

Element	Definition	Element Type	System Use / Functionality	Values	Option-ality	Repeat-ability	Notes / Examples
Interface In Process	The Interface for which the workflow is being controlled	pointer		ID from Interface entity	RA	N	Use either an Electronic Resource ID or an Interface ID but not both in one record
Electronic Resource In Process	The Electronic Resource for which the workflow is being controlled	pointer		ID from E-Resource entity	RA	N	Use either an Electronic Resource ID or an Interface ID but not both in one record

Processing Workflow Entity Pre-Selection Group

Definition:	Information necessary to manage the pre-selection process for an Electronic Product						
Elements	*Electronic Product Pre-Selection Expected Decision Date, Electronic Product Pre-Selection Cost Information, Electronic Product Evaluation History, Electronic Product Pre-Selection Note*						
Notes	Status for products in pre-selection can be found in the appropriate Electronic Resource or Interface Status elements in the Electronic Resource or Interface entities. FR23						

Element	Definition	Element Type	System Use / Functionality	Values	Option-ality	Repeat-ability	Notes / Examples
Electronic Product Pre-Selection Expected Decision Date	The date by which a decision to acquire the Electronic Product is to be made	date	FR29		R	N	A tickler for reminding staff about necessary decisions

Processing Workflow Entity Pre-Selection Group (continued)

Element	Definition	Element Type	System Use / Functionality	Values	Option-ality	Repeat-ability	Notes / Examples
Electronic Product Pre-Selection Cost Information	Pricing information for staff review	text	FR23		RA	N	May record several different pricing models from which an institution must choose
Electronic Product Evaluation History	Information regarding evaluations of the product made during the pre-selection process	text	May be a link to an outside record FR23		O	N	
Electronic Product Pre-Selection Note	Additional information pertaining to pre-selection actions and decisions	text	FR23		O	N	

Processing Workflow Entity In-Process Group

Definition:	Information necessary to manage the in-process part of an Electronic Product's lifecycle
Elements	*Order Request Date, Order Request Note, Authentication Status, Z39.50 Access Status, Cataloging Request Date, Cataloging Priority, Access Confirmation Indicator, Access Tested Date, Local Services Status, Interface Customization Status, Publicity Status, Instructional Tools Status, Public Display Release Status, Usage Data Setup Status, In Process Note*
Notes	FR30

Element	Definition	Element Type	System Use / Functionality	Values	Option-ality	Repeat-ability	Notes / Examples
Order Request Date	The date upon which a request is made for the production of a purchase order for the resource	date			O	N	Set by the system in response to system application functionality. This is included because we are expecting this to be a connection between two staff workflow units.
Order Request Note	Additional information about the request for order creation for an Electronic Product	text		Pending / Problem hold / Done	O	N	Could be used to clarify why an order has not yet been requested
Authentication Status	An indication that provided methods of authentication have been identified and accommodated	text		Pending / Other (free text)	O	N	e.g., if passwords have been posted internally, supplied to service points, etc.
Z39.50 Access Status	The status of setting up Z39.50 Access to the product	text	FR38.3.1	Pending / Done	O	N	

Processing Workflow Entity In-Process Group (continued)

Element	Definition	Element Type	System Use / Functionality	Values	Option-ality	Repeat-ability	Notes / Examples
Cataloging Request Date	The date when a request to catalog the product was made	date	FR38.5		O	N	Set by the system in response to system application functionality. This is included because we are expecting this to be a connection between two staff workflow units.
Cataloging Priority	The level of priority that the product should be assigned in the cataloging workflow	text	FR38.5	Low / Normal / Rush	O	N	
Access Confirmation Indicator	An indication that access to the product was functional when tested	logical	FR14	Yes / No	O	N	
Access Tested Date	The date on which access to the product was tested	date	FR14		O	N	
Local Services Status	The status of setting up access to the product in other local services	text	FR38.3	Not requested / Pending / Done	O	Y	e.g., OpenURL resolver, broadcast search, etc. Local institutions may want to specify statuses on these individually.
Interface Customization Status	The status of customizing the interface for the product	text	FR38.3	Pending / Done / Not applicable	O	N	Many products do not offer the capability to customize the interface
Publicity Status	The status of preparing publicity for the product	text	FR39	Pending / Done / Not applicable	O	N	
Instructional Tools Status	The status of instructional tools for the product	text	FR39	Pending / Done / Not applicable	O	N	
Public Display Release Status	The status of releasing the product to public display	text		Pending / Done / Not applicable	O	N	Used to indicate the status of having a resource show up on lists in webpages and in results from searches of electronic resources
Usage Data Setup Status	The status of the library's arrangement to receive usage data for the product	text	FR40	Pending / In process / Done / Not applicable	O	N	
In Process Note	Additional information regarding in process actions and decisions	text			O	N	

Processing Workflow Renewal and Termination Group

Definition:	Information necessary to manage the renewal or termination process for an Electronic Product
Elements	*Electronic Product Renewal Review Status, Electronic Product Renewal Expected Decision Date, Electronic Product Renewal Status Note, Electronic Product Evaluation History, Electronic Product Termination Status, Electronic Product Termination Status Note*
Notes	FR46, FR47

Element	Definition	Element Type	System Use / Functionality	Values	Option-ality	Repeat-ability	Notes / Examples
Electronic Product Renewal Review Status	The status of an E-Product that is undergoing renewal review	text	If value is Terminated or Expired, Electronic Product should not appear in any public lists of available resources FR46.5	Renewal pending / Under review / Comparison in progress / Approved for renewal / Renewal initiated / Renewal completed / Renewal rejected / Expired / Terminated	O	N	Values are examples and can/should be defined and/or expanded by local institutions
Electronic Product Renewal Expected Decision Date	The date by which a decision for renewal must be made	date	FR46.2		O	N	
Electronic Product Renewal Status Note	Detail on renewal or termination actions and decisions	text	FR46.5		O	N	
Electronic Product Evaluation History	Notes recorded about evaluations made by individuals in the renewal review process	text	May be a link to outside record FR46.6, FR47.4		O	N	
Electronic Product Termination Status	The current status in the workflow of the termination of an Electronic Product	text	FR47.3	Pending / Requirements fulfilled	O	N	e.g., certification that all institutional copies of product have been destroyed
Electronic Product Termination Status Note	Information regarding a decision to terminate the product	text	FR47.3		O	N	

Workflow Rules Entity

Definition:	Application logic; defines the possible statuses and next steps of the selection / acquisition / maintenance process
Note	The content and structure of this entity will be application-dependent, and its elements are not included in the Data Dictionary or this document. Examples of concepts that could be included: Acquisition Status, Acquisition Status Action, Acquisition Status Action Recipient, License Status Action, License Status Action Recipient, Troubleshooting Status, Troubleshooting Status Action, Troubleshooting Status Action Recipient, etc. FR24, FR25, FR26, FR27, FR28, FR29, FR30

Trial Entity

Definition:	Information necessary to manage a trial for an Electronic Product
Elements	*Trial ID, Electronic Resource On Trial, Interface On Trial, Trial Uniform Resource Indicator, Trial Uniform Resource Indicator Type, Trial Username, Trial Password, Trial Start Date, Trial Expire Date, Trial Available To Public Indicator, Trial License Required Indicator, Trial Note*
Note	FR28

Element	Definition	Element Type	System Use / Functionality	Values	Option-ality	Repeat-ability	Notes / Examples
Trial ID	The identification number assigned to the Trial record by the electronic resource management system	unique ID	system generated identifier		R	N	Links a Trial record to other data
Electronic Resource On Trial	The electronic resource for which a trial is arranged	pointer	FR28.2	ID from Electronic Resource entity.	RA	N	Use either an Electronic Resource ID or an Interface ID but not both in one record
Interface On Trial	The interface for which a trial is arranged	pointer	FR28.2	ID from Interface entity	RA	N	Use either an Electronic Resource ID or an Interface ID but not both in one record
Trial Uniform Resource Indicator	The URI used to access the product during the trial period	text	Hypertext link functionality. Paired element with Trial Uniform Resource Indicator type FR14.1, FR28.1	Layout: URI. Latest Draft: Uniform Resource Identifiers (URI): Generic Syntax (RFC 2396) (August 1998.)	RA	N	
Trial Uniform Resource Indicator Type	The type of URI that is being used for the trial	text	Paired element with Trial Uniform Resource Indicator FR28.1	URL, URN, etc.	O	N	

Trial Entity (continued)

Element	Definition	Element Type	System Use / Functionality	Values	Option-ality	Repeat-ability	Notes / Examples
Trial Username	The user name that must be used to access the product on trial	text	FR28.1		RA	N	
Trial Password	The password that must be used to access the product on trial	text	FR28.1		RA	N	
Trial Start Date	The date the trial begins or on which the product becomes available	date	FR28.2		R	N	
Trial Expire Date	The date on which the trial ends or that the product will no longer be accessible unless acquired	date	FR28.2, FR28.3		R	N	
Trial Available To Public Indicator	An indication of the availability of the trial product to the public	logical		Yes / No	R	N	
Trial License Required Indicator	Indicates whether a license is required for the product's trial period	logical		Yes / No	R	N	
Trial Note	Additional information about the trial access	text	FR7.2, FR28.2		O	N	

Consortium Entity

Definition:	Information about a consortium with whom the local institution cooperates
Elements	*Consortium ID, Consortium Name, Consortium Alternate Name, Consortium Address, Consortium Note*
Notes	A type of organization pulled out for convenience in managing data. FR19, FR45

Element	Definition	Element Type	System Use / Functionality	Values	Option-ality	Repeat-ability	Notes / Examples
Consortium ID	The identification number assigned to the Consortium by the electronic resource management system	unique ID	system generated identifier		R	N	Links a Consortium record to other data
Consortium Name	The official name of the consortium	text	FR45.1		R	N	
Consortium Alternate Name	Other names by which the consortium may be known	text	FR45.1		O	Y	Could be parent organization that has been absorbed or renamed
Consortium Address	The mailing address of the consortium	text	FR45.1		RA	N	
Consortium Note	Notes which clarify the consortium information	text	FR7.2, FR45.1		O	N	

Partner Library Entity

Definition:	Information about library partners who may cooperate in consortial deals
Elements	*Partner Library ID, Partner Library Name, Partner Library Alternate Name, Partner Library Address, Partner Library IP Ranges, Partner Library Note*
Note	A type of organization pulled out for convenience in managing data. FR19, FR45.1

Element	Definition	Element Type	System Use / Functionality	Values	Option-ality	Repeat-ability	Notes / Examples
Partner Library ID	The identification number assigned to the Partner Library by the electronic resource management system	unique ID	system assigned number		R	N	Links a Partner Library record to other data
Partner Library Name	The official name of the partner library	text	FR45.1		R	N	
Partner Library Alternate Name	Other name(s) by which the partner library is known	text	FR45.1		O	Y	
Partner Library Address	The mailing address of the partner library	text	FR45.1		RA	N	
Partner Library IP Ranges	The set of IP addresses associated with the partner library	text	FR45.1		O	N	To be used if a local institution or individual is serving in the point role for a consortial acquisition
Partner Library Note	Information needed to clarify the partner library or its role in the consortium	text	FR7.2, FR45.1		O	N	

Consortial Participation Bridge Entity

Definition:	Establishes relationships between an Acquisition, a Consortium, and possibly a Partner Library
Elements	*Consortium Participation ID, Consortial Acquisition, Consortium Acquiring, Consortial Partner, Consortial Fund Contribution, Number Of Consortial Participants, Consortial Issues Note*
Notes	Required only if an Acquisition is acquired in cooperation with a Consortium. FR19, FR45

Element	Definition	Element Type	System Use / Functionality	Values	Option-ality	Repeat-ability	Notes / Examples
Consortium Participation ID	The identification number assigned to the bridge by the electronic resource management system	unique ID	system assigned number		R	N	
Consortial Acquisition	The acquisition associated with a consortium	pointer		ID from Acquisition entity	R	N	

Consortial Participation Bridge Entity (continued)

Element	Definition	Element Type	System Use / Functionality	Values	Option-ality	Repeat-ability	Notes / Examples
Consortium Acquiring	The consortium that has arranged for the acquisition	pointer	May be used to generate reports about consortial agreements or to trigger certain actions, e.g. route messages to a consortial liaison FR45.1	ID from Consortium entity	R	N	The consortium may or may not serve in one or more of the following capacities: as negotiating intermediary, with or without a fee for services; as the vendor who accepts payment for the product; or as the named licensee for a particular agreement
Consortial Partner	The participating institution(s) in a consortial agreement	pointer	Paired element with Consortial Fund Contribution	ID from Partner Library entity	O	N	May be used to identify institutions with whom cost sharing and/or renewal decisions must be coordinated
Consortial Fund Contribution	The monetary contribution made by the partner library in a consortial purchase	text	Paired element with Consortial Partner FR44.2		O	N	Can be expressed as a percentage of the total amount or as a dollar figure. Would not be used if Partner Libraries are not tracked in general or for this product.
Number Of Consortial Participants	The number of library participants in a consortial deal	numeric	If Consortial Partner element is filled in for a particular Acquisition, system should automatically calculate this number FR45.1		RA	N	To be entered manually when the consortial partners are not tracked, but the number of participants need to be recorded for cost-sharing, etc.
Consortial Issues Note	Information relating to or clarifying consortial issues in this agreement	text	FR45.1		O	N	

Library Entity

Definition:	Records information about different libraries within an institution which may be acquiring the product
Elements	*Library ID, Library Name, Library Alternate Name, Library Address, Library Locations, Proxy Information, Library Note*
Note	FR18.1, FR19

Element	Definition	Element Type	System Use / Functionality	Values	Option-ality	Repeat-ability	Notes / Examples
Library ID	The identification number assigned to the Library by the electronic resource management system	unique ID	system assigned number		R	N	Links a Library record to other data
Library Name	The official name of the library	text			R	N	
Library Alternate Name	Other name(s) by which the library is known	text			O	Y	
Library Address	The mailing address of the library	text			RA	N	Can be an internal mailstop or other mailing address
Library Locations	Local locations associated with the library	pointer	Used for generating staff displays FR18.1.1	ID from Location entity	O	Y	
Proxy Information	The URI prefix used to direct access through a proxy server or other information needed to establish proxy connections in general	text	FR14.3		O	Y	
Library Note	Additional information needed to clarify the library data	text	FR7.2		O	N	

Library Acquisition Bridge Entity

Definition:	Used to identify which local libraries are cooperating in the acquiring of an Electronic Product
Elements	*Library Acquisition ID, Acquisition Coordinated, Library Cooperating, Cost Share, Cost Share Percentage, Cost Share Note*
Notes	FR19, FR44.2, FR44.3

Element	Definition	Element Type	System Use / Functionality	Values	Option-ality	Repeat-ability	Notes / Examples
Library Acquisition ID	The identification number assigned to each bridge record by the electronic resource management system	unique ID	system generated identifier		R	N	

Library Acquisition Bridge Entity (continued)							
Element	**Definition**	**Element Type**	**System Use / Functionality**	**Values**	**Option-ality**	**Repeat-ability**	**Notes / Examples**
Acquisition Coordinated	The business transaction that is being arranged	pointer		ID from Acquisition entity	R	N	
Library Cooperating	The library involved with the transaction	pointer		ID from Library entity	R	N	
Cost Share	Amount contributed by library to an electronic product acquisition	numeric	FR44.2		RA	N	For when a library is contributing a flat amount to the acquisition
Cost Share Percentage	The proportion of the funds contributed by the library to the cost of an Electronic Product	numeric	Recorded as a percentage FR44.2		RA	N	For when a library is contributing a percentage of the total to the acquisition
Cost Share Note	Other agreements regarding cost share	text	FR44.2		O	N	

Organization Entity

Definition:	Information about organizations with connections to electronic products
Elements	*Organization ID, Organization Name, Organization Alternate Name, Organization Address, Notice Address Licensor, Organization Note*
Types	Licensor, Vendor, Publisher, Agent, Provider
Note	Various other types of organizations are separated into their own entities for convenience in data management (e.g., Consortium, Partner Library, Library, etc.) FR19, FR42

Element	**Definition**	**Element Type**	**System Use / Functionality**	**Values**	**Option-ality**	**Repeat-ability**	**Notes / Examples**
Organization ID	The identification number assigned to the Organization by the electronic resource management system	unique ID	system assigned number		R	N	Links an Organization record to other data
Organization Name	The official name of the organization	text			R	N	
Organization Alternate Name	Other names by which the organization is known				O	Y	Could be parent organization or companies that have been absorbed or renamed
Organization Address	The mailing address of the organization	text	FR42.3		RA	N	
Notice Address Licensor	The notice address of the licensor	text	FR42.3		RA	N	To be used if organizational address differs for license purposes

Organization Entity (continued)

Element	Definition	Element Type	System Use / Functionality	Values	Option-ality	Repeat-ability	Notes / Examples
Organization Note	Additional information required to clarify the organization information	text	FR7.2		O	N	

Organization Library Bridge Entity

Definition:	Describes the relationship between an Organization and a Library
Elements	*Organization Library Bridge ID, Organization Working With Library, Library Working With Organization, Account Identifier Assigned To Library*
Notes	FR19

Element	Definition	Element Type	System Use / Functionality	Values	Option-ality	Repeat-ability	Notes / Examples
Organization Library Bridge ID	The identification number assigned to the bridge by the electronic resource management system	unique ID	system assigned number		R	N	
Organization Working With Library	The organization with whom a particular library has an established working relationship	pointer		ID from Organization entity	R	N	
Library Working With Organization	The library with whom a particular organization has an established working relationship	pointer		ID from Library entity	R	N	
Account Identifier Assigned To Library	Identifier assigned by an organization to a library's account	text			R	N	e.g., an organization may have account numbers for every ship-to address in their system

Contact Entity

Definition:	Information about individuals in the local setting or remote organizations who have a role in the lifecycle of an Electronic Product
Elements	*Contact ID, Contact Name, Contact Title, Contact Address, Contact Email Address, Contact Phone Number, Contact Fax Number, Contact Role, Organization Represented, Consortium Represented, Library Represented, Partner Library Represented*
Note	Contact information is for either local or remote individuals; the Contact Role specifies whether local or remote and which local or remote role the person is playing. FR26, FR28.3, FR42, FR45

Element	Definition	Element Type	System Use / Functionality	Values	Option-ality	Repeat-ability	Notes / Examples
Contact ID	The identification number assigned to the Contact by the electronic resource management system	unique ID	system generated identifier		R	N	Links a Contact record to other data
Contact Name	The name of the contact individual	text			R	N	For local information, it should be possible for this to hook into a CSO lookup. It is permissible to use a generic here if a name is unknown or inappropriate (e.g. Technical Support.)
Contact Title	The title of the contact individual	text			RA	N	
Contact Address	The mailing address of the contact	text			RA	N	May not be necessary if contact address is the same as the organization it represents. May be an internal address or a postal address.
Contact Email Address	The email address of the contact	text			R	N	
Contact Phone Number	The phone number of the contact	text			R	Y	
Contact Fax Number	The fax number of the contact	text			O	R	
Contact Role	The responsibility assigned to the contact person in general for electronic products	text	FR16.3, FR38.5.2, FR42.1, FR42.2	See Appendix A	R	Y	Roles should be site defined (examples might include Bibliographer, Selector, Product Sponsor, Interface Sponsor, Resource Steward, Billing Contact.) Note that this element is a generic situation apart from any Electronic Product and should be differentiated from Electronic Product Role, which is specific to a particular product.
Organization Represented	The organization that the contact represents	pointer		ID from the Organization entity	RA	N	Either an Organization ID or a Consortium ID or a Library Represented ID or Partner Library Represented ID but not more than one for any record in this entity

Contact Entity (continued)							
Element	**Definition**	**Element Type**	**System Use / Functionality**	**Values**	**Option-ality**	**Repeat-ability**	**Notes / Examples**
Consortium Represented	The consortium that the contact represents	pointer	FR45.2	ID from the Consortium entity	RA	N	Either an Organization ID or a Consortium ID or a Library Represented ID or Partner Library Represented ID but not more than one for any record in this entity
Library Represented	The local library that the contact represents	pointer		ID from the Library entity	RA	N	Either an Organization ID or a Consortium ID or a Library Represented ID or Partner Library Represented ID but not more than one for any record in this entity
Partner Library Represented	The consortial partner library that the contact represents	pointer		ID from the Partner Library entity	RA	N	Either an Organization ID or a Consortium ID or a Library Represented ID or Partner Library Represented ID but not more than one for any record in this entity

Contact Responsibilities Bridge Entity

Definition:	Information about which products a contact is responsible for and what roles a contact plays for a particular product
Elements	*Contact Responsibilities ID, Contact Responsible, Electronic Resource Under Care, Interface Under Care, License Under Care, Acquisition Under Care, Electronic Product Role*
Note	Contact responsibility information is for either local or remote individuals. The Contact Role specifies whether local or remote and which local or remote role the person is playing. FR19, FR26, FR42, FR45

Element	**Definition**	**Element Type**	**System Use / Functionality**	**Values**	**Option-ality**	**Repeat-ability**	**Notes / Examples**
Contact Responsibilities ID	The identification number assigned to the bridge record by the e-resource management system	unique ID	system generated identifier		R	N	
Contact Responsible	The individual assigned as contact for the Electronic Product	pointer		ID from Contact entity	R	N	
Electronic Resource Under Care	The e-resource assigned to the contact	pointer		ID from Electronic Resource entity	RA	N	Use either an E-Resource ID or an Interface ID but not both in one record. If a contact has role solely with a license or an acquisition for a product, that is recorded using the License Under Care or Acquisition Under Care options.

Contact Responsibilities Bridge Entity (continued)							
Element	Definition	Element Type	System Use / Functionality	Values	Option-ality	Repeat-ability	Notes / Examples
Interface Under Care	The interface assigned to the contact	pointer		ID from Interface entity	RA	N	Use either an E-Resource ID or an Interface ID but not both in one record. If a contact has role solely with a license or an acquisition for a product, that is recorded using the License Under Care or Acquisition Under Care options.
License Under Care	The license assigned to the contact	pointer		ID from License entity	RA	N	For when a contact has a role only in the license of a resource
Acquisition Under Care	The acquisition assigned to the contact	pointer		ID from Acquisition entity	RA	N	For when a contact has a role only in the business agreement for a resource
Electronic Product Role	The role that the contact is playing in the care of this Electronic Product	text		See Appendix A	RA	N	If contact is undertaking all roles, this may be left blank. Note that this element is specific to a particular product and should be differentiated from Contact Role, which is a generic situation apart from any Electronic Product.

Work Entity	
Definition:	Information about the intellectual work from which the resource has been derived
Elements	*Work ID, Electronic Resource Title Continues, Electronic Resource Title Continued By, International Standard Text Code, Subject, Uniform Title, Author*
Note	This entity is included in the data structure to indicate those elements associated with a work (regardless of the work's manifestation as an Electronic Product) that are needed for use by an electronic resource discovery tool. However, it is anticipated that in actual system implementations these elements will be derived from external systems. Alternatively, if no external system exists from which these elements could be derived, the elements could be incorporated into the Electronic Resource entity; in that case, some alternative structure must be created to relate different electronic resource manifestations of the same work with one another. Disclaimer: The authors are using the expression "work" in a non-FRBR sense in this data structure. FR8

Element	Definition	Element Type	System Use / Functionality	Values	Option-ality	Repeat-ability	Notes / Examples
Work ID	The identification number assigned to the Work by the electronic resource management system	unique ID	system generated identifier		R	N	Links a Work record to other data

Work Entity (continued)							
Element	**Definition**	**Element Type**	**System Use / Functionality**	**Values**	**Option-ality**	**Repeat-ability**	**Notes / Examples**
Electronic Resource Title Continues	The title immediately preceding the title of the resource	text	Used for display and resource discovery. May be derived from an external data source or locally assigned. May be created by system. FR5		O	Y	MARC equivalent 780. If the previous title was an electronic resource or a work identified in the ERMS, this should be a pointer to an Electronic Resource ID or a Work ID.
Electronic Resource Title Continued By	The title immediately succeeding the title of the resource	text	Used for display and resource discovery. May be derived from an external data source or locally assigned. May be created by system. FR5		O	Y	MARC equivalent 785. If the later title was an electronic resource or a work identified in the ERMS, this should be a pointer to an Electronic Resource ID or a Work ID.
International Standard Text Code	A voluntary numbering system for the identification of textual works	text		Layout: ISTC. Latest Draft: ISO Committee Draft 21047.	O	N	
Subject	The topic of the content of a resource, which may be expressed as keywords or terms from accepted classifications or thesauri	text	FR5	restricted to a canonical list of subject terms (site-defined or taken from an external authoritative source, e.g. LCSH)	R	Y	Source of definition: Dublin Core Metadata Initiative

Work Entity (continued)							
Element	Definition	Element Type	System Use / Functionality	Values	Option-ality	Repeat-ability	Notes / Examples
Uniform Title	A heading consisting of the title by which an item or a series is identified for cataloging purposes when the title is not entered under a personal, corporate, meeting, or jurisdiction name in a name / title heading construction	text	Used for display and resource discovery. May be derived from an external data source or locally assigned. FR5		O	Y	Source of definition: MARC 21
Author	The person or body that is identified as the creator of the electronic resource	text	FR5		O	Y	Usually present on single title resources

Related Version Entity

Definition:	Information about a related resource which is associated in some fashion with an electronic resource under control by the ERMS
Elements	*Related Version ID, Work Associated With Related Version, Related Version Title, Print International Standard Book Number, Print International Standard Serial Number, Local Record Number, Print Price, Print Subscription Identifier*
Note	A Related Version does not necessarily need to be one acquired by the local institution. If an instance of this data structure does not support a Related Version entity, then some of the elements stored here may need to become part of the Electronic Resource entity with some loss of functionality. May be recorded in an external system with which the ERM tool communicates. FR8, FR43.3, FR43.4.2, FR43.6

Element	Definition	Element Type	System Use / Functionality	Values	Option-ality	Repeat-ability	Notes / Examples
Related Version ID	The identification number assigned to the Related Version by the electronic resource management system	unique ID	system generated identifier		R	N	Links a Related Version record to other data
Work Associated With Related Version	The work from which the related resource was derived	pointer	FR8	ID from Work entity	R	N	
Related Version Title	Title for the print or other tangible version of the resource	text			O	N	
Print International Standard Book Number	A unique machine-readable identification number assigned to the print version of a resource	text		Layout: ISBN. ISO Standard 2108.	RA	Y	This is repeating, because the same book in print may have multiple ISBNs. (e.g., paperback, clothbound, etc.) Source of definition: ISBN Home page: http://www.isbn.org

Related Version Entity (continued)

Element	Definition	Element Type	System Use / Functionality	Values	Option-ality	Repeat-ability	Notes / Examples
Print International Standard Serial Number	A unique identification number assigned to each serial title by centers of the International Standard Serial Number Network	text		Layout: ISO Standard 3297-1975; ANSI Z39.9-1979	RA	N	Source of definition: CONSER Editing Guide
Local Record Number	The record number that is assigned by a local library management system to the bibliographic record of the related version	text			O	N	
Print Price	The price of the print version of the electronic resource	text	Preferably a link to an LMS system		RA	N	This link or recorded information is used only if the print price has an impact on the electronic version or vice versa
Print Subscription Identifier	An identifier associated with a print subscription that must be used to register the electronic version for online access	text	FR38.2		RA	N	e.g., a subscription number

Appendix A1 Contact Roles

Local Billing Contact	Vendor Billing Contact	Consortium Billing Contact
Local Instructional Contact	Vendor Contract Administration	Consortium Cataloging Contact
Local License Contact	Vendor Customer Support	Consortium General Contact
Local MARC Records Contact	Vendor General Contact	Consortium License Contact
Local Network Contact	Vendor IP Address Update Contact	Consortium MARC Records Contact
Local OpenURL Resolver Contact	Vendor MARC Records Contact	Consortium OpenURL Resolver Contact
Local Selector	Vendor Sales Representative	
Local Technical Contact	Vendor Technical Support	
Local Trial Contact	Vendor Training Representative	
Local Troubleshooter		

Appendix A2 User Groups

Role	Definition	Note
Faculty	Indicates faculty as a class of user	Includes current full-time, part-time and visiting faculty, as well as emeriti. Required for academic institutions only
Student	Indicates students as a class of user	Includes current full-and part-time students of the licensee and its participating institutions. Required for academic institutions only
Employee	Indicates employees as a class of user	Includes current full-and part-time employees of the licensee and its participating institutions, including temporary, contract and grant-funded employees
On-site library patron	Indicates walk-in users to the library as a class of user	
On-site institutional patron	Indicates walk-in users or other on-site visitors to the institution's premises, who have access to the licensee's public workstations and network facilities while physically present, as a class of user	
Alumni	Indicates former students who hold a degree from the participating licensed institution as a class of user	Required for academic institutions only
Affiliated researcher	Indicates persons other than current students, faculty, or employees, who by virtue of a specific research relationship with the licensed institution, its faculty or employees, are normally afforded access to institutional resources in the course of their work, as a class of user	
Retiree	Indicates former employees who have retired from the licensed institution as a class of user	
Registered library patron	Indicates an individual who is duly registered for access to the library's resources and services as a class of user	Chiefly used by public libraries
Adult library patron	Indicates an individual in the adult age category who is registered for access to the library's resources and services as a class of user	Chiefly used by public libraries
Child library patron	Indicates an individual in the child age category who is registered for access to the library's resources and services as a class of user	Chiefly used by public libraries
Senior library patron	Indicates an individual in the senior age category who is registered for access to the library's resources and services as a class of user	Chiefly used by public libraries
Young adult library patron	Indicates an individual in the young adult age category who is registered for access to the library's resources and services as a class of user	Chiefly used by public libraries
Note: While including more groups than those outlined as user privilege types in Z39.83 for circulation purposes, all Z39.83 types can be mapped here (http://www.niso.org/standards/resources/z3983pt1rev1.pdf).		

Notes

Electronic resource (Electronic resource): May require multiple iterations by format, if format has license/acquisition detail implications.

Terms: For those terms designated RA, some institutions may not want to track. The Data Structure only attempts to suggest Optionality, but there should certainly be leeway between R, RA, and O as a system is developed.

Country of implementation: The authors recognize that our collective area of experience is limited to the practice of ERM in libraries of the United States. We have tried to generalize elements for non- country specific use or indicate where elements may be solely of interest or use to U.S. libraries, but we have not attempted to map the universe of elements of interest to the practice of electronic resource management in other countries. System designers desiring to build products for international use should keep this in mind and research functional requirements beyond the United States.

Functional Requirement items not mapped above:

FR3 is not mapped above on the assumption that there is a higher level capability with system usernames that will permit view and editing of any grouping of the elements individually or together.

FR4 is not mapped above on the assumption that there is a higher level capability to accomplish reports.

FR12 implies connections between the above and other systems such as LMSs. There are indications in the above where such connections would be most logical or useful, but not all of them are fully annotated.

Nothing in the above precludes the specifications defined in FR14.5.

FR20 assumes a higher level capability to the ERMS.

FR31 implies archived data, which the above design does not go into.

FR34.2 implies a separate logging system not detailed above.

Nothing in the above precludes the specifications defined in FR40.4.

FR41.8 implies a sophisticated and calculable method for storing incidents and recording incident start and end times. This detailed functionality is not mapped in this document.

In order to facilitate FR42.4, the incident log functionality will need to record contact id for the appropriate vendor contact.

FR43.4.2 only applies where ERMS is interconnected with an LMS. The connection of which print cancellations to block would happen through the print version entity.

FR43.5.2 implies integration with a payment system where historical payment data is recorded and can be used as the basis for a calculation with the price cap.

FR46.3 is workflow functionality, and only the groundwork for workflow is laid above.

FR46.4 contains some workflow functionality, only the groundwork for which has been laid above.

Index to Entities, Groups, and Elements

Appendix F: XML Investigation

Adam Chandler, Sharon E. Farb, Angela Riggio, Nathan D. M. Robertson, Rick Silterra, Simon St. Laurent, and Robin Wendler

TABLE OF CONTENTS

Introduction

The scope of the DLF ERMI is wide-ranging, from a very large list of relevant data elements to workflow diagrams, functional requirements, and an abstract entity-relationship view of an ideal system. To round out the suite of deliverables the ERMI Steering Group felt it important to explore the use of XML as a wrapper for ERMI data elements. Within the library world, Roy Tennant may be the most vocal proponent of XML. In his editorial, "MARC Must Die," Tennant asserts that libraries risk technology fossilization unless they adopt XML as a replacement for the MARC standard (Tennant 2002a). In a follow-up piece, "MARC Exit Strategies," Tennant offers three strategies for moving from MARC to XML: (1) entombment—build a new parallel system along side MARC systems; (2) encapsulation—move MARC records into an XML structure such as MODS; or (3) migration—move everything into a new XML structure (Tennant 2002b). Tennant is not a lone voice in advocating the use of XML. The "Death of MARC" made the top of the ALA Library Information Technology Association's Top Trends in 2003. Work is underway in pushing this vision forward. For example, *XML in Libraries*, edited by Tennant, describes 13 innovative XML-based library projects. Kyle Banerjee's "How Does XML Help Libraries?" is another article advocating a transition to XML (Banerjee 2002). The point here is that XML is making significant inroads in libraries. Libraries are clearly in the midst of a transition from an environment with one primary exchange standard for bibliographic metadata (MARC) to one where specific application metadata (some bibliographic, some for administration) are exchanged according to a variety of standards, all packaged in XML. In the near future we will see ERM systems deployed across libraries. When that day comes, there will be a need for libraries to exchange XML data between other libraries, vendors, and from one software migration to the next.

Method

The steering group formed an XML subgroup in fall 2003 and followed two threads: (1) a prototype schema, and (2) possible use cases. To start, Robin Wendler created a partially completed ERMI XML schema module that would use or refer to extant XML schemas and/or semantics such as DC, MODS, VCard, etc, available from http://www.library.cornell.edu/cts/elicensestudy/dlfdeliverables/fallforum2003 /ermitest-rkw2.xsd.

The use cases the subgroup imagined in the first round of our discussions included:

- Link resolver data exchange between vendor and library. Possible elements: title, title level coverage, and user group license terms;

- Publisher e-resource title list. Possible elements include title, package name, title level coverage, discounts, and ISSN; and

- Possible exchange of data between the library ERM system and other campus systems such as course Web sites.

In January 2004, the steering group discussed the scope of the ongoing XML exploration and decided that it was too ambitious given the short amount of time available. Instead, the XML sub-group focused on creating a proof-of-concept schema that would be restricted to licensing-only data elements. Issues such as exchange of title level descriptive metadata within an XML container, while important, are better addressed in a separate, more specific initiative, such as the NISO/EDItEUR Joint Working Party for the Exchange of Serials Subscription Information (JWP).

Angela Riggio and Sharon Farb designed two relatively simple use cases, which both put the emphasis on exchanging license data. The *quick fix* use case (table 1) is a small list of elements which might be exchanged between librarians that need to communicate some essential details about a particular e-resource package. The second license-agreement use case (table 2) is a larger and more comprehensive list of elements, but the purpose is the same: to provide a vehicle for the exchange of metadata between libraries or consortia. Once we had restricted our attention to the two narrow use cases, we turned to developments in the dynamic and very complex fields of Digital Rights Management (DRM) and Rights Expression Languages (RELs), since it seemed that requirements for the expressions of license terms and digital rights might be similar. We reasoned that if existing rights expression languages could be used for license term expression, we could avoid reinventing the wheel.

Digital Rights Management and Rights Expression Languages

Karen Coyle's "The Technology of Rights: Digital Rights Management" provides us with an insightful and readable overview of DRM. Coyle begins the discussion by drawing a distinction between "thin copyright" and "thick copyright." The goal of thin copyright is to make works widely available to the public. The goal of thick copyright owners is to maximize profit. The core motivation behind DRM is the fact that making copies of digital works is trivial. Copyright, even thick copyright cannot technically prevent these copies from being made. DRM technology is based on the notion that digital works can and need to be protected by linking the rights to a work to a particular identification key. The first generation of DRM systems match the rights to use a work to a particular machine, such as an eBook reader. Second generation systems theoretically match the rights to a work to a particular person. Mike Godwin defines digital rights management as "technologies that prevent you from using copyrighted digital work beyond the degree to which the copyright owner wishes to allow you to use it" (Godwin 2003). (Microsoft's next generation operating system is expected to include DRM.)

The rules governing DRM technology are represented in a REL, "a different kind of language; it is a formal language like mathematics or like programming code; it is language that can be executed as an algorithm," (Coyle 2003). RELs work best with attributes that can be counted, i.e., time, units, or value exchange. In addition, Coyle notes that "where copyright law is an expression of 'everything that is not forbidden is permitted,' DRM takes the approach of 'everything that is not permitted is forbidden'." As a consequence, DRM and fair use as practiced in libraries may be incompatible.

Coyle has written a more recent report, "Rights Expression Languages: A Report for the Library of Congress," that according to Sally H. McCallum of the Library of Congress Network Development and MARC Standards Office was "commissioned to clarify the similarities and differences of various emerging RELs in order to assist users in making choices and to encourage cooperation among developers of the languages where feasible." It surveys the XML RELs from Creative Commons (CC), METSRights (METSR), Open Digital Rights Language (ODRL) and MPEG-21 Part 5 (MPEG-21/5). According to Coyle, each REL surveyed is designed for a specific purpose, and as a consequence, there will never be a universal REL. She offers the following insight on the relationship between RELs and fair use:

> Rights expression languages that are intended to be machine-actionable are expressly not intended to implement copyright law. Although some early researchers hoped to use RELs to express (and enforce) legal concepts like "fair use," that has not been the case in actual implementations. The copyright law, although carefully worded, simply cannot be expressed in the kind of algorithmic language that is required by computer programs to automate functionality like printing or copying. This is especially true of the key concept of "fair use." Fair use is a deliberately vague exception to the monopoly rights of the copyright holder. It says essentially that—although the copyright holder has the exclusive right to make copies of the work—members of the public can also make copies if their use is "fair." There is no a priori test for whether a use is fair; each such exercise of the public's right must be carefully scrutinized taking into account a number of factors. Even after such scrutiny, not everyone will agree on what is fair. Electronic systems need an unambiguous and quantitative definition that they can act on, and the copyright law does not provide that (Coyle 2004, p. 11).

As Coyle observes above, from a technical standpoint, fair use is difficult if not impossible to truly represent within a REL. More broadly, Lawrence Lessig argues in *Free Culture* that the electronic environment has in fact severely limited the available nonregulated uses of intellectual property. This is in part a consequence of a change in copyright law that eliminated the requirement that a work include a © symbol; that is, everything is now assumed to be copyrighted unless explicitly stated otherwise. Uses that were once unregulated are now regulated. Furthermore, within the electronic environment a copy is made each time a file is transferred; copy-and-paste may, in certain instances, be interpreted as a crime in this regulated system. In Lessig's view the reality of fair use today is that one must have a lawyer on retainer in order to make use of it; the scales are tipped overwhelming in favor of the copyright owner (Lessig 2004, pp. 116 – 173). We are quickly moving towards a fair use free world where copyright owners can simply assert control upfront within a DRM.

These considerations led the group to carefully consider whether or not to pursue the use of an existing REL, and if so, which one. Two of the better-established RELs described by Coyle, currently vie for recognition as the standard for media products such as movies in DVD format. The first of these is now referred to as MPEG-21/5, and grew out of the XrML language developed by a company named ContentGuard. ContentGuard is jointly controlled by Microsoft and Time Warner (Time Warner, 2004). The second is called the Open Digital Rights Language, or ODRL. These initiatives are intended both to enable a rights holder to describe what a user may do with a particular resource *and* to confer substantial control of user behavior on the implementing party. The XML group learned of the existence of extensive patent claims related to MPEG-21/5, and its strong preference for open standards led it to focus its work on use of ODRL.

Findings

OPEN DIGITAL RIGHTS LANGUAGE (ODRL)

What happens when ERMI data elements are placed within the ODRL framework? The following is a high-level description:

> The Open Digital Rights Language (ODRL) Initiative is an international effort of Supporters aimed at developing an open standard for the DRM sector and promoting the language at standards bodies.
>
> The ODRL specification supports an extensible language and vocabulary (data dictionary) for the expression of terms and conditions over any content including permissions, constraints, requirements, conditions, and offers and agreements with rights holders.
>
> ODRL is intended to provide flexible and interoperable mechanisms to support transparent and innovative use of digital resources in publishing, distributing and consuming of digital media across all sectors including publishers, education, entertainment, mobile, and software. ODRL also supports protected digital content and honors the rights, conditions and fees specified for digital contents (ODRL).

Our approach was to first mark up our use cases in ODRL Version 1.1 XML and then to create an ODRL schema supplement to validate them (figure 5). (The products of our ODRL experiment are figure 2, figure 4, and figure 5.) ODRL is a rich pre-defined data model. As a result, everything must fit into the model. Therefore, the first step in putting the ERMI elements into ODRL is to map the ERMI elements in the use case to the existing ODRL data dictionary. If the semantic content is the same, then the expectation is to use the existing element within the ODRL data dictionary thus enhancing the potential for interoperability. We offer the following observations on the results of this exercise:

1. The learning curve for using ODRL is steep. It is possible that accurate creation of our ODRL versions of the ERMI XML use cases and the associated ODRL XML schema might not have been completed without the generous assistance of Renato Iannella and Susanne Guth of the ODRL Initiative. If ODRL were to be used widely for exchanging metadata between different ERM systems, this cost would be internalized by the libraries and vendors.

2. The ERMI/ODRL schema we have created can only validate the form of the XML document, not the syntax or semantics of the values in the XML. For example, in figure 2, <ermi:assumed-permission> is actually a type of ODRL "permissionElement", as referenced in our supplement to the ODRL schema, figure 5. As such, it is not possible to define our new <ermi:assumed-permission> element in such a way to make only particular values valid. Any string would be valid. Iannella informed us after reading an earlier draft of this report that it is possible to validate more closely (Iannella 2004). He said, "You can support this by defining <ermi:assumed-permission> as a *restriction* of permissionType and then defining all the subelements that you want to limit to. (This is a strong feature of XML Schema.)"

3. ODRL does not allow the communication of negative values. For example, figure 1 is a very simple XML markup of some licensing elements. One of these elements is called <perpetualaccessright>undetermined</perpetualaccessright>. The value in this element, "undetermined," represents the idea that we don't always interpret everything in a license when it is signed, but if we were exchanging data between two libraries we would want to know that the answer to this question is essentially, "we don't know." ODRL does not permit this kind of communication. As you can see in figure 2, this element has been commented out. There was discussion about the lack of a "not" operator at the ODRL International Workshop held in Vienna in April, 2004. It appears that work will be underway to make that possible in ODRL Version 2.0 (ODRL Workshop 2004).

4. ODRL can only express customer rights and duties but not those pertaining to the rights holder. ODRL is moving to address this shortcoming. Guth presented a paper at the recent ODRL Workshop describing the need for ODRL to express rights and duties for both parties (Guth and Strembeck 2004).

It is worth observing that our frustration trying to work with negative, or interpreted, values in ODRL can be placed in the broader context of twenty-first century international property rights, as described by Christopher May. He writes, "one of the key elements of the 'problem' of DRM is therefore the solidification of aspects of copyright law which have hitherto been amenable to a certain amount of indeterminacy, which is to say there have been areas of legal grayness" (May 2003). With an REL like ODRL or XrML, there can be only black and white. ODRL appears to picture the contracts which define the relationships as a series of checkboxes rather than a complex legal document written in somewhat creative English, suggesting a very different view of information than that of

ERMI. Our experience trying to fit ERMI elements into ODRL makes it clear that more would be given up than gained by using it for our purpose. ODRL was designed for use cases very different than ours.

ERMI CREATIVE COMMONS CC RDF

Our experience attempting to work with ODRL raised a number of issues which led us to look for an REL that might better fit our needs. (The products of our CC RDF experiment are figure 6, figure 7, and figure 8.) The CC RDF license description approach attracted us. We were intrigued by the philosophy behind the Creative Commons, which is close to the traditional fair use ethic among librarians. Though the CC RDF is a REL, it is not intended to serve as a language to be embedded into a control structure that would lock down the content. On the contrary, "unlike Digital Rights Management (DRM) technology, which tries to restrict use of digital works, Creative Commons is providing ways to encourage permitted sharing and reuse of works" (CC Why). In contrast to ODRL, CC RDF is less rich, but also less constraining. With the Creative Commons approach, information is not lost. However, it is not clear what is gained. Certainly one of the purposes of an XML schema must be to validate the structure and data types within a particular XML document. Our CC RDF schema cannot really validate the syntax of an XML document. This is no fault of CC RDF: it was designed as a structure for content owners to place—with some qualifications—their content into the public domain. Our experience trying to adapt the CC RDF schema to our needs does not preclude the possibility of using the technology of RDF, but substantial work would be required and the benefits seem unclear. *Note* that in a related context, a recent RoMEO project study on rights metadata for open archiving recommends Creative Commons over ODRL (RoMEO Study 6).

ERMI *NATIVE* SCHEMAS

The third approach is a scaled down variation of where we started in the fall of 2003; we would use our own ERMI namespace exclusively and design two simple XML schemas, one for each use case. (The products of our ERMI *native* schema experiment are figure 9, figure 10, figure 11, and figure 12.) Following our experiments with ODRL and Creative Commons we learned that the costs of using an existing REL are higher than they may appear on the surface. Our native schema simply takes the existing ERMI data elements and treats them as their own namespace. No effort is made to try to map the elements to another namespace. As a consequence, ERMI native schemas offer the most rigid syntax for validation, and also happen to be the most compact.

Conclusion

The momentum to build ERM systems for libraries is building, and we will soon reach a point where there is a specific need for exchanging data between these systems. What the ERMI Steering Group envisioned and expressed in our two use cases is simply the exchange of metadata between two library entities.

Based on our investigation, we believe that placing ERMI metadata within an XML container would best be achieved without using a formal REL. Instead, using our own specific native schemas offers the best cost-benefit ratio. We have no desire to control the associated content—unlike, for example, in the case of a recording studio that is trying to lock down the latest Britney Spears release. Since we do not need to lock down the content, why bring along all the baggage that a commercially-oriented REL requires for those other purposes?

Nevertheless, it will probably be worthwhile to continue to monitor related initiatives. For example, more can be learned and gained from studying ODRL. Based on the positive experience we had working with Iannella, it is clear that he and others involved in ODRL development are interested in having their REL evolve to better accommodate the needs of all parties. There may also be some parallels between the need for an ERMI XML specification and the approach take by Publishing Requirements for Industry Standard Metadata (PRISM). According to Coyle, PRISM is "a good example of a REL that was developed for a specific situation where a more general rights language was not necessary" (Coyle 2004, p. 13). As Rick Silterra puts it, "We're looking for exchangeability, but not necessarily actionability."

William Moen says that a "standard represents an agreement by a community to do things in a specified way to address a common problem." In fact, he goes on to say, "developing standards can be viewed as a community-centric endeavor. It is first and foremost a social process" (Moen 2003, pp. 4, 5). Librarians should think very carefully about what they are trying to accomplish in the new ERM context, and take note of the caution delivered at the W3C Workshop on DRM for the Web in 2001, "There is some anxiety that the current balance may be off and that actual privileges (like those of Libraries) are not supported in such a system" (W3C DRM Workshop 2001). Until balance is achieved, we recommend that librarians and vendors pick out particular elements from the ERMI data dictionary and build a custom schema for validation. Other namespaces, such as Dublin Core, could be mixed in where appropriate. These application profiles could be posted to a Web site or registry and used as is or modified where needed (Heery 2000).

Acknowledgements

We would like to acknowledge the valuable role that Nancy Hoebelheinrich (Stanford) played in the early planning for this investigation. The ODRL exercise could not have been completed without the assistance of Susan Guth and Renato Iannella (ODRL). Tim Jewell pitched in with clear-headed editorial advice. Sarah Chandler proofread several final drafts.

Table 1. ERMI Use Case: Quick Fix Description

"Quick-fix" Scenario: Give Me the Essence of This Agreement

Stat!Ref Element Group/Element Name	Definition	Identifier	Element Value
Prevailing Digitally Copy	The right of the licensee and authorized users to download and digitally copy a reasonable portion of the licensed materials	digitallycopy	Permitted
Prevailing Print Copy	The right of the licensee and authorized users to print a reasonable portion of the licensed materials	pcopy	Permitted
Prevailing Scholarly Sharing	The right of authorized users and/or the licensee to transmit hard copy or electronic copy of reasonable amounts of licensed materials to a third party for personal, scholarly, educational, scientific or professional use	scholarlysharing	Permitted
Prevailing Interlibrary Loan Print or Fax	The right to use the licensed materials for interlibrary loan by way of print copies or facsimile transmission	illlporfax	Permitted
Prevailing Interlibrary Loan Electronic	The right to use the licensed materials for interlibrary loan by way of electronic copies	illelectronic	Silent, undertermined

Prevailing Interlibrary Loan Secure Electronic Transmission	The right to use the license materials for interlibrary loan by way of secure electronic transmission	illsecureetransmission	Silent, undertermined
Prevailing Interlibrary Loan Record Keeping Required	The requirement to keep records of interlibrary loan activity and provide reports to the licensor at periodic intervals or upon request	illrecordkeeping	No
Prevailing Electronic / Cached Copy for Library Reserve	The right to make electronic copies of the licensed materials and store them on a secure network	ecopylibreserve	Permitted
Prevailing Perpetual Access Right	The right to permanently access the licensed materials paid for during the period of the license agreement	perpetualaccessright	Undetermined

Figure 1. ERMI Use Case: Quick Fix XML

```
<?xml version="1.0" encoding="UTF-8"?>
<ERMI>
  <ERMIQuickFix>
    <eresourcetitle>Sample Aggregator</eresourcetitle>
    <digitallycopy>permitted</digitallycopy>
    <pcopy>permitted</pcopy>
    <scholarlysharing>permitted</scholarlysharing>
    <illlporfax>permitted</illlporfax>
    <illelectronic>Silent, undertermined</illelectronic>
    <illsecureetransmission>Silent, undertermined</illsecureetransmission>
    <illrecordkeeping>no</illrecordkeeping>
    <ecopylibreserve>permitted</ecopylibreserve>
    <perpetualaccessright>undetermined</perpetualaccessright>
  </ERMIQuickFix>
</ERMI>
```

Figure 2. ODRL Use Case: Quick Fix

```xml
<?xml version="1.0" ?>
<o-ex:rights xmlns:o-ex="http://odrl.net/1.1/ODRL-EX"
        xmlns:o-dd="http://odrl.net/1.1/ODRL-DD"
        xmlns:ermi="http://www.library.cornell.edu/cts/elicensestudy/dlfermi/xml/schema/0.1/"
        xmlns:onix="http://www.editeur.org/onix/ReferenceNames"
        xmlns:ebx="http://ebxwg.org/voucher/0.8/"
        xmlns:dc="http://purl.org/dc/elements/1.1/"
        >
  <o-ex:agreement>
    <o-ex:asset>
      <!--Title information etc. -->
      <dc:title>Sample Aggregator</dc:title>
    </o-ex:asset>
  <o-ex:permission>
    <o-dd:print>
      <!--expressing "reasonable portion permitted"? (pcopy)-->
      <o-ex:constraint>
        <o-dd:unit o-ex:type="onix:NumberOfPages">
          <o-ex:constraint>
            <o-dd:count>5<!--entered by librarian--></o-dd:count>
          </o-ex:constraint>
        </o-dd:unit>
      </o-ex:constraint>
    </o-dd:print>
    <ermi:scholarlysharing/>
    <ermi:illlporfax/>
    <!--<illrecordkeeping>no</illrecordkeeping>-->
    <o-dd:backup><!--a network backup-->
      <o-ex:constraint>
        <o-dd:network>
         <o-ex:context>
          <o-dd:uid>137.224.204.XXXX</o-dd:uid>
         </o-ex:context>
        </o-dd:network>
      </o-ex:constraint>
    </o-dd:backup>
    <o-dd:excerpt>
     <o-ex:constraint>
       <o-dd:unit o-ex:type="onix:Chapter">
         <o-ex:constraint>
           <o-dd:range>
             <o-dd:max>2<o-dd:max>
           </o-dd:range>
         </o-ex:constraint>
       </o-dd:unit>
     </o-ex:constraint>
    </o-dd:excerpt>
  </o-ex:permission>
  <ermi:assumed-permission>
```

```
<!--<perpetualaccessright>undetermined</perpetualaccessright>-->
<ermi:perpetualaccessright />
  <!--<illelectronic>Silent, undertermined</illelectronic>
  <illsecureetransmission>Silent, undertermined</illsecureetransmission>-->
<ermi:illelectronic />
<ermi:illsecureetransmission />
</ermi:assumed-permission>
</o-ex:agreement>
</o-ex:rights>
```

Table 2. ERMI Use Case: License Agreement Description

Library 1 wants to know the terms agreed to by Library 2 in a license agreement for a particular resource

After discussion following creation of the XML ODRL for the first case, the ERMI permission values were adjusted to make them less ambiguous.

permitted (explicit)
permitted (interpreted)
prohibited (explicit)
prohibited (interpreted)
silent (un-interpreted)
not applicable

License Agreement: Stat!Ref

Stat!Ref			
Element Group/Element Name	**Definition**	**Identifier**	**Element Value**
E-Resource Entity Title Group:			
E-Resource Title	The word or group of words that name an e-resource	eresourcetitle	Stat!Ref
License Entity Identifier Group:			
License Name	The locally-assigned name of the license agreement	licensename	Stat!Ref License Agreement
License Entity Review Group:			

License Reviewer	An individual reviewing the license for the local institution or consortium	licensereviewer	Barbara Schader
Terms Defined Entity Authorized User Group:			
Authorized User Definition	The language in the contract that defines the group of users allowed to use the e-resource(s)	authorizeduserdefinition	Persons affiliated with the University of California. Full and part time employees (including faculty, staff, and independent contractors) and students of company and the institution of which it is a part, regardless of the physical location of such persons.
Terms Defined Entity Terms of Use Group:			
Fair Use Clause	A clause that affirms statutory fair use rights under federal copyright law (17 USC Section 107), or that the agreement does not restrict or abrogate the rights of the licensee or its user community under copyright law	fairuseclauseindicator	absent
All Rights Reserved Clause Indicator	A clause stating that all intellectual property rights not explicitly granted to the	allrightsreservedindicator	absent

	licensee are retained by the licensor		
Anti-Database Protection Clause Indicator	A clause that provides fair use protections within the context of assertions of database protection or additional proprietary rights related to database content not currently covered by U.S. copyright law	antidbprotectionindicator	absent
Interlibrary Loan Print or Fax	The right to use the licensed materials for interlibrary loan by way of print copies or facsimile transmission	illprintorfax	permitted (explicit)
Interlibrary Loan Secure Electronic Transmission	The right to use the license materials for interlibrary loan by way of secure electronic transmission	illsecureetransaction	silent (uninterpreted)
Interlibrary Loan Electronic	The right to use the licensed materials for interlibrary loan by way of electronic copies	illelectronic	silent (uninterpreted)
Interlibrary Loan Record Keeping Required	The requirement to keep records of interlibrary loan activity and provide reports to the licensor at periodic intervals or upon request	illrecordkeepingreq	no

Electronic / Cached Copy for Library Reserve	The right to make electronic copies of the licensed materials and store them on a secure network	ecopylibreserve	permitted (explicit)
Print Course Pack	The right to use licensed materials in collections or compilations of materials assembled in a print format by faculty members for use by students in a class for purposes of instruction	pcoursepack	permitted (explicit)
Electronic Course Pack	The right to use licensed materials in collections or compilations of materials assembled in an electronic format by faculty members for use by students in a class for purposes of instruction	ecoursepack	prohibited (explicit)
Walk-In User Term Note**	Information which qualifies the status or permitted actions of walk-in users	walkinusertermnote	permitted (explicit)
Terms Defined Perpetual Rights Group:			
Perpetual Access Right	The right to permanently access the licensed materials paid for during the period of the license agreement	perpetualaccess	permitted (interpreted)

Perpetual Access Note	Other information related to perpetual access	perpetualaccessnote	<no value>
Archiving Right	The right to permanently retain an electronic copy of the licensed materials	archivingright	prohibited (interpreted)
Archiving Note	Information related to archiving rights, product and format	archivingnote	<no value>
Completeness of Content	The presence of a provision in the contract stating that the licensed electronic materials shall include all content found in the print equivalent	completenessofcontent	yes
Terms Defined Entity Mutual Obligations Group:			
Confidentiality of User Information	A clause that requires the privacy of terms of the license agreement	confidentialityofagreement	yes
Clickwrap Modification Clause	A clause indicating that the negotiated agreement supersedes any click-through, click-wrap, other user agreement, or terms of use residing on the provider's server that might	clickwrapmodification	yes

	otherwise function as a contract of adhesion		
Confidentiality of Agreement	A clause that requires the privacy of terms of the license agreement	confidentialityofagreement	no
Confidentiality of Agreement Note	Specific details of what aspects of the license are private		Here is a note about confidentiality.
Content Warranty	A clause that guarantees a remedy to the licensee if the quantity or quality of material contained within the resource is materially diminished	contentwarranty	Licensed materials are provided on an "as is" basis.
Administration Information Entity Usage Statistics Group:			
Usage Statistics Availability	The availability of usage statistics for the resource	usagestatsavail	no
Usage Statistics Delivery Method	The manner in which statistics are made available	usagestatsdelivery	unavailable
Usage Statistics Format	The format(s) in which statistics are made available	usagestatsformat	unavailable
Usage Statistics Frequency	The frequency with which statistics are made available	usagestatsfrequency	Quarterly

Figure 3. ERMI Use Case: License Agreement XML

```xml
<?xml version="1.0" encoding="UTF-8"?>
<ERMI>
  <ERMSharedLicense>
    <eresourcetitle>Stat!Ref</eresourcetitle>
    <licensename>Stat!Ref License Agreement</licensename>
    <licensereviewer>Barbara Schader</licensereviewer>
    <authorizeduserdefinition>Persons affiliated with the University of California. Full and part
time employees (including faculty, staff, and independent contractors) and students of company
and the institution of which it is a part, regardless of the physical location of such persons.
    </authorizeduserdefinition>
    <fairuseclauseindicator>absent</fairuseclauseindicator>
    <allrightsreservedindicator>absent</allrightsreservedindicator>
    <antidbprotectionindicator>absent</antidbprotectionindicator>
    <illprintorfax>permitted (explicit)</illprintorfax>
    <illrecordkeepingreq>no</illrecordkeepingreq>
    <ecopylibreserve>permitted (explicit)</ecopylibreserve>
    <pcoursepack>permitted (explicit)</pcoursepack>
    <ecoursepack>prohibited (explicit)</ecoursepack>
    <walkinusertermnote>permitted (explicit)</walkinusertermnote>
    <perpetualaccessnote>no value</perpetualaccessnote>
    <archivingnote>no value</archivingnote>
    <completenessofcontent>yes</completenessofcontent>
    <confidentialityofagreement>yes</confidentialityofagreement>
    <clickwrapmodification>yes</clickwrapmodification>
    <confidentialityofagreement>no</confidentialityofagreement>
    <confidentialityofagreementnote>Here is a note about confidentiality.
</confidentialityofagreementnote>
    <contentwarranty>Licensed materials are provided on an "as is" basis. </contentwarranty>
    <usagestatsavail>no</usagestatsavail>
    <usagestatsdelivery>unavailable</usagestatsdelivery>
    <usagestatsformat>unavailable </usagestatsformat>
    <usagestatsfrequency>Quarterly</usagestatsfrequency>
    <perpetualaccess>permitted (interpreted)</perpetualaccess>
    <illsecureetransaction>silent(uninterpreted)</illsecureetransaction>
    <illelectronic>silent (uninterpreted)</illelectronic>
    <archivingright>prohibited (interpreted)</archivingright>
  </ERMSharedLicense>
</ERMI>
```

Figure 4. ODRL Use Case: License Agreement

```xml
<?xml version="1.0" ?>
<o-ex:rights xmlns:o-ex="http://odrl.net/1.1/ODRL-EX"
        xmlns:o-dd="http://odrl.net/1.1/ODRL-DD"
        xmlns:ermi="http://www.library.cornell.edu/cts/elicensestudy/dlfermi/xml/schema/0.1/"
        xmlns:onix="http://www.editeur.org/onix/ReferenceNames"
        xmlns:ebx="http://ebxwg.org/voucher/0.8/"
        xmlns:dc="http://purl.org/dc/elements/1.1/">

  <o-ex:agreement>
    <o-ex:asset>
      <!--Title information etc. -->
      <dc:title>Stat!Ref</dc:title>
    </o-ex:asset>
    <o-ex:context><!--moved out of o-ex:asset per Renato-->
      <dc:relation>Stat!Ref License Agreement</dc:relation>
      <ermi:licensereviewer>Barbara Schader</ermi:licensereviewer>
    </o-ex:context>
    <o-ex:permission>
      <!--Following constraint meant equivalent to authorizeduserdefinition element in original-->
      <o-ex:constraint>
        <o-dd:group>
          <o-ex:context>
          <o-dd:remark>
Persons affiliated with the University of California. Full and part time employees
(including faculty, staff, and independent contractors) and students of company and the institution
of which it is a part, regardless of the physical location of such persons.
          </o-dd:remark>
          </o-ex:context>
        </o-dd:group>
      </o-ex:constraint>
      <!--<fairuseclauseindicator>absent</fairuseclauseindicator>-->
      <!--<allrightsreservedindicator>absent</allrightsreservedindicator>-->
      <!--<antidbprotectionindicator>absent</antidbprotectionindicator>-->
      <ermi:illprintorfax />
      <ermi:illrecordkeepingreq />
      <ermi:ecopylibreserve />
      <ermi:pcoursepack />
      <!--<ecoursepack>prohibited (explicit)</ecoursepack>-->
      <ermi:walkinusertermnote />
      <!--<perpetualaccessnote>no value</perpetualaccessnote>-->
      <!--<archivingnote>no value</archivingnote>-->
      <ermi:completenessofcontent />
      <ermi:contentwarranty>
    <o-ex:context>
      <o-dd:remark>Licensed materials are provided on an "as is" basis.</o-dd:remark>
    </o-ex:context>
    </ermi:contentwarranty>
```

```
<!--<usagestatsavail>no</usagestatsavail>-->
<!--<usagestatsdelivery>unavailable</usagestatsdelivery>-->
<!--<usagestatsformat>unavailable </usagestatsformat>-->
<!--<usagestatsfrequency>Quarterly</usagestatsfrequency>-->
<!--NEED to determine how to represent "Quarterly", but doesn't make sense when stats not
available.-->
</o-ex:permission>
<ermi:assumed-permission>
<!--<perpetualaccessright>permitted (interpreted)</perpetualaccessright>-->
<ermi:perpetualaccessright />
<!--UNCERTAIN how to handle silent (uninterpreted)-->
<!--<illsecureetransaction>silent (uninterpreted)</illsecureetransaction>-->
<!--<illelectronic>silent (uninterpreted)</illelectronic>-->
<!--<archivingright>prohibited (interpreted)</archivingright>-->
</ermi:assumed-permission>
<o-ex:condition>
<o-ex:constraint>
<ermi:clickwrapmodification />
<!--<confidentialityofagreement>no</confidentialityofagreement>-->
<ermi:confidentialityofagreementnote>
<o-ex:context>
<o-dd:remark>Here is a note about confidentiality.</o-dd:remark>
</o-ex:context>
</ermi:confidentialityofagreementnote>
</o-ex:constraint>
<o-ex:condition>
</o-ex:agreement>
</o-ex:rights>
```

Figure 5. Supplement to ODRL Schema for Both Use Cases

```
<xsd:schema
targetNamespace="http://www.library.cornell.edu/cts/elicensestudy/
dlfermi/xml/schema/0.1/" xmlns:o-ex="http://odrl.net/1.1/ODRL-EX">

<xsd:element name="assumed-permission" type="o-ex:permission"
substitutionGroup="o-ex:permissionElement" />

<xsd:element name="scholarlysharing" type="o-ex:permissionType"
substitutionGroup="o-ex:permissionElement" />

<!-- NOT USED: Equivalent to illprintorfax <xsd:element
name="illlporfax" type="o-ex:permissionType"
substitutionGroup="o-ex:permissionElement" />-->

<xsd:element name="illelectronic" type="o-ex:permissionType"
substitutionGroup="o-ex:permissionElement" />

<xsd:element name="illsecureetransmission" type="o-ex:permissionType"
substitutionGroup="o-ex:permissionElement" />

<xsd:element name="illrecordkeeping" type="o-ex:permissionType"
substitutionGroup="o-ex:permissionElement" />

<xsd:element name="fairuseclauseindicator" type="o-ex:permissionType"
substitutionGroup="o-ex:permissionElement" />

<xsd:element name="allrightsreservedindicator"
type="o-ex:permissionType" substitutionGroup="o-ex:permissionElement" />

<xsd:element name="antidbprotectionindicator" type="o-ex:permissionType"
substitutionGroup="o-ex:permissionElement" />

<xsd:element name="illprintorfax" type="o-ex:permissionType"
substitutionGroup="o-ex:permissionElement" />

<xsd:element name="illsecuretransaction" type="o-ex:permissionType"
substitutionGroup="o-ex:permissionElement" />

<xsd:element name="illelectronic" type="o-ex:permissionType"
substitutionGroup="o-ex:permissionElement" />

<xsd:element name="illrecordkeeping" type="o-ex:permissionType"
substitutionGroup="o-ex:permissionElement" />

<xsd:element name="ecopylibreserve" type="o-ex:permissionType"
substitutionGroup="o-ex:permissionElement" />

<xsd:element name="pcoursepack" type="o-ex:permissionType"
substitutionGroup="o-ex:permissionElement" />
```

```
<xsd:element name="ecoursepack" type="o-ex:permissionType"
substitutionGroup="o-ex:permissionElement" />

<xsd:element name="walkinusertermnote" type="o-ex:permissionType"
substitutionGroup="o-ex:permissionElement" />

<xsd:element name="perpetualaccessright" type="o-ex:permissionType"
substitutionGroup="o-ex:permissionElement" />

<xsd:element name="perpetualaccessnote" type="o-ex:permissionType"
substitutionGroup="o-ex:permissionElement" />

<xsd:element name="archivingright" type="o-ex:permissionType"
substitutionGroup="o-ex:permissionElement" />

<xsd:element name="archivingnote" type="o-ex:permissionType"
substitutionGroup="o-ex:permissionElement" />

<xsd:element name="completenessofcontent" type="o-ex:permissionType"
substitutionGroup="o-ex:permissionElement" />

<xsd:element name="confidentialityofuserinformation"
type="o-ex:conditionType" substitutionGroup="o-ex:conditionElement" />

<xsd:element name="clickwrapmodification" type="o-ex:conditionType"
substitutionGroup="o-ex:conditionElement" />

<xsd:element name="confidentialtyofagreement" type="o-ex:conditionType"
substitutionGroup="o-ex:conditionElement" />

<xsd:element name="confidentialityofagreementnote"
type="o-ex:permissionType" substitutionGroup="o-ex:permissionElement" />

<xsd:element name="contentwarranty" type="o-ex:permissionType"
substitutionGroup="o-ex:permissionElement" />

<xsd:element name="usagestatsavail" type="o-ex:permissionType"
substitutionGroup="o-ex:permissionElement" />

<xsd:element name="usagestatsdelivery" type="o-ex:permissionType"
substitutionGroup="o-ex:permissionElement" />

<xsd:element name="usagestatsformat" type="o-ex:permissionType"
substitutionGroup="o-ex:permissionElement" />

<xsd:element name="usagestatsfrequency" type="o-ex:permissionType"
substitutionGroup="o-ex:permissionElement" />
</xsd:schema>
```

Figure 6. ERMI Creative Commons RDF: Quick Fix

```
<?xml version="1.0" encoding="UTF-8"?>
<rdf:RDF xmlns="http://web.resource.org/cc/"
   xmlns:dc="http://purl.org/dc/elements/1.1/"
   xmlns:rdf="http://www.w3.org/1999/02/22-rdf-syntax-ns#"
   xmlns:ermi="http://www.library.cornell.edu/cts/elicensestudy/dlfdeliverables
   /xmlschema/rdf/">
<Work rdf:about="http://example.org/SampleAggregator">
 <dc:title>Sample Aggregator</dc:title>
 <dc:description>A lovely database of lovely data.</dc:description>
 <dc:creator><Agent>
  <dc:title>Sample  Aggregator</dc:title>
 </Agent></dc:creator>
 <dc:rights><Agent>
  <dc:title>A Database </dc:title>
 </Agent></dc:rights>
 <dc:date>2222</dc:date>
  <license rdf:resource="http://library.cornell.edu/licenses#License1" />
</Work>

<License rdf:about="http://library.cornell.edu/licenses#License1">
 <explicitlyPermits
rdf:resource="http://www.library.cornell.edu/cts/elicensestudy/dlfdeliverables/xmlschema/rdf/dig
itallycopy" />
 <explicitlyPermits
rdf:resource="http://www.library.cornell.edu/cts/elicensestudy/dlfdeliverables/xmlschema/rdf/pco
py" />
 <explicitlyPermits
rdf:resource="http://www.library.cornell.edu/cts/elicensestudy/dlfdeliverables/xmlschema/rdf/sch
olarlysharing" />
 <explicitlyPermits
rdf:resource="http://www.library.cornell.edu/cts/elicensestudy/dlfdeliverables/xmlschema/rdf/illp
orfax" />
 <explicitlyPermits
rdf:resource="http://www.library.cornell.edu/cts/elicensestudy/dlfdeliverables/xmlschema/rdf/eco
pylibreserve" />
 <requiresNot
rdf:resource="http://www.library.cornell.edu/cts/elicensestudy/dlfdeliverables/xmlschema/rdf/illr
ecordkeeping" />
 <dontKnow
rdf:resource="http://www.library.cornell.edu/cts/elicensestudy/dlfdeliverables/xmlschema/rdf/ille
lectronic" />
 <dontKnow
rdf:resource="http://www.library.cornell.edu/cts/elicensestudy/dlfdeliverables/xmlschema/rdf/ills
ecuretransmission" />
 <dontKnow
rdf:resource="http://www.library.cornell.edu/cts/elicensestudy/dlfdeliverables/xmlschema/rdf/per
petualaccessright" />
</License>
</rdf:RDF>
```

Figure 7. ERMI Creative Commons RDF: License Agreement

```
<?xml version="1.0" encoding="UTF-8"?>
<rdf:RDF xmlns="http://web.resource.org/cc/"
   xmlns:dc="http://purl.org/dc/elements/1.1/"
   xmlns:rdf="http://www.w3.org/1999/02/22-rdf-syntax-ns#"
   xmlns:ermi="http://www.library.cornell.edu/cts/elicensestudy/dlfdeliverables
   /xmlschema/rdf/">

<Work rdf:about="http://example.org/Somebody">
 <dc:title>Stat!Ref</dc:title>
 <dc:description>Just some data.</dc:description>
 <dc:creator><Agent>
  <dc:title>Whoever created the databse</dc:title>
 </Agent></dc:creator>
 <dc:rights><Agent>
  <dc:title>Whoever owns the rights to this database </dc:title>
 </Agent></dc:rights>
 <dc:date>1776</dc:date>
  <license rdf:resource="http://library.cornell.edu/licenses#License2" />
</Work>

<License rdf:about="http://library.cornell.edu/licenses#License2">
 <explicitlyPermits
rdf:resource="http://www.library.cornell.edu/cts/elicensestudy/dlfdeliverables/xmlschema/rdf/dig
itallycopy" />
 <explicitlyPermits
rdf:resource="http://www.library.cornell.edu/cts/elicensestudy/dlfdeliverables/xmlschema/rdf/pco
py" />
 <explicitlyPermits
rdf:resource="http://www.library.cornell.edu/cts/elicensestudy/dlfdeliverables/xmlschema/rdf/sch
olarlysharing" />
 <explicitlyPermits
rdf:resource="http://www.library.cornell.edu/cts/elicensestudy/dlfdeliverables/xmlschema/rdf/illp
orfax" />
 <explicitlyPermits
rdf:resource="http://www.library.cornell.edu/cts/elicensestudy/dlfdeliverables/xmlschema/rdf/eco
pylibreserve" />
  <explicitlyPermits
rdf:resource="http://www.library.cornell.edu/cts/elicensestudy/dlfdeliverables/xmlschema/rdf/pco
ursepack" />
 <explicitlyPermits
rdf:resource="http://www.library.cornell.edu/cts/elicensestudy/dlfdeliverables/xmlschema/rdf/wal
kinuserpermitted" />
 <explicitlyPermits
rdf:resource="http://www.library.cornell.edu/cts/elicensestudy/dlfdeliverables/xmlschema/rdf/clic
kwrapmodification" />

 <interpretedPermits
rdf:resource="http://www.library.cornell.edu/cts/elicensestudy/dlfdeliverables/xmlschema/rdf/per
petualaccess" />
```

```
    <explicitlyProhibits
rdf:resource="http://www.library.cornell.edu/cts/elicensestudy/dlfdeliverables/xmlschema/rdf/eco
ursepack" />
    <explicitlyProhibits
rdf:resource="http://www.library.cornell.edu/cts/elicensestudy/dlfdeliverables/xmlschema/rdf/usa
gestatsavail" />

    <interpretedProhibits
rdf:resource="http://www.library.cornell.edu/cts/elicensestudy/dlfdeliverables/xmlschema/rdf/arc
hivingright" />

    <requires
rdf:resource="http://www.library.cornell.edu/cts/elicensestudy/dlfdeliverables/xmlschema/rdf/co
mpletenessofcontent" />
    <requires
rdf:resource="http://www.library.cornell.edu/cts/elicensestudy/dlfdeliverables/xmlschema/rdf/con
fidentialityofagreement" />

    <requiresNot
rdf:resource="http://www.library.cornell.edu/cts/elicensestudy/dlfdeliverables/xmlschema/rdf/illr
ecordkeeping" />

  <dontKnow
rdf:resource="http://www.library.cornell.edu/cts/elicensestudy/dlfdeliverables/xmlschema/rdf/fair
useclauseindicator" />
  <dontKnow
rdf:resource="http://www.library.cornell.edu/cts/elicensestudy/dlfdeliverables/xmlschema/rdf/allr
ightsreservedindicator" />
  <dontKnow
rdf:resource="http://www.library.cornell.edu/cts/elicensestudy/dlfdeliverables/xmlschema/rdf/ant
idbprotection" />
  <dontKnow
rdf:resource="http://www.library.cornell.edu/cts/elicensestudy/dlfdeliverables/xmlschema/rdf/per
petualaccess" />
  <dontKnow
rdf:resource="http://www.library.cornell.edu/cts/elicensestudy/dlfdeliverables/xmlschema/rdf/ills
ecuretransaction" />
  <dontKnow
rdf:resource="http://www.library.cornell.edu/cts/elicensestudy/dlfdeliverables/xmlschema/rdf/ille
lectronic" />
  <dontKnow
rdf:resource="http://www.library.cornell.edu/cts/elicensestudy/dlfdeliverables/xmlschema/rdf/usa
gestatsdelivery" />
  <dontKnow
rdf:resource="http://www.library.cornell.edu/cts/elicensestudy/dlfdeliverables/xmlschema/rdf/usa
gestatsformat" />
    <!-- We are set up to permit,require, or prohibit actions.  This is not set up to
        actually give values to things, like "quarterly, or 1 dollar per copy. -->
```

```
    <dontKnow
rdf:resource="http://www.library.cornell.edu/cts/elicensestudy/dlfdeliverables/xmlschema/rdf/usa
gestatsdelivery" />

</License>
</rdf:RDF>
```

Figure 8. ERMI Creative Commons RDF Schema

```
<?xml version="1.0" encoding="UTF-8"?>
<!-- Creative commons based schema with additions  for ERMI.
    should cover use cases 1 and 2 -->

<rdf:RDF xmlns="http://web.resource.org/cc/"
    xmlns:dc="http://purl.org/dc/elements/1.1/"
    xmlns:rdf="http://www.w3.org/1999/02/22-rdf-syntax-ns#"
    xmlns:rdfs="http://www.w3.org/2000/01/rdf-schema#"

xmlns:ermi="http://www.library.cornell.edu/cts/elicensestudy/dlfdeliverables/xmlschema/rdf/">

<!-- Creative Commons permissions. -->

    <rdfs:Class rdf:about="http://web.resource.org/cc/Work">
        <dc:title>work</dc:title>
        <dc:description>a potentially copyrightable work</dc:description>
        <rdfs:seeAlso rdf:resource="http://www.w3.org/2000/10/swap/pim/doc#Work"/>
    </rdfs:Class>
    <rdfs:Class rdf:about="http://web.resource.org/cc/Agent">
        <dc:title>agent</dc:title>
        <dc:description>something (e.g. a person, corporation or computer) capable of creating
things</dc:description>
    </rdfs:Class>
    <rdfs:Class rdf:about="http://web.resource.org/cc/License">
        <dc:title>license</dc:title>
        <dc:description>a set of requests/permissions to users of a Work, e.g. a copyright license,
the public domain, information for distributors</dc:description>
    </rdfs:Class>
    <rdfs:Class rdf:about="http://web.resource.org/cc/Permission">
        <dc:title>permission</dc:title>
        <dc:description>an action that may or may not be allowed or desired</dc:description>
    </rdfs:Class>
    <rdfs:Class rdf:about="http://web.resource.org/cc/Requirement">
        <dc:title>requirement</dc:title>
        <dc:description>an action that may or may not be requested of you</dc:description>
    </rdfs:Class>
    <rdfs:Class rdf:about="http://web.resource.org/cc/Prohibition">
        <dc:title>prohibition</dc:title>
        <dc:description>something you may be asked not to do</dc:description>
    </rdfs:Class>

    <License rdf:about="http://web.resource.org/cc/PublicDomain">
        <dc:title>public domain</dc:title>
        <dc:description>no copyright; everything is permitted without restriction</dc:description>
    </License>

    <Permission rdf:about="http://web.resource.org/cc/Reproduction">
        <dc:title>reproduction</dc:title>
        <dc:description>making multiple copies</dc:description>
```

```
  </Permission>
  <Permission rdf:about="http://web.resource.org/cc/Distribution">
    <dc:title>distribution</dc:title>
    <dc:description>distribution, public display, and publicly performance</dc:description>
  </Permission>
  <Permission rdf:about="http://web.resource.org/cc/DerivativeWorks">
    <dc:title>derivative works</dc:title>
    <dc:description>creation and distribution of derivative works</dc:description>
  </Permission>

  <Requirement rdf:about="http://web.resource.org/cc/Notice">
    <dc:title>copyright notices</dc:title>
    <dc:description>copyright and license notices be kept intact</dc:description>
  </Requirement>
  <Requirement rdf:about="http://web.resource.org/cc/Attribution">
    <dc:title>attribution</dc:title>
    <dc:description>credit be given to copyright holder and/or author</dc:description>
  </Requirement>
  <Requirement rdf:about="http://web.resource.org/cc/ShareAlike">
    <dc:title>share alike</dc:title>
    <dc:description>derivative works be licensed under the same terms as the original
work</dc:description>
  </Requirement>
  <Requirement rdf:about="http://web.resource.org/cc/SourceCode">
    <dc:title>source code</dc:title>
    <dc:description>source code (the preferred form for making modifications) must be
provided for all derivative works</dc:description>
  </Requirement>

  <Prohibition rdf:about="http://web.resource.org/cc/CommercialUse">
    <dc:title>commercial use</dc:title>
    <dc:description>exercising rights for commercial purposes</dc:description>
  </Prohibition>

  <rdf:Property rdf:about="http://web.resource.org/cc/license">
    <dc:title>has license</dc:title>
    <rdfs:domain rdf:resource="http://web.resource.org/cc/Work"/>
    <rdfs:range rdf:resource="http://web.resource.org/cc/License"/>
    <rdfs:seeAlso rdf:resource="http://www.w3.org/2000/10/swap/pim/doc#ipr"/>
    <rdfs:subPropertyOf rdf:resource="http://purl.org/dc/elements/1.1/rights"/>
  </rdf:Property>
  <rdf:Property rdf:about="http://web.resource.org/cc/permits">
    <dc:title>permits</dc:title>
    <rdfs:domain rdf:resource="http://web.resource.org/cc/License"/>
    <rdfs:range rdf:resource="http://web.resource.org/cc/Permission"/>
  </rdf:Property>
  <rdf:Property rdf:about="http://web.resource.org/cc/requires">
    <dc:title>requires</dc:title>
    <rdfs:domain rdf:resource="http://web.resource.org/cc/License"/>
    <rdfs:range rdf:resource="http://web.resource.org/cc/Requirement"/>
  </rdf:Property>
```

```
<rdf:Property rdf:about="http://web.resource.org/cc/prohibits">
  <dc:title>prohibits</dc:title>
  <rdfs:domain rdf:resource="http://web.resource.org/cc/License"/>
  <rdfs:range rdf:resource="http://web.resource.org/cc/Prohibition"/>
</rdf:Property>


 <Prohibition rdf:about="http://web.resource.org/cc/CommercialUse">
  <dc:title>commercial use</dc:title>
  <dc:description>exercising rights for commercial purposes</dc:description>
</Prohibition>



<!-- New properties for ERMI exploration. In the ERMI name space. -->
<rdf:Property
rdf:about="http://www.library.cornell.edu/cts/elicensestudy/dlfdeliverables/xmlschema/rdf/explic
itlyProhibits">
    <dc:title>prohibited (explicit)</dc:title>
    <rdfs:domain rdf:resource="http://web.resource.org/cc/License"/>
    <rdfs:range rdf:resource="http://web.resource.org/cc/Prohibition"/>
</rdf:Property>


<rdf:Property
rdf:about="http://www.library.cornell.edu/cts/elicensestudy/dlfdeliverables/xmlschema/rdf/interp
retedProhibits">
    <dc:title>prohibited (interpreted)</dc:title>
    <rdfs:domain rdf:resource="http://web.resource.org/cc/License"/>
    <rdfs:range rdf:resource="http://web.resource.org/cc/Prohibition"/>
</rdf:Property>


<rdf:Property
rdf:about="http://www.library.cornell.edu/cts/elicensestudy/dlfdeliverables/xmlschema/rdf/explic
itlyPermits">
    <dc:title>permitted (explicit)</dc:title>
    <rdfs:domain rdf:resource="http://web.resource.org/cc/License"/>
    <rdfs:range rdf:resource="http://web.resource.org/cc/Permission"/>
</rdf:Property>

<rdf:Property rdf:about="http://www.ermi.org/erm/interpretedPermits">
    <dc:title>permitted (interpreted)</dc:title>
    <rdfs:domain rdf:resource="http://web.resource.org/cc/License"/>
    <rdfs:range rdf:resource="http://web.resource.org/cc/Permission"/>
</rdf:Property>

 <rdf:Property rdf:about="http://www.ermi.org/erm/dontKnow">
  <dc:title>silent (uninterpreted)</dc:title>
  <rdfs:domain rdf:resource="http://web.resource.org/cc/License"/>
  <rdfs:range rdf:resource="http://web.resource.org/cc/Permission"/>
</rdf:Property>

<rdf:Property rdf:about="http://www.ermi.org/erm/requiresNot">
  <dc:title>not required</dc:title>
```

```
    <rdfs:domain rdf:resource="http://web.resource.org/cc/License"/>
    <rdfs:range rdf:resource="http://web.resource.org/cc/Requirement"/>
  </rdf:Property>

  <!--- All the permissions and prohibitions. If these are shared by various institutions, they should
  be in the ermi namespace, or if institution specific, in the institution namespace.
  -->
  <Permission
rdf:about="http://www.library.cornell.edu/cts/elicensestudy/dlfdeliverables/xmlschema/rdf/scholarlysharing">
    <dc:title>scholarlysharing</dc:title>
    <dc:description>The right of authorized users
and/or the licensee to transmit hard copy or electronic copy of reasonable amounts of licensed materials to a third party for
personal, scholarly, educational, scientific or professional use</dc:description>
  </Permission>
  <Permission
rdf:about="http://www.library.cornell.edu/cts/elicensestudy/dlfdeliverables/xmlschema/rdf/digitallycopy">
    <dc:title>digitallycopy</dc:title>
    <dc:description>The right of the licensee and authorized users to download and
    digitally copy a reasonable portion of the licensed materials</dc:description>
      </Permission>
  <Permission
rdf:about="http://www.library.cornell.edu/cts/elicensestudy/dlfdeliverables/xmlschema/rdf/illelectronic">
    <dc:title>illelectronic</dc:title>
    <dc:description>The right to use the licensed materials for interlibrary loan by way of
electronic copies</dc:description>
  </Permission>
  <Permission
rdf:about="http://www.library.cornell.edu/cts/elicensestudy/dlfdeliverables/xmlschema/rdf/illsecureetransmission">
    <dc:title>illsecureetransmission</dc:title>
    <dc:description>The right to use the license materials for intcrlibrary loan by way of secure
electronic transmission</dc:description>
  </Permission>
  <Permission
rdf:about="http://www.library.cornell.edu/cts/elicensestudy/dlfdeliverables/xmlschema/rdf/illrecordkeeping">
    <dc:title>illrecordkeeping</dc:title>
    <dc:description>The requirement to keep records of interlibrary loan activity and provide
reports to the licensor at periodic intervals or upon request</dc:description>
  </Permission>
  <Permission
rdf:about="http://www.library.cornell.edu/cts/elicensestudy/dlfdeliverables/xmlschema/rdf/fairuseclauseindicator">
    <dc:title>fairuseclauseindicator</dc:title>
    <dc:description>A clause that affirms statutory fair use rights under federal copyright law (17
USC Section 107), or that the agreement does not restrict or
```

abrogate the rights of the licensee or its user community under copyright
law</dc:description>
  </Permission>
  <Permission
rdf:about="http://www.library.cornell.edu/cts/elicensestudy/dlfdeliverables/xmlschema/rdf/allrigh
tsreservedindicator">
    <dc:title>allrightsreservedindicator</dc:title>
    <dc:description>A clause stating that all intellectual property rights not explicitly
granted to the licensee are retained by the licensor </dc:description>
  </Permission>
  <Permission
rdf:about="http://www.library.cornell.edu/cts/elicensestudy/dlfdeliverables/xmlschema/rdf/antidb
protectionindicator">
    <dc:title>antidbprotectionindicator</dc:title>
    <dc:description> A clause that provides fair use protections within the context of assertions of
database protection or additional proprietary rights related to database content not currently
covered by U.S. copyright law </dc:description>
  </Permission>
  <Permission
rdf:about="http://www.library.cornell.edu/cts/elicensestudy/dlfdeliverables/xmlschema/rdf/illprin
torfax">
    <dc:title>illprintorfax</dc:title>
    <dc:description>The right to use the licensed materials for
 interlibrary loan by way of print copies or facsimile transmission </dc:description>
  </Permission>
  <Permission
rdf:about="http://www.library.cornell.edu/cts/elicensestudy/dlfdeliverables/xmlschema/rdf/ecopy
libreserve">
    <dc:title>ecopylibreserve</dc:title>
    <dc:description> The right to make electronic copies of the licensed
materials and store them on a secure network</dc:description>
  </Permission>
  <Permission
rdf:about="http://www.library.cornell.edu/cts/elicensestudy/dlfdeliverables/xmlschema/rdf/pcour
sepack">
    <dc:title>pcoursepack</dc:title>
    <dc:description> The right to use licensed materials in collections or
compilations of materials assembled in a print format by faculty members for use by students in a
class for purposes of instruction</dc:description>
  </Permission>
  <Permission
rdf:about="http://www.library.cornell.edu/cts/elicensestudy/dlfdeliverables/xmlschema/rdf/ecours
epack">
    <dc:title>ecoursepack</dc:title>
    <dc:description> The right to use licensed materials in collections or
compilations of materials assembled in an electronic format by faculty members for use by
students in a class for purposes of instruction</dc:description>
  </Permission>
  <Permission
rdf:about="http://www.library.cornell.edu/cts/elicensestudy/dlfdeliverables/xmlschema/rdf/walki
nusertermnote">

```
    <dc:title>walkinusertermnote</dc:title>
    <dc:description> </dc:description>
  </Permission>
  <Permission
rdf:about="http://www.library.cornell.edu/cts/elicensestudy/dlfdeliverables/xmlschema/rdf/perpet
ualaccessright">
    <dc:title>perpetualaccessright</dc:title>
    <dc:description>The right to permanently access the licensed materials paid
for during the period of the license agreement</dc:description>
  </Permission>

  <Permission
rdf:about="http://www.library.cornell.edu/cts/elicensestudy/dlfdeliverables/xmlschema/rdf/archiv
ingright">
    <dc:title>archivingright</dc:title>
    <dc:description>The right to permanently retain an electronic copy of the licensed materials
</dc:description>
  </Permission>

  <Permission
rdf:about="http://www.library.cornell.edu/cts/elicensestudy/dlfdeliverables/xmlschema/rdf/compl
etenessofcontent">
    <dc:title>completenessofcontent</dc:title>
    <dc:description> The presence of a provision in the contract stating that the licensed
electronic materials shall include all content found in the print equivalent</dc:description>
  </Permission>
  <Permission
rdf:about="http://www.library.cornell.edu/cts/elicensestudy/dlfdeliverables/xmlschema/rdf/confid
entialityofuserinformation">
    <dc:title>confidentialityofuserinformation</dc:title>
    <dc:description> </dc:description>
  </Permission>
  <Permission
rdf:about="http://www.library.cornell.edu/cts/elicensestudy/dlfdeliverables/xmlschema/rdf/click
wrapmodification">
    <dc:title>clickwrapmodification</dc:title>
    <dc:description> A clause indicating that the negotiated agreement supersedes any click-
through, click-wrap, other user agreement, or terms of use residing on the provider's server that
might otherwise function as a contract of adhesion</dc:description>
  </Permission>
  <Permission
rdf:about="http://www.library.cornell.edu/cts/elicensestudy/dlfdeliverables/xmlschema/rdf/confid
entialtyofagreement" >
    <dc:title>confidentialtyofagreement</dc:title>
    <dc:description>A clause that requires the privacy of terms of the license agreement
</dc:description>
  </Permission>

  <Permission
rdf:about="http://www.library.cornell.edu/cts/elicensestudy/dlfdeliverables/xmlschema/rdf/conte
ntwarranty">
```

```
    <dc:title>contentwarranty</dc:title>
    <dc:description> A clause that guarantees a remedy to the licensee if the quantity or
quality of material contained within the resource is materially diminished</dc:description>
    </Permission>
    <Permission
rdf:about="http://www.library.cornell.edu/cts/elicensestudy/dlfdeliverables/xmlschema/rdf/usage
statsavail">
    <dc:title>usagestatsavail</dc:title>
    <dc:description>The availability of usage statistics for the resource</dc:description>
    </Permission>
    <Permission
rdf:about="http://www.library.cornell.edu/cts/elicensestudy/dlfdeliverables/xmlschema/rdf/usage
statsdelivery">
    <dc:title>usagestatsavail</dc:title>
    <dc:description>The manner in which statistics are made available </dc:description>
    </Permission>
    <Permission
rdf:about="http://www.library.cornell.edu/cts/elicensestudy/dlfdeliverables/xmlschema/rdf/usage
statsformat">
    <dc:title>usagestatsformat</dc:title>
    <dc:description>The format(s) in which statistics are made available </dc:description>
    </Permission>
    <Permission
rdf:about="http://www.library.cornell.edu/cts/elicensestudy/dlfdeliverables/xmlschema/rdf/usage
statsfrequency">
    <dc:title>usagestatsfrequency</dc:title>
    <dc:description> The frequency with which statistics are made available</dc:description>
    </Permission>


    <Prohibition
rdf:about="http://www.library.cornell.edu/cts/elicensestudy/dlfdeliverables/xmlschema/rdf/schola
rlysharing">
    <dc:title>scholarlysharing</dc:title>
    <dc:description>The right of authorized users
and/or the licensee to transmit hard copy or electronic copy of reasonable amounts of licensed
materials to a third party for
personal, scholarly, educational, scientific or professional use</dc:description>
    </Prohibition>
    <Prohibition
rdf:about="http://www.library.cornell.edu/cts/elicensestudy/dlfdeliverables/xmlschema/rdf/illelec
tronic">
    <dc:title>illelectronic</dc:title>
    <dc:description>The right to use the licensed materials for interlibrary loan by way of
electronic copies</dc:description>
    </Prohibition>
    <Prohibition
rdf:about="http://www.library.cornell.edu/cts/elicensestudy/dlfdeliverables/xmlschema/rdf/illsecu
reetransmission">
    <dc:title>illsecureetransmission</dc:title>
    <dc:description>The right to use the license materials for interlibrary loan by way of secure
electronic transmission</dc:description>
```

```
</Prohibition>
<Prohibition
rdf:about="http://www.library.cornell.edu/cts/elicensestudy/dlfdeliverables/xmlschema/rdf/illreco
rdkeeping">
    <dc:title>illrecordkeeping</dc:title>
    <dc:description>The requirement to keep records of interlibrary loan activity and provide
reports to the licensor at periodic intervals or upon request</dc:description>
</Prohibition>
<Prohibition
rdf:about="http://www.library.cornell.edu/cts/elicensestudy/dlfdeliverables/xmlschema/rdf/fairus
eclauseindicator">
    <dc:title>fairuseclauseindicator</dc:title>
    <dc:description>A clause that affirms statutory fair use rights under federal copyright law (17
USC Section 107), or that the agreement does not restrict or
            abrogate the rights of the licensee or its user community under copyright
law</dc:description>
</Prohibition>
<Prohibition
rdf:about="http://www.library.cornell.edu/cts/elicensestudy/dlfdeliverables/xmlschema/rdf/allrigh
tsreservedindicator">
    <dc:title>allrightsreservedindicator</dc:title>
    <dc:description>A clause stating that all intellectual property rights not explicitly
granted to the licensee are retained by the licensor </dc:description>
</Prohibition>
<Prohibition
rdf:about="http://www.library.cornell.edu/cts/elicensestudy/dlfdeliverables/xmlschema/rdf/antidb
protectionindicator">
    <dc:title>antidbprotectionindicator</dc:title>
    <dc:description> A clause that provides fair use protections within the context of assertions of
database protection or additional proprietary rights related to database content not currently
covered by U.S. copyright law </dc:description>
</Prohibition>
<Prohibition
rdf:about="http://www.library.cornell.edu/cts/elicensestudy/dlfdeliverables/xmlschema/rdf/illprin
torfax">
    <dc:title>illprintorfax</dc:title>
    <dc:description>The right to use the licensed materials for
 interlibrary loan by way of print copies or facsimile transmission </dc:description>
</Prohibition>
<Prohibition
rdf:about="http://www.library.cornell.edu/cts/elicensestudy/dlfdeliverables/xmlschema/rdf/ecopy
libreserve">
    <dc:title>ecopylibreserve</dc:title>
    <dc:description> The right to make electronic copies of the licensed
materials and store them on a secure network</dc:description>
</Prohibition>
<Prohibition
rdf:about="http://www.library.cornell.edu/cts/elicensestudy/dlfdeliverables/xmlschema/rdf/pcour
sepack">
    <dc:title>pcoursepack</dc:title>
    <dc:description> The right to use licensed materials in collections or
```

compilations of materials assembled in a print format by faculty members for use by students in a class for purposes of instruction</dc:description>
    </Prohibition>
    <Prohibition
rdf:about="http://www.library.cornell.edu/cts/elicensestudy/dlfdeliverables/xmlschema/rdf/ecoursepack">
        <dc:title>ecoursepack</dc:title>
        <dc:description> The right to use licensed materials in collections or
compilations of materials assembled in an electronic format by faculty members for use by students in a class for purposes of instruction</dc:description>
    </Prohibition>
    <Prohibition
rdf:about="http://www.library.cornell.edu/cts/elicensestudy/dlfdeliverables/xmlschema/rdf/walkinusertermnote">
        <dc:title>walkinusertermnote</dc:title>
        <dc:description> </dc:description>
    </Prohibition>
    <Prohibition
rdf:about="http://www.library.cornell.edu/cts/elicensestudy/dlfdeliverables/xmlschema/rdf/perpetualaccessright">
        <dc:title>perpetualaccessright</dc:title>
        <dc:description>The right to permanently access the licensed materials paid
for during the period of the license agreement</dc:description>
    </Prohibition>

    <Prohibition
rdf:about="http://www.library.cornell.edu/cts/elicensestudy/dlfdeliverables/xmlschema/rdf/archivingright">
        <dc:title>archivingright</dc:title>
        <dc:description>The right to permanently retain an electronic copy of the licensed materials </dc:description>
    </Prohibition>

    <Prohibition
rdf:about="http://www.library.cornell.edu/cts/elicensestudy/dlfdeliverables/xmlschema/rdf/completenessofcontent">
        <dc:title>completenessofcontent</dc:title>
        <dc:description> The presence of a provision in the contract stating that the licensed
electronic materials shall include all content found in the print equivalent</dc:description>
    </Prohibition>
    <Prohibition
rdf:about="http://www.library.cornell.edu/cts/elicensestudy/dlfdeliverables/xmlschema/rdf/confidentialityofuserinformation">
        <dc:title>confidentialityofuserinformation</dc:title>
        <dc:description> </dc:description>
    </Prohibition>
    <Prohibition
rdf:about="http://www.library.cornell.edu/cts/elicensestudy/dlfdeliverables/xmlschema/rdf/clickwrapmodification">
        <dc:title>clickwrapmodification</dc:title>

<dc:description> A clause indicating that the negotiated agreement supersedes any click-through, click-wrap, other user agreement, or terms of use residing on the provider's server that might otherwise function as a contract of adhesion</dc:description>
  </Prohibition>
  <Prohibition
rdf:about="http://www.library.cornell.edu/cts/elicensestudy/dlfdeliverables/xmlschema/rdf/confidentialtyofagreement" >
    <dc:title>confidentialtyofagreement</dc:title>
    <dc:description>A clause that requires the privacy of terms of the license agreement </dc:description>
  </Prohibition>

  <Prohibition
rdf:about="http://www.library.cornell.edu/cts/elicensestudy/dlfdeliverables/xmlschema/rdf/contentwarranty">
    <dc:title>contentwarranty</dc:title>
    <dc:description> A clause that guarantees a remedy to the licensee if the quantity or quality of material contained within the resource is materially diminished</dc:description>
  </Prohibition>
  <Prohibition
rdf:about="http://www.library.cornell.edu/cts/elicensestudy/dlfdeliverables/xmlschema/rdf/usagestatsavail">
    <dc:title>usagestatsavail</dc:title>
    <dc:description>The availability of usage statistics for the resource</dc:description>
  </Prohibition>
  <Prohibition
rdf:about="http://www.library.cornell.edu/cts/elicensestudy/dlfdeliverables/xmlschema/rdf/usagestatsdelivery">
    <dc:title>usagestatsavail</dc:title>
    <dc:description>The manner in which statistics are made available </dc:description>
  </Prohibition>
  <Prohibition
rdf:about="http://www.library.cornell.edu/cts/elicensestudy/dlfdeliverables/xmlschema/rdf/usagestatsformat">
    <dc:title>usagestatsformat</dc:title>
    <dc:description>The format(s) in which statistics are made available </dc:description>
  </Prohibition>
  <Prohibition
rdf:about="http://www.library.cornell.edu/cts/elicensestudy/dlfdeliverables/xmlschema/rdf/usagestatsfrequency">
    <dc:title>usagestatsfrequency</dc:title>
    <dc:description> The frequency with which statistics are made available</dc:description>
  </Prohibition>

<!-- Statistics keeping that might be imposed upon the database provider, OR upon the licensee, will need some different way of encoding upon whom a requirement is imposed. At the moment, the requirements embed within themselves the agent imposing the requirement, and the agent upon whom the requirement is imposed.
This is a problem in general with the requirements, prohibitions, and permission, but they all seem to have implicit statements of who is involved in what role with this action. -->

```
  <Requirement
rdf:about="http://www.library.cornell.edu/cts/elicensestudy/dlfdeliverables/xmlschema/rdf/compl
etenessofcontent">
    <dc:title>completenessofcontent</dc:title>
    <dc:description> The presence of a provision in the contract stating that the licensed
electronic materials shall include all content found in the print equivalent.</dc:description>
  </Requirement>
  <Requirement
rdf:about="http://www.library.cornell.edu/cts/elicensestudy/dlfdeliverables/xmlschema/rdf/confid
entialityofagreement">
    <dc:title>confidentialityofagreement</dc:title>
    <dc:description> The presence of a provision in the contract stating that the terms of this
agreement are confidential. This is a mutual requirement. </dc:description>
  </Requirement>
  <!-- If there are different kinds of warranty's maybe they would have to be sub classes, -->
  <Requirement
rdf:about="http://www.library.cornell.edu/cts/elicensestudy/dlfdeliverables/xmlschema/rdf/conte
ntwarranty">
    <dc:title>contentwarranty</dc:title>
    <dc:description>Materials are provided on an as-is basis.</dc:description>
  </Requirement>

  <!-- Utility Terms -->

  <rdf:Property rdf:about="http://web.resource.org/cc/derivativeWork">
    <dc:title>has a derivative work</dc:title>
    <rdfs:domain rdf:resource="http://web.resource.org/cc/Work" />
    <rdfs:range rdf:resource="http://web.resource.org/cc/Work" />
    <rdfs:seeAlso rdf:resource="http://purl.org/dc/elements/1.1/source" />
  </rdf:Property>
</rdf:RDF>
```

Figure 9. ERMI Native XML for Quick Fix Use Case

```xml
<?xml version="1.0" encoding="UTF-8"?>
<ERMI xmlns:xsi="http://www.w3.org/2001/XMLSchema-instance"
xsi:noNamespaceSchemaLocation="qf.xsd">
    <ERMIQuickFix>
        <eresourcetitle>Sample Aggregator</eresourcetitle>
        <digitallycopy>no</digitallycopy>
        <pcopy>permitted</pcopy>
        <scholarlysharing>permitted</scholarlysharing>
        <illlporfax>permitted</illlporfax>
        <illelectronic>undetermined</illelectronic>
        <illsecureetransmission>undetermined</illsecureetransmission>
        <illrecordkeeping>no</illrecordkeeping>
        <ecopylibreserve>permitted</ecopylibreserve>
        <perpetualaccessright>undetermined</perpetualaccessright>
    </ERMIQuickFix>
</ERMI>
```

Figure 10. ERMI Native Schema for Quick Fix Use Case

```xml
<?xml version="1.0" encoding="UTF-8"?>
<!--W3C Schema generated by XMLSPY v5 rel. 4 U (http://www.xmlspy.com)-->
<xs:schema xmlns:xs="http://www.w3.org/2001/XMLSchema"
elementFormDefault="qualified">
    <xs:simpleType name="perms">
        <xs:annotation>
            <xs:documentation>The only values associated with a permission.</xs:documentation>
        </xs:annotation>
        <xs:restriction base="xs:string">
            <xs:enumeration value="permitted">
                <xs:annotation>
                    <xs:documentation>Permitted</xs:documentation>
                </xs:annotation>
            </xs:enumeration>
            <xs:enumeration value="prohibited">
                <xs:annotation>
                    <xs:documentation>Prohibited</xs:documentation>
                </xs:annotation>
            </xs:enumeration>
            <xs:enumeration value="no">
                <xs:annotation>
                    <xs:documentation>Prohibited</xs:documentation>
                </xs:annotation>
            </xs:enumeration>
            <xs:enumeration value="undetermined">
                <xs:annotation>
                    <xs:documentation>We don't know.</xs:documentation>
                </xs:annotation>
            </xs:enumeration>
```

```
        </xs:restriction>
    </xs:simpleType>
    <xs:element name="ERMI">
        <xs:complexType>
            <xs:sequence>
                <xs:element ref="ERMIQuickFix"/>
            </xs:sequence>
        </xs:complexType>
    </xs:element>
    <xs:element name="ERMIQuickFix">
        <xs:complexType>
            <xs:sequence>
                <xs:element ref="eresourcetitle"/>
                <xs:element ref="digitallycopy"/>
                <xs:element ref="pcopy"/>
                <xs:element ref="scholarlysharing"/>
                <xs:element ref="illlporfax"/>
                <xs:element ref="illelectronic"/>
                <xs:element ref="illsecureetransmission"/>
                <xs:element ref="illrecordkeeping"/>
                <xs:element ref="ecopylibreserve"/>
                <xs:element ref="perpetualaccessright"/>
            </xs:sequence>
        </xs:complexType>
    </xs:element>
    <xs:element name="digitallycopy" type="perms"/>
    <xs:element name="ecopylibreserve" type="perms"/>
    <xs:element name="eresourcetitle" type="xs:string"/>
    <xs:element name="illelectronic" type="perms"/>
    <xs:element name="illlporfax" type="perms"/>
    <xs:element name="illrecordkeeping" type="perms"/>
    <xs:element name="illsecureetransmission" type="perms"/>
    <xs:element name="pcopy" type="perms"/>
    <xs:element name="perpetualaccessright" type="perms"/>
    <xs:element name="scholarlysharing" type="perms"/>
</xs:schema>
```

Figure 11. ERMI Use Case: License Agreement XML

```xml
<?xml version="1.0" encoding="UTF-8"?>
<ERMI xmlns:xsi="http://www.w3.org/2001/XMLSchema-instance"
xsi:noNamespaceSchemaLocation="C:\datax\dlfermi\xmlschema\native\license.xsd">
    <ERMSharedLicense>
        <eresourcetitle>Stat!Ref</eresourcetitle>
        <licensename>Stat!Ref License Agreement</licensename>
        <allrightsreservedindicator>unknown</allrightsreservedindicator>
        <antidbprotectionindicator>unknown</antidbprotectionindicator>
        <archivingnote>unknown</archivingnote>
        <archivingright>prohibited (interpreted)</archivingright>
        <authorizeduserdefinition>Persons affiliated with the University of California. Full and
part time employees (including faculty, staff, and independent contractors) and students of
company and the institution of which it is a part, regardless of the physical location of such
persons.</authorizeduserdefinition>
        <clickwrapmodification>permitted (explicit)</clickwrapmodification>
        <completenessofcontent>permitted (explicit)</completenessofcontent>
        <confidentialityofagreement>permitted (explicit)</confidentialityofagreement>
        <confidentialityofagreementnote>Here is a note about confidentiality.
</confidentialityofagreementnote>
        <contentwarranty>Licensed materials are provided on an "as is" basis. </contentwarranty>
        <ecopylibreserve>permitted (explicit)</ecopylibreserve>
        <ecoursepack>prohibited (explicit)</ecoursepack>
        <fairuseclauseindicator>unknown</fairuseclauseindicator>
        <illelectronic>silent (uninterpreted)</illelectronic>
        <illprintorfax>permitted (explicit)</illprintorfax>
        <illrecordkeepingreq>prohibited (explicit)</illrecordkeepingreq>
        <illsecureetransaction>silent (uninterpreted)</illsecureetransaction>
        <licensereviewer>Barbara Schader</licensereviewer>
        <pcoursepack>permitted (explicit)</pcoursepack>
        <perpetualaccess>permitted (interpreted)</perpetualaccess>
        <perpetualaccessnote>unknown</perpetualaccessnote>
        <usagestatsavail>prohibited (explicit)</usagestatsavail>
        <usagestatsdelivery>unknown</usagestatsdelivery>
        <usagestatsformat>unknown </usagestatsformat>
        <usagestatsfrequency>Quarterly</usagestatsfrequency>
        <walkinusertermnote>permitted (explicit)</walkinusertermnote>
    </ERMSharedLicense>
</ERMI>
```

Figure 12. ERMI Native Schema for License Agreement Use Case

```xml
<?xml version="1.0" encoding="UTF-8"?>
<!--W3C Schema generated by XMLSPY v5 rel. 4 U (http://www.xmlspy.com)-->
<xs:schema xmlns:xs="http://www.w3.org/2001/XMLSchema"
elementFormDefault="qualified">
    <xs:simpleType name="perms">
        <xs:annotation>
            <xs:documentation>The only values associated with a permission.</xs:documentation>
        </xs:annotation>
        <xs:restriction base="xs:string">
            <xs:enumeration value="permitted (explicit)">
                <xs:annotation>
                    <xs:documentation>permitted (explicit)</xs:documentation>
                </xs:annotation>
            </xs:enumeration>
            <xs:enumeration value="permitted (interpreted)">
                <xs:annotation>
                    <xs:documentation>permitted (interpreted)</xs:documentation>
                </xs:annotation>
            </xs:enumeration>
            <xs:enumeration value="prohibited (explicit)">
                <xs:annotation>
                    <xs:documentation>prohibited (explicit)</xs:documentation>
                </xs:annotation>
            </xs:enumeration>
            <xs:enumeration value="prohibited (interpreted)">
                <xs:annotation>
                    <xs:documentation>prohibited (interpreted)</xs:documentation>
                </xs:annotation>
            </xs:enumeration>
            <xs:enumeration value="silent (uninterpreted)">
                <xs:annotation>
                    <xs:documentation>silent (uninterpreted)</xs:documentation>
                </xs:annotation>
            </xs:enumeration>
            <xs:enumeration value="not applicable">
                <xs:annotation>
                    <xs:documentation>not applicable</xs:documentation>
                </xs:annotation>
            </xs:enumeration>
            <xs:enumeration value="unknown">
                <xs:annotation>
                    <xs:documentation>unknown</xs:documentation>
                </xs:annotation>
            </xs:enumeration>
        </xs:restriction>
    </xs:simpleType>
    <xs:element name="ERMI">
        <xs:complexType>
            <xs:sequence>
                <xs:element ref="ERMSharedLicense" maxOccurs="unbounded"/>
```

```
            </xs:sequence>
        </xs:complexType>
    </xs:element>
    <xs:element name="ERMSharedLicense">
        <xs:complexType>
            <xs:sequence>
                <xs:element ref="eresourcetitle"/>
                <xs:element ref="licensename"/>
                <xs:element ref="allrightsreservedindicator"/>
                <xs:element ref="antidbprotectionindicator"/>
                <xs:element ref="archivingnote"/>
                <xs:element ref="archivingright"/>
                <xs:element ref="authorizeduserdefinition"/>
                <xs:element ref="clickwrapmodification"/>
                <xs:element ref="completenessofcontent"/>
                <xs:element ref="confidentialityofagreement"/>
                <xs:element ref="confidentialityofagreementnote"/>
                <xs:element ref="contentwarranty"/>
                <xs:element ref="ecopylibreserve"/>
                <xs:element ref="ecoursepack"/>
                <xs:element ref="fairuseclauseindicator"/>
                <xs:element ref="illelectronic"/>
                <xs:element ref="illprintorfax"/>
                <xs:element ref="illrecordkeepingreq"/>
                <xs:element ref="illsecureetransaction"/>
                <xs:element ref="licensereviewer"/>
                <xs:element ref="pcoursepack"/>
                <xs:element ref="perpetualaccess"/>
                <xs:element ref="perpetualaccessnote"/>
                <xs:element ref="usagestatsavail"/>
                <xs:element ref="usagestatsdelivery"/>
                <xs:element ref="usagestatsformat"/>
                <xs:element ref="usagestatsfrequency"/>
                <xs:element ref="walkinusertermnote"/>
            </xs:sequence>
        </xs:complexType>
    </xs:element>
    <xs:element name="eresourcetitle"/>
    <xs:element name="licensename"/>
    <xs:element name="authorizeduserdefinition"/>
    <xs:element name="allrightsreservedindicator" type="perms"/>
    <xs:element name="antidbprotectionindicator" type="perms"/>
    <xs:element name="archivingnote" type="perms"/>
    <xs:element name="archivingright" type="perms"/>
    <xs:element name="clickwrapmodification" type="perms"/>
    <xs:element name="completenessofcontent" type="perms"/>
    <xs:element name="confidentialityofagreement" type="perms"/>
    <xs:element name="confidentialityofagreementnote"/>
    <xs:element name="contentwarranty"/>
    <xs:element name="ecopylibreserve" type="perms"/>
    <xs:element name="ecoursepack" type="perms"/>
```

```
    <xs:element name="fairuseclauseindicator"/>
    <xs:element name="illelectronic" type="perms"/>
    <xs:element name="illprintorfax" type="perms"/>
    <xs:element name="illrecordkeepingreq" type="perms"/>
    <xs:element name="illsecureetransaction" type="perms"/>
    <xs:element name="licensereviewer"/>
    <xs:element name="pcoursepack" type="perms"/>
    <xs:element name="perpetualaccess" type="perms"/>
    <xs:element name="perpetualaccessnote"/>
    <xs:element name="usagestatsavail"/>
    <xs:element name="usagestatsdelivery"/>
    <xs:element name="usagestatsformat"/>
    <xs:element name="usagestatsfrequency"/>
    <xs:element name="walkinusertermnote"/>
</xs:schema>
```

References

Banerjee, Kyle. "How Does XML Help Libraries?" *Computers in Libraries* 22, no. 8 (September 2002). Available at: http://www.infotoday.com/cilmag/sep02/Banerjee.htm.

Coyle, Karen. "The Technology of Rights: Digital Rights Management." Based on a talk originally given at the Library of Congress, November 19, 2003. http://www.kcoyle.net/drm_basics1.html.

———. "Rights Expression Languages: A Report for the Library of Congress." February, 2004. Available at: http://www.loc.gov/standards/Coylereport_final1single.pdf.

Creative Commons. Website. http://creativecommons.org/.

———. "Why We Have Creative Commons Metadata." Creative Commons. http://creativecommons.org/technology/metadata/why.

EDItEUR. "Onix for Serials." http://www.editeur.org/.

Godwin, Mike. "What Every Citizen Should Know about DRM, a.k.a. 'Digital Rights Management'." Public Knowledge. http://www.publicknowledge.org/content/overviews/citizens-guide-to-drm/view.

Gadd, Elizabeth, Charles Oppenheim, Steve Probets. "Romeo Studies 6: Rights Metadata for Open Archiving." http://www.lboro.ac.uk/departments/ls/disresearch /romeo/index.html.

Guth, Susanne, Strembeck. "A Proposal for the Evolution of the ODRL Information Model." *Proceedings of the First International ODRL Workshop, Vienna, Austria, April 22-23, 2004.* Eds. Renato Iannella and Susanne Guth). http://odrl.net/workshop2004/paper/odrl-guth-paper.pdf.

Heery, Rachel, Patel, Manjula. "Application Profiles: Mixing and Matching Metadata Schemas." *Ariadne* 25 (2000). http://www.ariadne.ac.uk /issue25/app-profiles/intro.html.

Iannella, Renato. Email correspondence. June 8, 2004.

National Information Standards Organization. "NISO/EDItEUR Joint Working Party for the Exchange of Serials Subscription Information." http://www.fcla.edu/%7Epcaplan/jwp/.

Library and Information Technology Association (LITA). "The Top Trends [of 2003]." http://www.ala.org/ala/lita/litaresources/toptechtrends/annual2003.htm.

———. "The Top Trends" [of 2004]. http://www.ala.org/ala/lita/litaresources /toptechtrends/midwinter2004.htm.

Lagoze, Carl, Herbert van de Sompel, Michael Nelson, Simeon Warner. "OAI-Rights White Paper." http://www.openarchives.org/documents/OAIRightsWhitePaper.html.

Lessig, Lawrence. *Free Culture*. New York: Penguin, Press, 2004.

Martin, Mairéad, et al. "Federated Digital Rights Management: A Proposed DRM Solution for Research and Education." *D-Lib Magazine* 8, no. 7/8 (July/August 2002). http://www.dlib.org/dlib/july02/martin/07martin.html.

May, Christopher. "Digital Rights Management and the Breakdown of Social Norms." *First Monday* 8, no. 11 (November 2003).

Moen, William. "No Longer Under Our Control: The Nature and Role of Standards in the 21st Century Library." Presentation at the Library of Congress, Luminary Lecture Series, December 3, 2003. Washington, DC. http://www.unt.edu/wmoen/presentations /LuminaryLectureDecember2003.pdf.

ODRL (Open Digital Rights Language). http://www.odrl.net/.

————"ODRL International Workshop 2004, Vienna, Austria." http://odrl.net/workshop2004/report.html.

Publishing Requirements for Industry Standard Metadata (PRISM). http://www.prismstandard.org/.

Renato, Iannella. "Digital Rights Management Architectures," *D-Lib Magazine,* June 2001. http://www.dlib.org/dlib/june01/iannella/06iannella.html.

Tennant, Roy. "MARC Must Die," *Library Journal* 127, no. 17 (Oct. 15, 2002).

————. "MARC Exit Strategies," *Library Journal* 127, no. 19 (Nov. 15, 2002).

————, ed. *XML in Libraries*. New York: Neal-Schuman Publishers, Inc., 2002.

"Time Warner Invests in ContentGuard," *The Register*. April 13, 2004. http://www.theregister.co.uk/2004/04/13/time_warner_invests/.

Vestavik, Oyvind. "REAP: A System for Managing Rights Management in Digital Libraries." http://odrl.net/workshop2004/paper/odrl-vestavik-paper.pdf.

W3C. "W3C Workshop on Digital Rights Management for the Web: Workshop Report." January 22-23, 2001. http://www.w3.org/2000/12/drm-ws/workshop-report.html.

XRML (eXtensible Rights Markup Language) http://www.xrml.org/.